Carolyn Hilarski, PhD, LCSW
John S. Wodarski, PhD, MSSW
Editors

Comprehensive Mental Health Practice with Sex Offenders and Their Families

*Pre-publication
REVIEWS,
COMMENTARIES,
EVALUATIONS...*

"*Comprehensive Mental Health Practice with Sex Offenders and Their Families* is nicely positioned to fill a significant gap in the psychotherapy and behavior change field, that of the lack of evidence-based approaches to assessment and treatment of sex offenders. The international cast of contributing authors adds a useful element of diversity to the chapters. This book does not shrink from especially difficult topics, such as sexually aggressive children, female sex offenders, or sex offenders with developmental disabilities. Epidemiological and descriptive information is provided on the major categories of sex offenders, as is the most contemporary information on treatment approaches best supported by empirical research. The familial focus on assessment and intervention with sex offenders is another strength of this considerably impressive book. I consider this new book essential reading for mental health practitioners serving sex offenders."

Bruce A. Thyer, PhD
*Professor,
College of Social Work,
Florida State University*

More pre-publication
REVIEWS, COMMENTARIES, EVALUATIONS . . .

"This text delivers as stated in its title. It is an impressive text in which the authors thoroughly explore the wide range and types of sex offenders and their families. The authors provide an internally consistent format for addressing sex offenders across the life span, such as child, adolescent, adult male, women, professional perpetrators, intellectually and developmentally challenged sex offenders, and violent sex offenders.

Drs. Hilarski and Wodarski have brought together an outstanding group of international contributors to focus attention on an area of mental health practices long overlooked in the helping profession. They are to be congratulated for their extensive coverage of this field in an accessible and surprisingly easy-to-understand text. This is an extremely valuable addition to students and professionals alike who must deal with these offenders on a daily basis."

Marvin D. Feit, PhD
*Dean and Professor,
Norfolk State University,
Ethelyn R. Strong
School of Social Work*

"This is an accessible and ultimately practical text which many practitioners working with sexual offenders will find of direct benefit to their practice. Hilarski and Wodarski have assembled an impressive range of contributors who address with skill and confidence an important area of offender assessment and treatment. This book will be valuable to new practitioners working in this field, offering as it does comprehensive background literature on a range of offender profiles coupled with the application of this knowledge to typical case examples. The text manages the difficult task of balancing the needs of offenders in treatment without losing sight of the victims of these offenses and this is a real achievement."

Michael Coffey, RN, MSc
*Lecturer in Community
Mental Health Nursing,
University of Wales,
Swansea, United Kingdom*

The Haworth Press
New York • London • Oxford

NOTES FOR PROFESSIONAL LIBRARIANS AND LIBRARY USERS

This is an original book title published by The Haworth Press, Inc. Unless otherwise noted in specific chapters with attribution, materials in this book have not been previously published elsewhere in any format or language.

CONSERVATION AND PRESERVATION NOTES

All books published by The Haworth Press, Inc., and its imprints are printed on certified pH neutral, acid-free book grade paper. This paper meets the minimum requirements of American National Standard for Information Sciences-Permanence of Paper for Printed Material, ANSI Z39.48-1984.

DIGITAL OBJECT IDENTIFIER (DOI) LINKING

The Haworth Press is participating in reference linking for elements of our original books. (For more information on reference linking initiatives, please consult the CrossRef Web site at www.crossref.org.) When citing an element of this book such as a chapter, include the element's Digital Object Identifier (DOI) as the last item of the reference. A Digital Object Identifier is a persistent, authoritative, and unique identifier that a publisher assigns to each element of a book. Because of its persistence, DOIs will enable The Haworth Press and other publishers to link to the element referenced, and the link will not break over time. This will be a great resource in scholarly research.

Comprehensive Mental Health Practice with Sex Offenders and Their Families

THE HAWORTH PRESS
Titles of Related Interest

How to Work with Sex Offenders: A Handbook for Criminal Justice, Human Service, and Mental Health Professionals by Rudy Flora

Identifying and Treating Sex Offenders: Current Approaches, Research, and Techniques edited by Robert Geffner, Kristina Crumpton Franey, Terri Geffner Arnold, and Bob Falconer

Identifying and Treating Youth Who Sexually Offend: Current Approaches, Techniques, and Research edited by Robert Geffner, Kristina Crumpton Franey, Terri Geffner Arnold, and Bob Falconer

Sex Offender Treatment: Accomplishments, Challenges, and Future Directions edited by Michael H. Miner and Eli Coleman

Treating Sex Offenders: A Guide to Clinical Practice with Adults, Clerics, Children, and Adolescents, Second Edition by William E. Prendergast

Treating Youth Who Sexually Abuse: An Integrated Multi-Component Approach by Paul Stephen Lundrigan

Identifying Child Molesters: Preventing Child Sexual Abuse by Recognizing the Patterns of the Offenders by Carla van Dam

The Socially Skilled Child Molester: Differentiating the Guilty from the Falsely Accused by Carla van Dam

Comprehensive Mental Health Practice with Sex Offenders and Their Families

Carolyn Hilarski, PhD, LCSW
John S. Wodarski, PhD, MSSW
Editors

The Haworth Press
New York • London • Oxford

For more information on this book or to order, visit
http://www.haworthpress.com/store/product.asp?sku=5260

or call 1-800-HAWORTH (800-429-6784) in the United States and Canada
or (607) 722-5857 outside the United States and Canada

or contact orders@HaworthPress.com

© 2006 by The Haworth Press, Inc. All rights reserved. No part of this work may be reproduced or utilized in any form or by any means, electronic or mechanical, including photocopying, microfilm, and recording, or by any information storage and retrieval system, without permission in writing from the publisher. Printed in the United States of America.

The Haworth Press, Inc., 10 Alice Street, Binghamton, NY 13904-1580.

PUBLISHER'S NOTES
The development, preparation, and publication of this work has been undertaken with great care. However, the Publisher, employees, editors, and agents of The Haworth Press are not responsible for any errors contained herein or for consequences that may ensue from use of materials or information contained in this work. The Haworth Press is committed to the dissemination of ideas and information according to the highest standards of intellectual freedom and the free exchange of ideas. Statements made and opinions expressed in this publication do not necessarily reflect the views of the Publisher, Directors, management, or staff of The Haworth Press, Inc., or an endorsement by them.

Identities and circumstances of individuals discussed in this book have been changed to protect confidentiality.

Cover design by Jennifer M. Gaska.

Library of Congress Cataloging-in-Publication Data

Comprehensive mental health practice with sex offenders and their families / Carolyn Hilarski, John S. Wodarski, editors.
    p. cm.
Includes bibliographical references and index.
ISBN-13: 978-0-7890-2542-5 (hard : alk. paper)
ISBN-10: 0-7890-2542-6 (hard : alk. paper)
ISBN-13: 978-0-7890-2543-2 (soft : alk. paper)
ISBN-10: 0-7890-2543-4 (soft : alk. paper)
  1. Sex offenders. 2. Psychosexual disorders—Treatment. I. Hilarski, Carolyn. II. Wodarski, John S.
  [DNLM: 1. Child Abuse, Sexual—psychology. 2. Child Abuse, Sexual—statistics & numerical data. 3. Family Therapy—methods. 4. Psychopathology—methods. WM 610 C737 2006]

RC560.S47C663 2006
616.85'83—dc22

2005022894

This book is dedicated to those who live each day
with the consequences of abusive behavior.

CONTENTS

About the Editors	xi
Contributors	xiii
Acknowledgments	xv

Chapter 1. Child Sex Offenders   1
    Peggy P. Keller
    Matthew T. Theriot
    Catherine N. Dulmus

Introduction	1
Prevalence of Child Sexual Offending	3
Characteristics of Child Sex Offenders	4
Family Characteristics	6
Offense Characteristics	6
Etiology	7
Assessment	8
Empirical Interventions	12
Case Example	13
Conclusion	17

Chapter 2. Adolescent Sex Offending   21
    Matthew T. Theriot

Introduction	21
Overview of Adolescent Sex Offending	22
Demographics	23
Deviant Sexual Behavior Characteristics	24
Traumatic Victimization History	27
Cognitive and Psychiatric Characteristics	28
Social and Environmental Dynamics	29
Assessment	31
Treatment	40
Case Example	41

Chapter 3. Adult Male Sex Offenders   47
Carolyn Hilarski
Carl W. Christensen

Introduction	47
Prevalence	48
Personal Characteristics	48
Etiology	49
The Consequences of Sexual Offending	50
Risk Factors	51
Assessment	51
Interventions	54
Therapy Groups	55
Treatment	55
Case Example	59

Chapter 4. Women Who Sexually Abuse Children   71
Myriam S. Denov
Franca Cortoni

Introduction	71
Etiology	72
Prevalence	74
Long-Term Consequences of Child Sexual Abuse by Females	77
Assessment	82
Treatment	86
Case Example	92
Conclusion	94

Chapter 5. Perpetrators Within Professions   101
Joe Sullivan
Anthony Beech

Introduction	101
Overview of the Typical Perpetrator Within Professions	102
Abuse Settings	104
Etiology of Abuse	107
Behavioral Consequences	109
Current Empirical Assessment	112
Empirical Interventions for Perpetrators Within Professions	117
Relapse Prevention	120
Case Example	122

Chapter 6. Intellectually and Developmentally Challenged Sex Offenders — 133
William R. Lindsay
Lesley Steptoe
Kathleen Quinn

Introduction	133
Prevalence and Characteristics	133
Typologies of Offenders	137
Assessment Issues	142
Issues for Families	149
Interventions	151
Case Example	156
Conclusion	158

Chapter 7. Violent Sex Offenders — 167
Devon L. L. Polaschek
Tony Ward
Theresa A. Gannon

Introduction	167
The Nature of Violence	168
Offender Characteristics	170
Rapist Typologies and Violence	172
Etiology of Violent Sex Offending	178
Current Empirical Assessment Issues with Violent Sex Offenders	179
Current Empirically Supported Interventions	182
Relapse Prevention	184
Case Example	185
Conclusion	187

Chapter 8. Comorbid Psychopathology in Child, Adolescent, and Adult Sexual Offenders — 193
David P. Fago

Introduction	193
Comorbidity in a Developmental Context	194
Child and Adolescent Sexual Offenders	195
Adult Sexual Offenders	198
Etiological Implications	200
Mood Dysregulation and the "Monoamine Hypothesis"	200

The "Executive Dysfunction" Hypothesis 201
Assessment and Treatment: A Multimodal Approach 204
Case Example 209

Index **219**

ABOUT THE EDITORS

Carolyn Hilarski, PhD, LCSW, ACSW, is in the Department of Social Work at North Carolina State University in Raleigh. She is editor of *Addiction, Assessment, and Treatment with Adolescents, Adults, and Families* and serves on the editorial boards of *Stress, Trauma, and Crisis: An International Journal* and the *Journal of Evidenced-Based Social Work: Advances in Practice, Programming, and Research Policy.* Dr. Hilarski also serves as a research consultant and co-investigator for several grants concerning youth substance abuse and trauma.

John S. Wodarski, PhD, MSSW, is Professor in the College of Social Work at the University of Tennessee in Knoxville. He is co-editor of the *Journal of Human Behavior in the Social Environment,* the *Journal of Social Service Research,* and the *Journal of Evidence-Based Social Work,* and has authored or co-authored nearly 200 publications, including 21 books. Dr. Wodarski was honored as Social Work Professor of the Year in 1988 at the University of Georgia. His strengths are in child welfare and alcohol abuse problems and his commitment to empirically based practice.

CONTRIBUTORS

Anthony Beech, PhD, The School of Psychology; University of Birmingham, UK.

Carl W. Christensen CSW, ACSW, Department of Social Work, Rochester Institute of Technology.

Franca Cortoni, PhD, Director of Programming Research, Correctional Service of Canada.

Myriam S. Denov, PhD, Department of Criminology, University of Ottawa.

Catherine N. Dulmus, PhD, ACSW, School of Social Work, State University of New York at Buffalo.

David P. Fago, PhD, University of Maryland, College Park and Maryland Institute for Individual and Family Therapy.

Theresa A. Gannon, PhD, Victoria University of Wellington, New Zealand.

Peggy P. Keller, MS, RN, CCBT, Nurse Manager, Inpatient Behavioral Health, Jamestown, NY.

William R. Lindsay, PhD, NHS Tayside and University of Abertay, Dundee, Scotland.

Devon L. L. Polaschek, PhD, School of Psychology, Victoria University of Wellington.

Kathleen Quinn, MB, ChB, NHS Tayside, Scotland.

Lesley Steptoe, BA, NHS Tayside and University of Abertay, Dundee, Scotland.

Joe Sullivan, MA, The Lucy Faithful Foundation, The University of Birmingham, UK.

Matthew T. Theriot, PhD, The University of Tennessee, College of Social Work.

Tony Ward, PhD, Psychology, Victoria University, New Zealand.

Acknowledgments

The editors wish to thank all of the authors for their graciousness and willingness to join this project and contribute their experience, knowledge, and wisdom to this vital effort. We also want to thank our partners, Chris and Lois Ann, for enduring the long hours . . . alone . . . Finally, we want to express our deepest gratitude to the publisher who offered the opportunity for this information to be shared, the readers who gave us valuable feedback, and the staff members who packaged it brilliantly.

Chapter 1

Child Sex Offenders

Peggy P. Keller
Matthew T. Theriot
Catherine N. Dulmus

INTRODUCTION

Of all of the sex-offending typologies profiled in this book, perhaps none has received less research attention than child sex offenders (i.e., sex offenders under age twelve). This may result from the difficulty researchers often encounter when attempting to study vulnerable populations (e.g., children, offenders, and especially offending children). Another reason for this limited research may be society's general unwillingness to acknowledge sexual behavior among children. After all, children are innocent and pure, playful, and nonsexual.

Although this view of children is not incorrect, it does fail to recognize myriad sexual behaviors, both normal and otherwise, exhibited by children. Despite popular perceptions and the lack of public awareness, research shows that certain sexual behaviors are an important part of normal child development. These behaviors provide an opportunity for children to learn more about their bodies and the bodies of others (Johnson, 2002). Normal sexual behaviors include children's games (e.g., "playing doctor"), the use of sexually explicit words, kissing nonfamily peers and adults, undressing in front of others, and peeking at, touching, or exposing genitals (Horton, 1996). These behaviors involve voluntary participation from children of similar age and physical size (Horton, 1996); children do not feel anger, shame, or fear following such behavior (Johnson, 1991); and children will usually cease such actions when asked to stop (Gil & Johnson, 1993).

Comprehensive Mental Health Practice with Sex Offenders and Their Families
© 2006 by The Haworth Press, Inc. All rights reserved.
doi:10.1300/5260_01

Of course, not all sexual behavior by children is normal. A range of sexual activities among children are indeed abnormal. In light of this possible variation in behavior, it has been suggested that sexual behavior by children is best viewed along a continuum. Horton (1996), for example, describes a continuum model originally developed by Berliner and Rawlings (1991). In their arrangement, the continuum begins with *normal sexual behavior,* then moves to *inappropriate sexual behavior, developmentally precocious sexual behavior,* and finally *coercive* or *aggressive sexual behavior.*

The initial point on this continuum, *normal sexual behavior,* includes those behaviors previously described. The next step, *inappropriate sexual behavior,* is the first (and least severe) category of abnormal sexual misconduct. Examples include highly sexualized play or art, touching others or asking to be touched, and the repeated public exposure of genitals (Horton, 1996). Gil and Johnson (1993) believe that this behavior is often "sexually reactive," or stemming from the child's own sexual abuse or exposure to sexual situations (such as adult sexual activity or sexually explicit television). This stage does not necessarily involve sexual contact between children and certainly does not involve coercive or assaultive behavior (Horton, 1996).

This is also true of the third stage on the continuum, *developmentally precocious sexual behavior* (Horton, 1996), or *extensive mutual sexual behavior* (Gil & Johnson, 1993). In this stage, children engage in explicit sexual activity, but not behaviors that are coercive or aggressive. This activity may include oral-genital contact or vaginal and anal penetration. Horton notes that siblings experiencing a stressful or sexually abusive home life may engage in this type of sexual activity.

The final stage on this continuum, *coercive* or *aggressive sexual behavior,* is the most problematic and serious form of abnormal sexual behavior. As implied in the name, this stage is defined by engagement in sexual activity with others using coercion or force (Horton, 1996). In using force, the child may hit, restrain, or threaten violence to achieve the desired sexual outcome. He or she may similarly use threats against others, bribery, or deception (Horton, 1996).

The remainder of this chapter focuses on these most serious and troubled children. Their use of aggression, violence, and force makes them the most offensive group among those children with sexual behavior problems. Subsequently, in a book such as this one (with its focus on "sex offenders"), these children are the most appropriate group for inclusion and discussion herein. Future use of the term "child sex offenders" in this chapter will be in specific reference to these aggressive and assaultive child perpetrators.

PREVALENCE OF CHILD SEXUAL OFFENDING

Unfortunately, the true scope of child sex offending is difficult to estimate. This may result from the aforementioned unwillingness of many people to attribute sexual behavior to children. Araji (1997) also notes that many people view preadolescence as a period when children are not interested in sex or sexual exploration. People holding this opinion would be less likely to recognize sexual behavior problems in children. Other factors that may contribute to the lack of available information on child sex offending (including prevalence data) are mislabeling of children's behavior (such as confusing aggressive and normal sexual behavior or labeling child sexual misconduct as fighting or rough play), the unwillingness of many to apply the "sex offender" label to children, the lack of available treatment services, and people's unwillingness to report sexual offenses by children (Araji, 1997). Regardless of the specific reasons, the truth remains that there are no known reliable estimates on the annual occurrence of child sex offending in the United States.

One of the most commonly utilized sources for estimating annual crime rates among adolescents and adults is the Federal Bureau of Investigation's (FBI) Uniform Crime Report. This document is a generally reliable source for comprehensive data on reported crime in the United States. Accordingly, excluding forcible rape and prostitution, 2,571 children aged twelve or younger were arrested for a sex offense in 2002 (FBI, 2002). This equates to approximately 3.8 percent of all sex offense arrests for the year. Likewise, 1.9 percent of arrestees for forcible rape were children, or 378 out of 20,162 total arrests (FBI, 2002).

These figures undoubtedly underestimate the number of sex offenses perpetrated annually by children. Given the aforementioned reluctance of many to attribute sexually aggressive behavior to preadolescents, one would expect that even more people are unwilling to seek arrest and formal criminal processing for such behavior. However, it may not be unreasonable to assume that very young children actually arrested for a sex offense are among the most problematic and aggressive offenders. Thus, while these figures may underestimate the overall occurrence of sexual misbehavior by children, they may be more accurate for those specific child sex offenders highlighted in this chapter. Some child sex offenders are arrested for assault or other related offenses involving aggression or violence.

Despite the lack of reliable prevalence data, child welfare and law enforcement groups report encountering escalating numbers of child sex offenders (Gil & Johnson, 1993). Suggestive of either an increase in occurrence or growing awareness of this important topic, child welfare, mental health, and criminal justice professionals will likely be called upon to intervene with these offending children. As a result, a better understanding of this population must be developed, including their characteristic information as well as empirically supported assessment and treatment methods.

CHARACTERISTICS OF CHILD SEX OFFENDERS

Just as it is difficult to report reliable data on the occurrence of child sex offending, the reporting of child sex offender characteristics is equally challenging. Practically, the detailing of characteristics is hindered by many of the limitations described in previous sections of this chapter. Once again, these include the misidentification and mislabeling of offending behavior and an unwillingness to attribute such behavior to children, among other limitations. From a research perspective, more attention has been paid to studying sexually aggressive behavior among minors in general (eighteen years of age and younger) than among young children specifically. Likewise, several research articles that purport to focus on sexually aggressive *children* or *youths* often include children older than twelve years in the study samples. Consequently, it is difficult to differentiate the characteristics of younger study participants from those of their adolescent counterparts. Most studies on child sex offenders are also further limited by small sample sizes, which restrict analyses and the generalization of study findings. Regardless, the available literature on child sex offenders does provide a useful introduction to the most important characteristics of these young offenders.

Gender Issues

Among nine studies on sexually aggressive children reviewed by Araji (1997), the majority of the different study samples included more males than females, and only one of these studies focused entirely on female children (Johnson, 1989). Pithers, Gray, Busconi, and Houchens (1998) found that male children were overrepresented in a group of sexually aggressive children while females were overrepresented in less extreme groups of children with sexual behavior problems. Similarly, Miranda, Begler, Davis, Frevert, & Taylor (2001) summarize a handful of studies reporting that male children exhibit more sexually aggressive behavior than female children do. According to the authors, this may be because males are socialized to externalize behaviors while females are socialized to internalize them. However, since males are overrepresented in almost all offending populations, an alternative explanation for this gender difference may be that males are more likely to be perceived as offensive than female children are. This may be especially true regarding sexual aggression, which is often perceived as an exclusively male activity.

Psychological and Cognitive Characteristics

In a study of seventy-two children and adolescents referred for outpatient treatment, Fago (2003) found that 82 percent of the sample was diagnosed with attention-deficit/hyperactivity disorder (ADHD) or another neurodevelopmental disorder. This was especially true for the younger sexually aggressive children (thirteen years old or younger). In this subgroup, 89 percent of the study subjects had such a diagnosis. Pithers et al. (1998) also noted a high percentage of ADHD among the sexually aggressive children in their sample as well as a high percentage of children diagnosed with conduct disorder. Other studies have likewise identified a high prevalence of conduct disorder as well as oppositional and defiant disorder, adjustment disorder, or a concurrent diagnosis of ADHD and these latter two disorders in samples of child sex offenders (Friedrich & Luecke, 1988; Miranda et al., 2001).

In terms of intelligence and emotional well-being, studies summarized by Araji (1997) show that child sex offenders generally have IQ scores in the average to low-average range, yet their behavior problems and aggressive actions often put these children at a high risk for peer rejection and school failure (Miranda et al., 2001). In Fago's (2003) study, 55 percent of the subjects had a history of peer rejection and/or social skills deficits (though only 44 percent had a documented history of school failure or learning disability). Furthermore, child sex offenders often suffer from low self-esteem, feelings of inadequacy and vulnerability, a lack of empathy, and other relationship difficulties (Horton, 1996; Miranda et al., 2001).

FAMILY CHARACTERISTICS

The families of child sex offenders are generally dysfunctional (Araji, 1997; Fago, 2003; Horton, 1996; Johnson, 1989), involving caregiver violent behavior (Pithers & Gray, 1996) and/or alcohol and drug abuse (Johnson, 1988). Among forty-seven male child sex offenders, Johnson found that 73 percent of parents or grandparents abused alcohol and/or drugs. Friedrich and Luecke (1988) found that the majority of mothers of child sex offenders in their sample were chemically dependent whereas a very small minority received good emotional support. Many child sex offenders often come from single-parent homes and may not know the whereabouts of the absent parent (Horton, 1996).

Pithers et al. (1998) labeled the families of children with sexual behavior problems as "multiply entrapped" (p. 129). According to the authors, high levels of distress and some level of isolation characterize these families.

One additional characteristic of family relationships that requires further discussion relates to the sexual interaction between family members. Johnson (1988) reported that 64 percent of sampled male sex offenders victimized immediate (46 percent) or extended (18 percent) family members. In a similar study of female child sex offenders, 77 percent sexually victimized a sibling or cousin (Johnson, 1989).

OFFENSE CHARACTERISTICS

Although the majority of children in Johnson's (1988, 1989) studies victimized family members, other victim groups included neighbors, schoolmates, children in foster homes, and other nonfamilial people. In completing the sexual assault, the majority of offending children used verbal coercion while 23 to 38 percent used physical coercion or force. Furthermore, the most common types of sexual activity were fondling, genital contact without penetration, oral sex, simulating intercourse, penetration of the anus with penis (or finger for female perpetrators), and penetration of the vagina with penis. These offense types are consistent with those reported in other studies. For example, the most common types of sexual activity in the study by Friedrich and Luecke (1988) were oral sex and fondling. Anal and vaginal penetration occurred with considerably less frequency.

Child sex offenders also tend to victimize others close to their own age. When compared to children with less extreme sexual behavior problems, Pithers et al. (1998) found that a greater percentage of sexually aggressive children penetrated their victim and that these children had the highest average number of penetrative acts. The sexually aggressive children were also more likely to utilize aggression in their sexual assault.

ETIOLOGY

With rare exception, one consistent finding across studies of child sex offenders is the alarmingly high rate of sexual abuse victimization among these children. This may be especially true for female child sex offenders (Gordon & Schroeder, 1995). In a study of thirteen female child sex offenders, 100 percent had been sexually abused (Johnson, 1989). Although the impact of this finding may be curtailed somewhat by the relatively small sample, numerous other studies have reported similar figures. In the studies reviewed by Araji (1997), most estimated that approximately 75 to 80 percent of the different study participants had a history of sexual abuse victimization.

Other studies have shown high rates of sexual abuse in addition to physical abuse. Among seventy-two children with sexual behavior problems, Pithers et al. (1998) found that approximately 60 percent of the sample had experienced multiple forms of abuse. Physical abuse was also prevalent in many of the studies cited in the aforementioned review by Araji (1997).

The accumulation of such study findings have led many people both in the general public and in mental health and law enforcement circles to believe that all child sex offenders have a history of sexual abuse victimization (Johnson, 2002). However, this erroneous view is countered by a handful of evidence to the contrary. In one such piece of research, Fago (2003) found that 18 percent (or 13 of 72 study respondents) had been sexually abused. This number, it is argued, does not differ from sexual abuse estimates for the general population. Likewise, English and Ray (1991, as cited by Araji, 1997) reported that only 6 percent of the eighty-nine children in their sample had been sexually abused.

In considering causal factors for sexually aggressive behavior in children, the high rate of sexual abuse among samples of child sex offenders lends support for social or observational learning theories. Specifically, these offending children may be acting out sexually abusive behaviors that have been modeled for them in their own molestation. However, this is not true for all child sex offenders since some sexually aggressive children have no history of sexual abuse. Instead, cognitive or psychological disorders may be a causal factor (Fago, 2003). Yet, some children with the cognitive or developmental disorders previously described do not perpetrate sexual aggressive behaviors. Familial issues in addition to other factors must also be considered. The cautious conclusion then is that there is not enough known yet about child sex offenders or offending categories and subgroups to make specific theoretical statements, assumptions, or predictions.

ASSESSMENT

As the previous section clearly portrayed, child sex offenders present with an array of individual and familial problems, often including a history of sexual abuse. Thus, sexually offensive conduct is really one behavioral piece of a larger, more complicated problem; so comprehensive assessment of the child and the family system is critical (Perry & Orchard, 1992). The current trend is to view the child sex offender as an emotionally disturbed child, who is both an offender and a victim, and to provide assessment and intervention within this context. Thus, to fully assess and intervene with the child sex offender, data must be collected from a variety of sources, across a range of topics, utilizing a variety of tools. Since no specific assessment protocol has been determined for assessment of this specific population, an approach to assessing children with emotional and behavioral problems suggested by Merrell (1994) is suggested and reviewed in the following text.

The Model

In the past two decades, significant advances have been made in the research and technology base for conducting assessments with children (Merrell, 1994). One of the major developments has been the articulation of the multimethod, multisource, multisetting assessment model. The critical feature of this model is that it dictates obtaining assessment data through a number of different instruments, methods, sources, informants, and settings. Such an approach is essential for assessing child sex offenders as the model allows for a comprehensive approach to assessing the referred child's behavioral, social, and emotional functioning (Merrell, 1994).

The assessment components of this model include methods, sources, and settings. Application of this model to assessment of child sex offenders would include the following:

Methods
- Direct observation
- Behavior rating scales
- Interviews
- Record reviews
- Sociometric assessment
- Self-report measures

Sources
- The child client
- Parents
- Other family members
- Teachers
- Other school personnel
- The peer group
- Community-based informants
- Law officials

Settings
- Home
- School

- Clinic
- Play
- Community

Accurate assessment is critical as it dictates treatment. In reality though, it is often difficult or impossible to include all of the relevant sources and settings. Every attempt should be made to incorporate as many as possible, though, as the broader and more diverse the assessment, the better the clinical picture of the child's behavioral, social, and emotional functioning (Merrell, 1994). At a minimum, the assessment must incorporate a psychosocial assessment, a psychological evaluation, a psychiatric evaluation, and a risk assessment (Rich, 2003), which incorporates as many of the methods, sources, and settings as possible in the previous model.

The Assessment

Psychosocial Assessment

A psychosocial assessment is an assessment of the offender's developmental, contextual, psychological, social, and relational history. Most important, there needs to be an assessment of the child's current referral offense as well as a recounting of past sexually offensive behavior (both reported and unreported). When inquiring about the current offense of record and past sexual deviance, ask detailed questions about each offense and note similarities in each that suggest a pattern of sexually abusive activity. Some key points to focus on are level of aggression, frequency of sexually abusive behaviors, preferred victim type, and sexual arousal patterns (Lane, 1997).

Other areas to be assessed in a comprehensive psychosocial assessment are developmental history, family characteristics, social relationships, substance use, and traumatic victimization history. Pay special attention to those attributes with an empirical connection to child sexual offending, and consider the child's exposure to family violence, the type of discipline used in the family, past and current nonsexual delinquent behavior, previous experiences with mental health treatment, the child's own sexual or physical abuse victimization, and peer relationships. Given the importance of each of these topics, utilization of a structured interview schedule helps to insure that no relevant areas are missed or forgotten.

Family Assessment

In addition to the items previously listed, another important element of a comprehensive psychosocial assessment is an interview with the offender's family. Besides being a crucial source of collateral information, this engages the family in the assessment process as well as establishes a working relationship for treatment.

In terms of data collection in family assessment, family members should be asked about their perceptions of both the child's sexual offense as well as the overall functioning of the child. The family should also be encouraged to provide information on the roles and expectations for each family member, any abuse or violence occurring in the home, substance use or abuse in the family, other incidents of sexual offending in the nuclear or extended family, and the family's attitudes about counseling and mental health treatment (Perry & Orchard, 1992). Beginning research by Gray and Pithers (as cited in Araji, 1997) indicates that families of child sex offenders have an array of characteristics indicative of parental and familial distress, including high rates of poverty, violence between parents, sexual victimization and perpetration within the extended family, physical abuse of the child, and parental arrest. The assessment process should incorporate these family issues as well.

Without a doubt, family involvement is an important aspect of treatment. Therefore, members should be encouraged to participate in the assessment process and subsequent treatment planning to facilitate optimal commitment to treatment.

Psychological Evaluation

Similar to psychosocial assessment, multiple areas should be considered when undertaking a comprehensive psychological evaluation, including educational measures, level of intelligence, and various tests of functioning, attitudes, and interests (Rich, 2003).

In assessing educational factors, for example, one should assess for possible learning disabilities. Correspondingly, the Weschler Adult Intelligence Scale-Revised (WAIS-R) is an instrument for assessing intelligence that has been promoted for use on adolescent sex offenders (Perry & Orchard, 1992). Keeping in mind that poor school performance does not always equate to low intelligence or a learning disability, academic and discipline records from the adolescent's school may yield useful information about possible educational and learning difficulties.

Standardized psychological measures must be developmentally appropriate and have acceptable reliability and validity. Few instruments have been developed specifically for children under age twelve, and even less specific to sex offending behaviors among this population. As previously indicated, a high percentage of child sex offenders have ADHD, low self-esteem, feelings of inadequacy and vulnerability, a lack of empathy, social skills deficits, and other relationship difficulties. Standardized instruments to assist in assessment of these, as well as other areas of concern, are available for use with children.

Psychiatric Evaluation

Building on the psychological evaluation previously described, a psychiatric evaluation will determine the need for psychiatric medications (Rich, 2003). Depending on the child's psychiatric diagnosis, medication may be an important first step in treatment, especially if the child experiences behaviors or cognitive impairments that will interfere with counseling or other treatments. Only a psychiatrist or certified medical professional should conduct a psychiatric evaluation.

Risk Assessment

Assessing risk is attempting to predict a child's likelihood of future sexual offending or delinquency. Research has done a fair job in identifying common traits and characteristics among child sex offenders, but few characteristics have been consistently linked to sexual re-offending in the empirical literature for adolescents, let alone for children (Righthand & Welch, 2001). Likewise, no empirically based risk assessment instruments have been developed (Becker & Hunter, 1997; Beckett, 1999). Further research is necessary to develop instruments and protocols related to children who sexually offend.

EMPIRICAL INTERVENTIONS

Unfortunately, a treatment approach to working with child sexual offenders that has empirical support is nonexistent. Some research on specific interventions are in progress, but outcome study results are not yet available. Keeping this in mind, the following approaches to treatment are suggested approaches, not best practices.

One of the primary goals of treatment is teaching the child to recognize the abuse cycle. The child is taught to identify each phase of the abuse cycle as it pertains to his or her individual situation. He or she is taught to recognize trigger situations and to interrupt the cycle by using appropriate skills.

Family

One of the first obligations of a clinician working with a family is to assess the safety of the environment and to educate the involved family members sufficiently to ensure their ability to recognize the antecedent behaviors and to provide security. The clinician should conduct a thorough assessment prior to making a recommendation regarding identification, level of risk, placement options, and case management needs (Henderson, English, & MacKenzie, 1988). The entire nuclear family is likely to be impacted by a sexual abuser. The clinician should consider the potential that other children in the family may have been victims or may be experiencing the effects of the abusive behavior of their sibling. Often, the initial meeting with family members centers on managing the shock of learning that their child is an offender. A parent may express denial regarding the sexual behavior of his or her child.

Because the victim/abuser are often related or are friends, conflictual dynamics may be present when working with the involved families. Families may express a feeling of powerlessness to control the behavior of their child. Inclusion of the parents in the treatment process empowers them to be a part of the solution process. It gives them a forum to express their concern and is a safe place to express feelings of shame and failure. They may experience grief and loss issues and look to the clinician to assist in resolving these feelings.

CASE EXAMPLE

Pedro is a twelve-year-old male child referred to an outpatient clinic by his mother. Pedro was suspended from school for two weeks. He is accused of lighting a wastebasket afire in the boys' bathroom. He has been suspended from school several times in the past for aggressive behavior, bringing cigarettes to school, teacher disrespect, and failure to complete assignments. There may be charges filed for the fire setting.

Pedro is a well-nourished twelve-year-old male who looks his age. He is appropriately dressed and tidy. He exhibits poor eye contact. He is alert and oriented. Speech is clear, coherent, and nonspontaneous. It is goal directed. He denies any suicidal or homicidal ideation. He does not present any hallucinations or delusions. He appears sad, but adamantly denies depression.

Initially, Pedro is uncooperative to interview. He speaks in a rapid, clipped manner. He refuses to discuss school and will not talk about his friends. He speaks with a Hispanic accent and does not seem to fully understand questions posed to him. He does not request clarification. He frequently refers to himself as the "man of the house."

Pedro's mother is a soft-spoken, attractive, thirty-year-old single parent. She reports that her family moved to this country twenty-four months ago, but has recently relocated to this area six months ago to be with a boyfriend. The family consists of Pedro, a four-year-old sister, mother, and her new boyfriend. Mother works evenings doing a housekeeping job at a local department store. Until recently, Pedro and his sister were home alone after school daily.

Mother admits that she has been very dependent on Pedro over the past two years to help her with babysitting while she works. She states that he has always been very dependable and adult for his age. She notes that her daughter is always obedient and "minds Pedro." Mother claims that their family is "very close." She states that she is now frightened because Pedro will not "listen to" her. She states that he does not respect her rules and that he now often stays out too late. He refuses to attend mass with her. Pedro has always been an outstanding student. His grades at the new school have been poor. He is disrespectful to her and to her boyfriend.

Pedro attended a small Catholic school before moving to this area. Pedro's mother indicates that he has no friends and has not been invited to any activities at his new school. She notes that he prefers to spend time on the computer. She states that she does not supervise his computer use since it seems to make him angry.

Throughout the assessment process, Pedro admits that he did set the fire in the boys' bathroom. He admits that he has been rude and disrespectful at school. He states that he hates his new school and everybody there. He says that he has threatened some of the students to prove that he is "tough." He also reveals that he has touched his sister sexually and has forced her to touch him. He says that this behavior has been occurring for about a year. Initially his sister (age three) was cooperative with his requests, but has been more resistive recently (age four). Pedro has used verbal coercion to persuade her to participate. Pedro denies that he has ever been a sex abuse victim.

Pedro also indicates that he has been accessing pornographic material on the Internet. He states that he was uncomfortable asking his mother about this type of information and had been curious. He notes that the after-school independence offered opportunity on a regular basis.

Treatment Plan

First, the safety of the four-year-old sister must be addressed immediately. A safety plan to ensure that Pedro no longer sexually abuses her must be instituted.

Concerning developing a treatment plan for Pedro, every aspect of the comprehensive assessment must be taken into account. The clinician will have evaluated many areas of the child using knowledge of normal development as the measure. Depending on the available treatment milieu and the outcome of the assessments, group, individual, family, or a combination therapy may be selected. The treatment program must be flexible, in order to address the individual needs of a patient.

Information should be drawn from the interview, school records, criminal records, medical history, previous psychological tests, and collateral interviews to understand the child's struggles. Areas to consider are emotional status, family-of-origin issues, other environments (school, church, etc.), social conflicts, self-esteem, anger management, substance abuse, and coping skills.

The treatment plan should incorporate and utilize to the fullest an understanding of the child's individual strengths. An assessment of strengths should examine talents, skills, and resources. Intelligence, support systems, communication skills, duration of problem, previously successful coping strategies, and self-concept are also very important in the planning process.

Recognize and compensate for any noted impediments to treatment. These might include a language barrier, significant cultural beliefs that may impede the treatment process, inadequate familial support systems, transportation issues, unsafe living environment, etc.

Once an assessment of these areas is completed, the clinician and the child can work together at identifying treatment goals. The child must be fully involved in this process. His or her age and developmental level should be considered; use language and explanations that are appropriate and understandable. Solicitation of feedback from both child and parent is also important.

Plan Specifics: Goals and Objectives

A treatment plan for Pedro would necessarily address his sex-offending behavior. The long-term goal identified for him would be to decrease the intensity and frequency of feelings of desire to sexually offend, to teach him to control his acting on those feelings, to increase the ability to recognize and appropriately express thinking errors, and to identify antecedent behaviors. Short-term objectives would focus on learning the various aspects of the abuse cycle, the idea of victim empathy, and a development of the concept of thinking errors. Interventions would be to teach Pedro about appropriate sexual functioning for a child his age and to introduce him to the concept of the abuse cycle.

Pedro has not developed appropriate peer relationships at his new school. Learning about age-appropriate peer relationships is another intervention that might be included. Pedro's after-school responsibilities may have interfered with his participation in school activities and the development of those normal relationships. This issue could be addressed in collateral meetings with Pedro's mother. A long-term goal for Pedro would be for him to become involved in an age-appropriate supervised school sport or activity. Short-term objectives would include exploration of interests, past enjoyed activities, and perceived talents. Interventions would focus on assisting Pedro in investigating opportunities available and ways to access them.

Pedro is unable to identify his feelings of anger and resentment toward his mother's new relationship. He may be feeling that he has lost his role in the family. These concerns should be addressed, and additional work could involve identifying emotions.

Long-term goals to improve anger-management skills would be to decrease intensity and frequency of angry feelings, and to increase Pedro's ability to recognize and appropriately express angry feelings as they occur. Short-term objectives would be to acknowledge feeling angry, to identify targets of anger, to identify causes of anger, and to identify a pattern in feelings.

Pedro has not acknowledged his emotions, and as a result has developed some maladaptive coping mechanisms. He uses isolation in his room and distraction with the computer. Pedro has not developed any healthy, age-appropriate outlets such as sports, visiting with friends, or a suitable hobby. Long-term goals for Pedro regarding coping skills would be to develop age-appropriate coping strategies. Poor self-esteem is a significant issue for Pedro. His marginal language skills have prevented him from forming friendships at his new school and have been at the core of the dramatic decrease in his grades. His response to these issues has been to become a behavior problem, acting out and being disrespectful in an overcompensation for the embarrassment he feels. In addition, Pedro feels displaced in his role within his nuclear family. He is threatened by the appearance of a new male figure in the household.

The long-term goal for Pedro is to elevate his self-esteem. Short-term objectives might include acknowledging his feelings of incompetence, decreasing feelings of rejection, increasing his insight into current feelings of low self-esteem, and identifying accomplishments that will improve his self-image and making a plan to achieve that goal.

The clinician may choose a combination of individual, group, and family therapy for this case. When making this decision the child's ability to participate successfully in a group setting must be assessed. Language skills would be of major concern as well as developmental level and the blend of other group participants.

CONCLUSION

Current education and awareness programs for children utilized in the United States include information regarding appropriate peer interactions as well as focusing on warning children about the danger of adult strangers. They do not introduce the concept that a known person or a peer might be an offender. Children are not taught how to cope with peer pressure and its use to coerce unwilling participation in sexual behaviors. Both assertiveness training and role-playing could be helpful in preparing a child to manage a peer situation. Teaching children about normal sexuality would provide them a baseline and appropriate language to describe their experiences.

Parents and other caregivers should be taught how to discuss sexuality issues with children and to recognize and investigate possible abusive situations. Children need to be taught to seek an adult's assistance when faced with an abusive situation. Parents or care providers must understand what is normal sexual behavior and what is inappropriate behavior. Too often, adults do not recognize and/or acknowledge abusive behavior as being outside the norm. This can result in a child being repeatedly exposed to abusive behavior and to the child not trusting the adult to keep him or her safe. Adults must know how to respond to inappropriate behavior.

Finally, we would be remiss not to acknowledge that child sex offending is a societal problem, not an individual one (Araji, 1997). A theme throughout this chapter has been that many young offenders are victims of child abuse themselves and are being reared in homes plagued by poverty, parental alcohol and drug abuse, child access to pornography, and domestic violence. A preventive approach requires a societal response, with development and implementation of community-based interventions, to address the contributing factors to child sex offending.

REFERENCES

Araji, S.K. (1997). Sexually aggressive children: Social demographics and psychological characteristics. In S. K. Araji (Ed.), *Sexually aggressive children: Coming to understand them* (pp. 50-54). Thousand Oaks, CA: Sage Publications.

Becker, J.V. & Hunter Jr., J. A. (1997). Understanding and treating child and adolescent sexual offenders. In T. H. Ollendick & R. J. Prinz (Eds.), *Advances in clinical child psychology* (Vol. 19, pp. 177-197). New York: Plenum Press.

Beckett, R. (1999). Evaluation of adolescent sexual abusers. In M. Erooga & H. Masson (Eds.), *Children and young people who sexually abuse others: Challenges and responses* (pp. 204-224). London: Routledge.

Berliner, L. & Rawlings, L. (1991). *A treatment manual: Children with sexual behavior problems.* Seattle, WA: Harborview Sexual Assault Center.

Fago, D.P. (2003). Evaluation and treatment of neurodevelopmental deficits in sexually aggressive children and adolescents. *Professional Psychology: Research and Practice, 34*(3), 248-257.

Federal Bureau of Investigation. (2002). *Crime in the United States: Persons arrested 2002.* Washington, DC: Author.

Friedrich, W.N. & Luecke, W.J. (1988). Young school-age sexually aggressive children. *Professional Psychology: Research and Practice, 19*(2), 155-164.

Gil, E. & Johnson, T.C. (1993). *Sexualized children: Assessment and treatment of sexualized children who molest.* Rockville, MD: Launch Press.

Gordon, B.N. & Schroeder, C.S. (1995). *Sexuality: A developmental approach to problems.* New York: Plenum.

Henderson, J.E., English, D.J., & MacKenzie, W.R. (1988). Family centered casework practice with sexually aggressive children. *Journal of Social Work and Human Sexuality, 7*(2), 89-108.

Horton, C.B. (1996). Children who molest other children: The school psychologist's response to the sexually aggressive child. *School Psychology Review, 25*(4), 540-557.

Johnson, T.C. (1988). Child perpetrators—children who molest other children: preliminary findings. *Child Abuse & Neglect, 12,* 219-229.

Johnson, T.C. (1989). Female child perpetrators: Children who molest other children. *Child Abuse & Neglect, 13,* 571-585.

Johnson, T.C. (1991, August/September). *Understanding the sexual behavior problems of young children.* SEICUS report, pp. 8-15.

Johnson, T.C. (2002). Some considerations about sexual abuse and children with sexual behavior problems. *Journal of Trauma & Dissociation: The Official Journal of the International Society for the Study of Dissociation (ISSD), 3*(4), 83-105.

Lane, S. (1997). Assessment of sexually abusive youth. In G. Ryan & S. Lane (Eds.), *Juvenile sexual offending: Causes, consequences, and correction* (pp. 219-263). San Francisco, CA: Jossey-Bass Publishers.

Merrell, K.W. (1994). *Assessment of behavioral, social, and emotional problems: Direct and objective methods for use with children and adolescents.* White Plains, NY: Longman.

Miranda, A.O., Biegler, B.N., Davis, K., Frevert, V.S., & Taylor, J. (2001). Treating sexually aggressive children. *Journal of Offender Rehabilitation, 33*(2), 15-32.

Perry, G.P. & Orchard, J. (1992). *Assessment and treatment of adolescent sex offenders.* Sarasota, FL: Professional Resource Press.

Pithers, W.D. & Gray, A.S. (1996). Utility of relapse prevention in treatment of sexual abusers. *Sexual Abuse: Journal of Research and Treatment, 8*(3), 223-239.

Pithers, W.D., Gray, A., Busconi, A., & Houchens, P. (1998). Five empirically derived subtypes of children with sexual behavior problems: Characteristics potentially related to juvenile delinquency and adult criminality. *The Irish Journal of Psychology, 19*(1), 49-67.

Rich, P. (2003). *Juvenile sexual offenders: Understanding, assessing, and rehabilitating.* Hoboken, NJ: John Wiley & Sons, Inc.

Righthand, S. & Welch, C. (2001). *Juveniles who have sexually offended: A review of the professional literature.* Office of Juvenile Justice and Delinquency Prevention. Washington, DC: USGPO.

Chapter 2

Adolescent Sex Offending

Matthew T. Theriot

INTRODUCTION

This chapter concerns adolescent sex offenders, with a specific emphasis on empirically based assessment and treatment approaches. Such an empirically based, or evidence-based, approach guides the interviewer in data collection, provides the context for a better understanding of adolescent sex offenders and their offending, and directs practitioners in the ethical *best practices* for treatment and intervention with the adolescent and his or her family. Given that adolescent sex offenders historically have received only limited and occasional scholarly study, an empirically based emphasis would have been suspect and less informative in decades past, yet the past twenty years have seen a virtual explosion in research devoted to this population, thus, increasing the knowledge base and making this emphasis feasible. This chapter begins with a brief introduction to the size and scope of adolescent sex offending before moving to a review of the research describing this group. By providing a comprehensive overview of adolescent sex offenders and highlighting key research findings, this review is intended to provide a contextual foundation for understanding these offending youths. Following this, the next section outlines a framework for empirically based assessment. The chapter concludes with an appraisal of effective treatment approaches and a brief case example.

OVERVIEW OF ADOLESCENT SEX OFFENDING

Whereas adolescence is often romanticized as a time of budding social skills, nervous school dances, and the awkward first kiss, reports on the number of youths arrested for sexual offenses show that sexual offending by adolescents is a serious and sizable problem. According to the Federal Bureau of Investigation (2002), 20.5 percent of all arrests for sex offenses (excluding forcible rape and prostitution) occurring in 2002 involved people under the age of eighteen. This equates to 13,877 actual arrests. Juveniles also accounted for 16.7 percent of all forcible rape arrests (or 3,361 actual arrests).

Unfortunately, as disturbing as these numbers may be, these statistics probably underreport the true occurrence of adolescent sexual offending. Given the young age of offenders, a large number of offenses may go either unreported or excused as a simple act of sexual curiosity (Aljazireh, 1993; Lab, Shields, & Schondel, 1993; Masson, 1995; National Adolescent Perpetrator Network, 1993). Likewise, because many juvenile perpetrators target young children who they know or are related to, it may be more difficult for the victims, the family, or others to pursue the proper legal channels (Aljazireh, 1993). Moreover, criminal sexual acts committed by juveniles were often described historically as an "adolescent adjustment reaction" or the result of an emotional disturbance (National Adolescent Perpetrator Network, 1993, p. 5). This may be especially true of sexual offenses that do not include violence or physical harm (e.g., fondling or voyeurism). Many date rapes may also go unreported. Finally, sexual assaults involving violence or other criminal misconduct may result in criminal charges of a nonsexual nature, such as assault or battery (National Adolescent Perpetrator Network, 1993). Faced with such a myriad of considerations and potential limitations, many researchers estimate that adolescents may be responsible for as much as 25 to 33 percent of all sexual offenses (Masson, 1995; Messerschmidt, 1999; Rutter, Giller, & Hagell, 1998). According to estimates, adolescents are responsible for approximately 50 percent of all sexual abuse of children (Cellini, 1995; Davis & Leitenberg, 1987; Ertl & McNamara, 1997; Fehrenbach, Smith, Monastersky, & Deisher, 1986; Katz, 1990; Kavoussi, Kaplan, & Becker, 1988; Messerschmidt, 1999; Shaw et al., 1993).

DEMOGRAPHICS

Age

A sex offender under age eighteen is a *juvenile* sex offender. However, the time from early childhood to late adolescence is one of tremendous change and development. Therefore, simply defining juvenile sex offenders (or adolescent sex offenders) as being under the age of eighteen conceals pieces of the larger picture. Although most studies have a mean, median, or modal age of fourteen to fifteen years, offender ages range from five to eighteen years in the scholarly literature (Aljazireh, 1993; Awad & Saunders, 1991; Becker, Kaplan, Cunningham-Rathner, & Kavoussi, 1986; Cellini, 1995; Hawkes, Jenkins, & Vizard, 1997; Kahn & Chambers, 1991; Katz, 1990; Kavoussi, Kaplan, & Becker, 1988; Ryan, Miyoshi, Metzner, Krugman, & Fryer, 1996; Smith & Monastersky, 1986; Weinrott, Riggan, & Frothingham, 1997). In other studies, the median age is as young as eleven to thirteen years (Ray & English, 1995; Shaw et al., 1993).

Recent studies have shown the emergence of a differentiation between adolescent sex offenders and *sexually aggressive children* (Araji, 1997). Although this division is clinical and not legal, the latter category usually refers to children twelve years of age and younger that demonstrate some form of sexually deviant behavior. They are not included in this chapter.

Gender

Consistent with most other offending groups, adolescent sex offenders are predominantly male (Aljazireh, 1993; Greenfeld, 1997; Masson, 1995; Rutter, Giller, & Hagell, 1998; Schwartz, 1995). In fact, this dominance is such that one study of 221 adolescent sex offenders found that male perpetrators outnumbered females by a ratio of 20 to 1 (Kahn & Chambers, 1991). Nonetheless, evidence suggests that females account for a small but significant proportion of sex offending with minors (Aljazireh, 1993; Corcoran, Miranda, Tenukas-Steblea, & Taylor, 1999; Schwartz, 1995). Estimates on the number of adolescent female perpetrators range from 1 to 7 percent in some studies (Corcoran et al., 1999; Greenfeld, 1997; Rutter et al., 1998), to a larger minority of 10 percent (Cellini, 1995) or 5 to 15 percent

(Aljazireh, 1993). According to FBI (2002) statistics, females accounted for 9.2 percent of all adolescent arrests for sex offenses (or 1,276 arrests) in 2002. Females accounted for a much smaller percentage of all adolescent arrests for forcible rape (3.2 percent, or 109 arrests).

Considering the popular perception that sex offending in general is an almost exclusively male crime, these low figures and small numbers regarding adolescent females may not be representative of the true extent of female sexual offending. Instead, people may be unwilling or unable to recognize the contribution of women to sexual offending. Thus, sex offenses committed by females may be underreported. Similarly, activities involving young children that are traditionally performed by females, including bathing or dressing children, may serve as a covert outlet for sexually offensive behavior (Groth & Birnbaum, 1979; Travin, Cullen, & Protter, 1990).

Ethnicity

Although criminal justice statistics show that racial minorities are more likely to be charged and incarcerated for sex offenses than majority adolescents, research on adolescent sex offenders has used predominantly white samples. This is probably the result of sampling methods, which more often draw subjects from treatment settings rather than the criminal justice system. Racial stratification in these studies ranges from "typical study participant" to 79 percent white compared with only 5 percent African American (Kahn & Chambers, 1991; Katz, 1990). Nonetheless, a handful of studies with samples are comprised of more African Americans than Whites (e.g., Kavoussi et al., 1988; Becker et al., 1986). There does not appear to be any significant differences in race or ethnicity regarding adolescent sex offenders.

DEVIANT SEXUAL BEHAVIOR CHARACTERISTICS

The Offense

The types of sexual acts perpetrated by adolescent sex offenders differ from study to study. Becker (1988) found that in a sample of offenders who had also been sexually abused, the most common types of deviant sexual acts were genital fondling, anal penetration, and rubbing bodies. The most common nongenital offenses were voyeurism, frottage (without genital contact), and exhibitionism. Similarly, in an analysis of intake data for 1,616 sexually offending youths referred to treatment programs, 68 percent of the adolescents had committed one or more acts of vaginal or anal penetration and/or oral-genital contact (Ryan et al., 1996). Likewise, Fehrenbach et al. (1986) reported that the most common offense was fondling (59 percent of 297 adolescent male offenders), followed by rape (23 percent), and exhibitionism (11 percent).

In terms of more general criminality, approximately half of all adolescent sex offenders commit crimes of a nonsexual nature in addition to their sexual offense, especially among those offenders committing a sexual offense involving a major assault (Fehrenbach et al., 1986; Rutter et al., 1998; Ryan et al., 1996). This supports the notion that, for many adolescent sex offenders, sexual misconduct is just one specific outlet in a more general pattern of delinquency.

Victims

Once again, it must be stated that adolescents are responsible for approximately 50 percent of all cases of child sexual abuse. It is not surprising then that the median age of victims tends to be quite young. In some studies, the median age of victims is seven to nine years (Cellini, 1995; Shaw et al., 1993; Smith & Monastersky, 1986). In another study, Kahn and Chambers (1991) found that 95 percent of the victims were between one to eighteen years of age, with 35 percent being between the ages of three to four years. Fehrenbach et al. (1986) reported that 62 percent of victims were aged twelve years or younger and 44 percent were under age six.

In these assaults involving young children, the victim is generally a known acquaintance or relative, usually a younger full or half-sibling and sometimes a cousin (Awad & Saunders, 1991; Davis & Leitenberg, 1987; Kahn & Chambers, 1991; Katz, 1990; Smith & Monastersky, 1986). Male adolescent sex offenders are more likely to choose female victims, yet when the victim is a young child, more males are victimized (Aljazireh, 1993; Davis & Leitenberg, 1987; Ryan et al., 1996). The most common offense situation for adolescent sex offenders involving younger children is babysitting (Fehrenbach et al., 1986; Righthand & Welch, 2001; Smith & Monastersky, 1986). When adolescents do rape adults, the victim is usually a stranger. "Noncontact" offenses, such as voyeurism and obscene phone calls, also victimize strangers (Aljazireh, 1993).

Recidivism

Study after study has shown that adolescent sex offenders are more likely to reoffend nonsexually than with another sexual offense. This statement is supported by numerous studies and literature reviews (Righthand & Welch, 2001). Hagan and Gust-Brey (2000), for example, followed fifty adolescent sex offenders for ten years after their release from a treatment facility. During the follow-up period, 12 percent reoffended sexually, 66 percent reoffended nonsexually, and 22 percent did not reoffend. In general, sexual reoffending is reported for approximately 8 to 14 percent of adolescent sex offenders (Righthand & Welch, 2001).

Of course, besides illustrating the very low rates of sexual recidivism, these studies also speak to the tendency of these adolescents to engage in nonsexual delinquency. In combination, these two outcomes (low sexual recidivism and high nonsexual offending) suggest that the especially young age of victims is a function of opportunity and availability rather than preference (as with adult pedophiles). This is probably accurate for many adolescent sex offenders, especially since these juveniles often more closely resemble juvenile nonsexual offenders than they do adult pedophiles.

Nevertheless, it is worth mentioning that there is a small body of research noting differences between adolescents who target children and those who assault peers or older victims. In one study, the single predictor of sexual recidivism was a sexual interest in children (Worling & Curwen, 2000). In a different study, Awad and Saunders (1991) compared twenty-four adolescent "sexual assaulters," forty-five juvenile child molesters (those with victims four or more years younger than they were), and twenty-four nonsexual juvenile delinquents. They found that the victims of the adolescent child molesters were more likely to have known the offender prior to being molested, to have been repeatedly molested, and to be male. These adolescent child molesters were also more likely to demonstrate sexually deviant behavior before the age of twelve, less likely to use or threaten violence against their victims, and more likely to have been sexually abused. In a study comparing adolescent males who sexually assaulted children to those who assaulted older females (pubescent and postpubescent), Hunter, Figueredo, Malsmuth, & Becker (2003) found that adolescents targeting children had greater deficits in psychosocial functioning, used less aggression in their assault, and were more likely to victimize relatives.

Studies such as this suggest that there may be two important subtypes of adolescent sex offenders—youths who commit sex crimes only in addition to other delinquent behaviors and those youths who are truly sexually deviant (Becker, 1988). This differentiation may be important for assessing needs, developing interventions, and predicting recidivism. This area needs more research, especially longitudinal studies with large samples of juvenile sex offenders drawn from residential care, criminal justice, and community-based treatment settings.

TRAUMATIC VICTIMIZATION HISTORY

When describing adolescent sex offenders, one of the most recurring and consistent research findings is the unusually high incidence of sexual or physical abuse victimization among these youths. Generally, estimates on the percentage of adolescent sex offenders who have experienced sexual abuse in their own childhood range from 9 to 47 percent in some studies (Aljazireh, 1993; Kahn & Chambers, 1991; Ryan et al., 1996; Schwartz, 1995), to estimates as high as 50 to 94 percent in others (Becker & Hunter, 1997; Corcoran et al., 1999; Katz, 1990; Ray & English, 1995; Weinrott et al., 1997). In one study, adolescents who molested children were more likely to have been sexually abused than adolescents who assaulted older victims or other adolescent delinquents (Awad & Saunders, 1991).

Likewise, estimates on the incidence of physical abuse among this population range from approximately 13 to 47 percent (Aljazireh, 1993; Ryan et al., 1996). Regarding both sexual *and* physical abuse, one study of seventy-two children with sexual behavior problems found that approximately 59 percent of boys and 63 percent of girls were victims of both physical and sexual abuse (Pithers Gray, Busconi, Houchens, 1998). Ray and English (1995) reported that approximately

90 percent of the sex offenders in their sample were multiple-abuse victims (usually physical and sexual abuse). Adolescent sex offenders may experience high levels of family violence (Pithers, Gray, Busconi, & Houchens, 1998). Davis and Leitenberg (1987), for example, found that 79 percent of adolescent sex offenders had witnessed violence at home compared to only 20 percent of nonviolent juvenile offenders.

The Family

In addition to high rates of family violence, research on the families of adolescent sex offenders has revealed several other problems. For example, adolescent sex offenders and their mothers have reported high rates of neurotic symptoms (Blaske, Borduin, Henggler, & Mann, 1989). These families have also been shown to be highly distressed and somewhat isolated (Pithers et al., 1998). Moreover, after reviewing the literature, Burton and Meezan (2004) concluded that the families of adolescent sex offenders are characterized by difficult relationships among family members and a lack of parental nurturance and supervision of the offender. Adolescent sex offenders are also exposed to higher levels of criminality and more substance abuse within their family (Burton & Meezan, 2004).

COGNITIVE AND PSYCHIATRIC CHARACTERISTICS

One of the most frequent psychiatric disorders in samples of adolescent sex offenders is conduct disorder. Although this is a common disorder in juvenile offending groups across a variety of offense categories, estimates on the incidence of conduct disorder among adolescent sex offenders generally range from 39 to 60 percent depending on the diagnostic techniques and criteria being used by the clinician (Kavoussi et al., 1988). Regarding other specific psychiatric diagnoses, research indicates that many adolescent sex offenders meet the diagnostic criteria for antisocial personality disorder, other personality disorders, a major depressive disorder, or posttraumatic stress disorder (PTSD) (Shaw et al., 1993; Cellini, 1995; Corcoran et al., 1999; Schwartz, 1995). ADHD has also been linked to sexually offensive behavior (Becker et al., 1986), especially among offenders under age thirteen (Fago, 1999).

Socially, many adolescent sex offenders are marked by a genuine lack of empathy for others, especially their victims (Corcoran et al., 1999). This lack of empathy may allow the offender to maintain sexual arousal during the attack despite the victim's pain or pleas for the attack to stop. The lack of empathy also allows the attacker to ignore the tremendous violation of the victim's personal space during and after the assault (Corcoran et al., 1999). Along the same lines, adolescent sex offenders also demonstrate problems controlling their impulses and anger, problems of low self-esteem, high anxiety, less emotional bonding with peers, unhealthy and inappropriate social skills, social isolation, substantial fear of peer rejection, and a sense of powerlessness (Cellini, 1995; Corcoran et al., 1999; Katz, 1990; Miner & Crimmins, 1997; Schwartz, 1995; Shaw et al., 1993). Adolescent sex offenders are also twice as likely to be aroused by environmental stimuli than individuals in the general population are. This "hypersensitivity" may help to explain the lack of proper impulse control (Corcoran et al., 1999).

SOCIAL AND ENVIRONMENTAL DYNAMICS

Education and School Performance

Most adolescent sex offenders attend school and achieve at least average grades (Cellini, 1995; Miner & Crimmins, 1997). For example, Fehrenbach et al. (1986) found that in a sample of 305 adolescent sex offenders, 55 percent were on schedule in terms of their grade placement while 2 percent were ahead of schedule, 27 percent were behind in school, and 5 percent had dropped out of school completely. However, looking beyond academics, a significant number of juvenile sex offenders demonstrate problems such as truancy, classroom behavioral problems, and learning disabilities (Kahn & Chambers, 1991; Cellini, 1995; Becker & Hunter, 1997). These difficulties, depending on the particular study, have been estimated in 30 to 50 percent of adolescent sex offenders.

Adolescent sex offenders often perceive their teachers as having excessively negative attitudes toward them (Miner & Crimmins, 1997). A substantial proportion also reports being socially isolated (Fehrenbach et al., 1986). Along with deficits in social skills, such social isolation has been shown to be a risk factor that may predispose some adolescents to molest younger children (Katz, 1990). In sum, however, no universal academic or social markers for adolescent sexual offending are available, leading Cellini (1995) to conclude that the social characteristics of juvenile sex offenders would seem to range from "popular athletes and/or academically gifted students to tough, delinquent youth" (p. 6-3).

Substance Use and Abuse

Although alcohol plays a significant role in adult offending (sexually or otherwise), a limited body of research has assessed this problem among adolescent sex offenders (Schwartz, 1995; Becker & Hunter, 1997). One review of the literature found studies reporting that as few as 3.4 percent and as much as 72 percent of adolescent sex offenders were under the influence of alcohol and drugs at the time of their offense (Lightfoot & Barbaree, 1993). Kahn and Chambers (1991) found that 37 percent of their sample had a problem with substance abuse, and Becker and Stein (1991) reported that 61 percent of their sample admitted using alcohol although 49 percent stated that alcohol had "no effect on their sexual arousal." Nonetheless, this study did find a significant relationship between alcohol use and a higher number of victims. This relationship was not true for the 39 percent of the sample admitting to drug use.

Yokley (1999) suggests that adolescent sex offenders exhibit numerous similarities to substance abusers in terms of personality and behavior. To support this, Yokley found that adolescent sex offenders tend to be multiple abusers (e.g., of people, property, and substances) with a substance abuse rate of approximately 8 percent in the sample from which these conclusions were drawn. Considering this finding, in conjunction with the varied reports of alcohol use in other studies, whether or not substance use is really a risk factor for offending must be assessed. It may simply be that substance abuse and dependence are just another problem demonstrated by these already deeply troubled adolescents (Lightfoot & Barbaree, 1993).

ASSESSMENT

Lanyon (2001) suggests that a very general model of assessment may have the greatest utility. Given the complicated nature of sex offending, such a general model would be applicable across a variety of settings and assessment situations. Although Lanyon is describing the assessment of adult sex offenders rather than juveniles, this approach may have special relevance for assessing a heterogeneous group such as adolescent sex offenders. Unfortunately, such a model has not yet been established for this group.

A review of several previously published models for assessing adolescent sex offenders (Becker & Hunter, 1997; Perry & Orchard, 1992; Rich, 2003; Lane, 1997; Will, 1999) does reveal some fundamental commonalities. For instance, each model highlights the importance of a comprehensive assessment that includes a clinical interview with the adolescent, the administration of standardized assessment measures, an interview with the offending youth's family, and an assessment of the adolescent's risk for reoffending. In the absence of a universally accepted general assessment model, these shared components provide a useful framework for the forthcoming discussion of the assessment process.

Prior to exploring any particulars of assessment, however, it is critical to highlight that the assessment must be *comprehensive*. Sexually offensive conduct is really one behavioral piece of a larger, more complicated problem (Perry & Orchard, 1992). Thus, to fully understand adolescent sex offenders and their offending and to develop appropriate intervention plans, data must be collected across a variety of topics and with a variety of tools. Without such a comprehensive approach, vital information may be missed that could later derail or sabotage treatment. Likewise, the provision of any services without first conducting a complete and thorough assessment is both unethical and potentially harmful to the offender, his or her family, and the community.

With that said, the duty to perform such a comprehensive assessment can be understandably overwhelming. Frankly, it can be dizzying to think about the myriad of different avenues and axes for information gathering. For these reasons, the assessment process must be approached with some structure and basic organization. To this end, perhaps Rich (2003) provides the most useful conceptualization of a comprehensive assessment. In Rich's structure, the following are five basic components of the assessment process.

1. Psychosocial assessment
2. Psychological evaluation
3. Physiological measurement
4. Psychiatric evaluation
5. Risk assessment

Each of these pieces will be discussed later in this chapter.

The Clinical Interview

Much of the assessment of an adolescent sex offender will take place within the bounds of a *semistructured clinical interview.* This meeting with the adolescent is not only an opportunity for asking questions, gathering information, and administering assessment instruments, but also an opportunity to build rapport with the youth and engage him or her in assessment and treatment. Techniques for building rapport include acknowledging that the interview may be anxiety provoking for the adolescent, complimenting the adolescent when he or she discloses details of the offense, and making a distinction between the adolescent as a sex offender and the adolescent as a person (Perry & Orchard, 1992).

The clinical interview also provides an occasion to assess the quality, context, and meaning of the adolescent's statements by adding the element of personal observation (Rich, 2003). For all of these reasons, a well-developed and comprehensive interview may be the most important tool for assessing adolescent sex offenders (Perry & Orchard, 1992).

In conducting a clinical interview, the interviewer should maintain a nonjudgmental attitude that is respectful of the adolescent but also aware of the youth's level of denial and the potential power struggles that may emerge in the interview (Lane, 1997). The offending youth will generally be motivated to establish power and maintain control during the assessment process. This motivation may be manifested through the adolescent's denial, repeated lying, minimizing and rationalizing of his or her offensive acts, being uncooperative, or becoming agitated during the interview (Perry & Orchard, 1992).

When encountering such reactions, the interviewer must maintain control of the interview while still encouraging the adolescent to participate honestly and openly. Perry and Orchard (1992) suggest presenting collateral documents to counter the adolescent's denial. They also state that use of a structured interview helps to keep the assessment focused. Structured interviewing increases the clinical and formal nature of the interview, thus adding distance between the interviewer and interviewee. This may decrease the adolescent's feelings of embarrassment and anxiety when asked to discuss personal topics, such as his or her own sexual experiences, feelings, and arousal patterns (Will, 1999).

The interviewer should begin with introductions, an orientation to the assessment process, a discussion of confidentiality, and an explanation of the limits to confidentiality. A common language for sexual organs and acts must also be established (Will, 1999). This will curb future misunderstandings and miscommunication while adding more structure to the interview. Moreover, at least part of the interview (if not all) should be conducted apart from the adolescent's parents or other family since their presence may inhibit the adolescent from openly discussing difficult or embarrassing topics.

As the interview moves forward from this point, there is no consensus regarding which topics to cover first. Will (1999) believes that a good interview begins with less threatening topics then gradually climbs to more difficult ones. Conversely, Perry and Orchard (1992) argue that beginning with less threatening topics only increases the adolescent's anxiety since he or she now must wait and wonder when the stressful topics will be addressed. Instead, they suggest assessing the adolescent's current referral offense and sexual offending history first. Regardless of assessment organization, the interview should be driven by one's knowledge of the empirical research in the field, one's own personal style, and a clear understanding of the expectations that one's agency or setting has for the assessment. In many settings, there will be a standard protocol for data collection and information gathering. To view a sample interview guide, please refer to Perry and Orchard (1997, Appendix A, p. 111).

Preassessment Considerations

Before pushing forward with the actual assessment, the vital first step in any assessment is a review of all available records and collateral reports related to the adolescent and his or her offense (Lane, 1997; Will, 1999). Besides being an invaluable source of information, these documents may suggest areas for follow-up inquiry during the subsequent stages of assessment. In addition, these records can be a powerful tool in the assessment and treatment of the offender's denial. *Denial,* a common defense mechanism for offenders in general and adolescent sex offenders in particular, may be a denial of the assault, a denial of ever harming or violating others, a denial of past offensive behavior, or another type of denial (Perry & Orchard, 1992; Rich, 2003). In working with such denial, a significant part of both the assessment process and later treatment will be comparing the offender's recounting of the sexual offense to information stated in collateral documents such as police reports and victim statements. Without congruence between the offender's version of the events and these other recorded versions, treatment will be more difficult and most likely ineffective. Similarly, in confronting the adolescent with these discrepancies, the opportunity arises to assess the level of responsibility that the adolescent is assuming as well as how he or she handles disagreement, conflict, and criticism (Lane, 1997). Other examples of collateral reports include court documents, school records, and reports prepared by other mental health professionals who may have worked previously with the adolescent.

In addition to recognizing and confronting denial, *cultural issues* must also be assessed. After all, as sexual norms can differ across cultural groups, so too do views on sexual behavior and sexuality (Lane, 1997). Thus, by placing information gathered throughout the assessment process into a cultural context, the interviewer may develop a better understanding of the adolescent's views on such topics as sex, social relationships, or family situation. Understanding the influence of culture and ethnicity may also help the interviewer comprehend behavior during the interview, including the youth's levels of denial, trust and comfort, views of family, and so on.

Psychosocial Assessment

A psychosocial assessment is an assessment of the offender's developmental, contextual, psychological, social, and relational history. This includes a Mental Status Examination (MSE) (Rich, 2003). In keeping with Perry and Orchard's (1992) recommendations, the first topic to cover would be the psychosexual evaluation. This assesses the adolescent's sexual feelings, knowledge, interests, and experiences (including consensual sexual activity and dating). The content and frequency of sexual fantasy must also be assessed since the adolescent may fantasize about various sexual acts before actually engaging in such behaviors (Becker & Hunter, 1997).

Most important, the adolescent's current referral offense as well as a recounting of past sexually offensive behavior (both reported and unreported) must be assessed. When inquiring about the current offense of record and past sexual deviance, ask detailed questions about each offense and note similarities in each that suggest a pattern of sexually abusive activity. Some key points to focus on are level of aggression, frequency of sexually abusive behaviors, preferred victim type, and sexual arousal patterns (Lane, 1997).

Other areas of evaluation include developmental history, family characteristics, social relationships, substance use, and a traumatic victimization history. Paying special attention to those attributes with an empirical connection to adolescent sexual offending, consider the adolescent's exposure to family violence, the type of discipline used in the family, past and current nonsexual delinquent behavior, previous experiences with mental health treatment, the adolescent's own sexual or physical abuse victimization, and peer relationships. Given the importance of each of these topics, utilization of a structured interview schedule helps to insure that no relevant areas are missed or forgotten.

Rich (2003) also promotes including the MSE in the psychosocial assessment. This popular brief assessment tool gauges the adolescent's mental condition at the time of the interview. Based on interviewer impressions, the MSE assesses the adolescent's physical appearance, mood, thought content, speech, and concentration, among other factors. For more information on the MSE, please refer to Trzepacz and Baker (1993).

In considering the use of standardized psychological measures, use only those instruments that have been found to have acceptable reliability and validity with adolescent sex offenders. Although there are countless tools for use with adult sex offenders, only a handful offer empirical support for use on adolescent sex offenders. In psychosexual assessment, the Adolescent Sexual Interest Card Sort (ASIC) is a sixty-four-item self-report measure of sexual interest and arousal (Hunter, Becker, & Kaplan, 1995). The Math Tech Sex Education Test (Kirby, 1984, as cited by Beckett, 1999) is another option. This test is designed to assess adolescents' attitudes and beliefs toward sex and relationships. Phallometric assessment (the measurement of penile responses to different stimuli) has been widely used with both adult and adolescent sex offenders. However, research offers only limited support for the use of this assessment technique with adolescent sex offenders (Becker & Hunter, 1997). Finally, other instruments are available for measuring drug and alcohol abuse, rape attitudes, and victim empathy. For an in-depth review of these instruments, please refer to Beckett (1999).

Family Assessment

In addition to the items previously listed, another important element of a comprehensive psychosocial assessment is an interview with the offender's family. Besides being a crucial source of collateral information, this is also an opportunity to engage the family in the assessment process as well as establish a working relationship for treatment. The timing of the family assessment is somewhat flexible, although the assessor may need to meet with the parents first if their consent is required before initiating contact with the adolescent. Assessors must know and understand all consent laws and guidelines pertaining to assessment and pursue the proper channels to obtain consent as needed. Regardless, meet with the family sooner rather than later since part of the family assessment requires explaining and orienting the family to the full assessment process.

Similar to initializing an assessment with the adolescent, family assessment should begin with introductions, a review of the interviewer's qualifications and experience working with adolescent sex offenders, and an explanation of confidentiality and its limits. Since many family members will be confused, scared, or have misperceptions about the youth's offending, interviewers should educate the family about adolescent sex offenders and offending patterns (Perry & Orchard, 1992).

In terms of data collection in family assessment, family members should be asked about their perceptions of both the adolescent's sexual offense as well as the overall functioning of the adolescent. The family should also be encouraged to provide information on the roles and expectations for each family member, any abuse or violence occurring in the home, substance use or abuse in the family, other incidents of sexual offending in the nuclear or extended family, and the family's attitudes about counseling and mental health treatment (Perry & Orchard, 1992). Family involvement is an important aspect of treatment. Therefore, members should be encouraged to participate in treatment planning and be committed to following through with the treatment plan.

Psychological Evaluation

Similar to psychosocial assessment, multiple areas should be considered when undertaking a comprehensive psychological evaluation, including educational measures, level of intelligence, and various tests of functioning, attitudes, and interests (Rich, 2003). In approaching this evaluation, recognize that not all adolescent sex offenders have severe psychological problems (Gray & Pithers, 1993). Given the heterogeneity that defines this population, psychological tests may not expose a major mental disorder, an acute psychosis, or another grave psychological impairment. Although offenders should be screened for psychological disorders, a psychological evaluation driven by empirical research will probably have better utility for identifying areas for treatment and intervention.

In assessing educational factors, for example, one should assess for possible learning disabilities. Correspondingly, the WAIS-R is an instrument for assessing intelligence that has been promoted for use on adolescent sex offenders (Perry & Orchard, 1992). Keeping in mind that poor school performance does not always equate to low intelligence or a learning disability, academic and discipline records from the adolescent's school may yield useful information about possible educational and learning difficulties.

Moving now to the assessment of functioning, attitudes, and interests, the Adolescent Cognition Scale (Becker & Hunter, 1997) is a thirty-two-item forced-choice inventory measuring the adolescent's number of cognitive distortions. The empirical literature on adolescent sex offenders also suggests that a comprehensive psychological evaluation must include the adolescent's level of self-esteem, social isolation, peer relationships, feelings of anger, and social skills. In measuring social skills, social competence, and peer relationships, Beckett (1999) recommends a modified version of the Fear of Negative Evaluation Scale (Watson & Friend, 1964, as cited by Beckett, 1999) and the Child Assertive Behavior Scale (Mitchelson & Wood, 1982, as cited by Beckett, 1999). For measuring self-esteem, Beckett recommends the Harter Self-Esteem Questionnaire (Harter, 1985, as cited by Beckett, 1999). This thirty-six-item questionnaire measures overall self-esteem in addition to focusing on academic achievement, social acceptance, athletic ability, and physical appearance.

Valid and reliable instruments measuring feelings, attitudes, and perceptions in adolescents are far more common than instruments assessing sexual deviance and risk for reoffending. The scales previously cited are just a sampling of such instruments and are included here because they have been referenced or developed for use with adolescent sex offenders. For a list of psychological tests recommended for use in forensic interviews with juveniles, please refer to Ackerman (1999). In addition to using standardized instruments, assess each of these topics with open-ended questions during a clinical interview. For instance, the adolescent can be asked to describe his or her friends or to describe how he or she feels about himself or herself.

Psychiatric Evaluation

Building on the psychological evaluation previously described, a psychiatric evaluation will determine the need for psychiatric medications (Rich, 2003). Depending on the adolescent's psychiatric diagnosis, medication may be an important first step in treatment, especially if the adolescent experiences behaviors or cognitive impairments that will interfere with counseling or other treatments.

Physiological Measurement

Physiological, or psychophysiological, measures examine the connection of mental and bodily processes. Examples relevant to adolescent sex offenders include physical reactions such as changes in blood pressure, pulse rate, breathing, or penile arousal in response to different sexual scenarios, sexual stimuli, or confrontation. The aforementioned phallometric assessments are a form of physiological measure. Another measure of this type is a polygraph test, which attempts to measure honesty by monitoring bodily changes during questioning. Though this technique is frequently used with adolescent sex offenders, little evidence supports its utility, reliability, or validity with this population (Righthand & Welch, 2001). Although some informal physiological measurement may be taken as part of the traditional clinical interview (e.g., noting changes in breathing when discussing particular topics), more formal measures require specialized devices and trained administrators. This may limit their accessibility for many mental health professionals.

Risk Assessment

Risk assessment is attempting to predict an adolescent's likelihood of future sexual offending or delinquency. Although research has done a fair job in identifying common traits and characteristics among adolescent sex offenders, few characteristics have been consistently linked to sexual reoffending in the empirical literature (Righthand & Welch, 2001). Likewise (or maybe consequently), no empirically based risk assessment instruments are available (Becker & Hunter, 1997; Beckett, 1999). Comparatively, several such instruments are available for adult male sex offenders. Suggestions for future research then may be developing predictive instruments for use with adolescent sex offenders as well as evaluating the utility of existing measures.

Without the availability of reliable and valid instrumentation, Becker and Hunter (1997, pp. 192-193) suggest six criteria on which to formulate a risk assessment. These criteria relate not just to level of risk for reoffending, but are also useful in identifying those adolescents needing inpatient or residential care as opposed to outpatient treatment. The six criteria are:

1. number of arrests (more arrests = greater risk),
2. number of victims (more victims = greater risk),
3. level of psychopathy (a history of conduct-disordered behavior = greater risk),
4. distortions in thinking patterns (more cognitive distortions = greater risk),
5. type of offense (offenses involving premeditation, the use of force, or penetration = greater risk), and
6. the degree of compulsivity and deviant arousal (a higher degree of either = greater risk).

In addition to these criteria, risk assessment should also incorporate an evaluation of the adolescent's *motivation for treatment* and willingness to participate in treatment (Cellini, 1995; Will, 1999). Such information may directly predict the youth's successful or unsuccessful completion of treatment as well as his or her risk for reoffending. When assessing motivation for treatment, consider the level of denial that the adolescent exhibits about his or her offending behaviors, the frequency of the offending behaviors, level of empathy for the victim or victims, and self-professed interest in receiving treatment (Cellini, 1995; Lane, 1997; Perry & Orchard, 1992).

TREATMENT

Despite the low rate of sexual recidivism by adolescent sex offenders, relapse prevention is still the primary goal of any intervention. In reaching this goal, several specific objectives have been identified. These include confronting and reducing denial and increasing acceptance of responsibility, increasing victim empathy, cognitive restructuring, decreasing deviant sexual arousal, instruction in anger management, sex education, training in vocational and living skills, and the development of social and impulse control skills (Becker & Hunter, 1997; Ertl & McNamara, 1997). Another important treatment objective is working with the family. Besides promoting healthier relationships between family members, interventions involving adolescent sex offenders and their families will also increase the family's knowledge and understanding of sex offending thus making recidivism less likely (Burnham, Moss, deBelle, & Jamieson, 1999).

Currently, the treatment landscape is dominated by a cognitive behavioral orientation (Burton & Meezan, 2004). Although there is increasing evidence that this practice model is effective for treating both adult (Hall, 1995) and adolescent sex offenders (Burton & Meezan, 2004), Rich (2003) endorses a theoretically integrated model of treatment for adolescent sex offenders. Rich's model promotes using cognitive-behavioral interventions for relapse prevention and cognitive restructuring while also incorporating a psychoeducational component for skill-building, a psychodynamic approach for reaching insight and discovering feelings, and a psychiatric method in regard to psychopharmacology and medical care.

Regardless of differing opinions or divergent practice orientations, adolescent sex offenders are a heterogeneous group. Although this may complicate the development of a universally accepted treatment model, it would certainly seem to support the use of an individually based treatment model. This is accomplished by using the information gained through an evidence-based assessment to develop a treatment plan that will address the specific needs of the individual adolescent and his or her family.

CASE EXAMPLE

Anthony, a sixteen-year old African-American male, was suspended from his high school after grabbing a female classmate's vagina and squeezing her breast in the hallway between classes. Believing that the school's disciplinary actions were not harsh enough, the assaulted female's mother filed a formal complaint with the local police department. Anthony has been under the supervision of Child Protective Services since he was removed from his mother's care at the age of ten. His mother admitted to physically abusing Anthony and readily surrendered her parental rights. At the time of the assault, Anthony was living with his fourth foster care family. However, fearing for the safety of their other children, the family insisted that he be removed from their care following this incident. Anthony was placed with a new family and, after agreeing to participate in mental health treatment, the assaulted female and her mother agreed not to pursue any further legal action. Although he had been arrested twice before for petty theft, Anthony did not have any juvenile convictions or a known history of sexually assaultive behavior. He was also not considered a discipline problem in school, where he was enrolled in mostly remedial courses and earned average grades.

Treatment Plan

In developing a treatment plan for Anthony, the primary long-term goal is to eliminate further sexually offensive behavior. Other long-term goals include eliminating Anthony's nonsexual delinquent behavior, reducing the negative impact that his own physical abuse and subsequent abandonment has on his daily life, and developing appropriate healthy relationships with family members and peers. A final long-term goal is that Anthony must accept responsibility for all of his actions, especially those that hurt or violate others.

To reach these goals, several short-term objectives must be met. First, Anthony must confront his denial of the assault. A key step in this objective requires that Anthony candidly describe the assault and openly identify his offending actions. A second short-term objective is that Anthony must get involved in a program that will teach him appropriate social skills. Third, Anthony needs counseling to address his history of physical abuse, his abandonment by his birth mother, and the causes and issues underlying his sexual misconduct. Finally, Anthony's new foster family may benefit from education on adolescent sexual offending and relapse prevention. Anthony and his foster family should also participate in counseling together to increase their sense of family unity and bonding.

The delivery of services to accomplish these objectives will depend on several variables, including the presence of specialized adolescent sex offender treatment programs or other specialized service providers in the area in addition to the availability and accessibility of complementary mental health services. Regardless of these factors, Anthony must complete a comprehensive assessment to determine his exact needs and treatment requirements. Given Anthony's background, assessing his history of abuse and other acts of sexual deviance that he may have committed prior to his current offense is important. Moreover, if Anthony needs services from several different providers, his case manager or primary mental health care provider will need to closely monitor his attendance and progress at these other locations. Treatment is also best provided by professionals who have both experience working with adolescent sex offenders and a solid understanding of their characteristics, problems, and needs.

REFERENCES

Ackerman, M. J. (1999). *Essentials of forensic psychological assessment.* New York: John Wiley & Sons, Inc.

Aljazireh, L. (1993). Historical, environmental, and behavioral correlates of sexual offending by male adolescents: A critical review. *Behavioral Sciences and the Law, 11,* 423-440.

Araji, S. K. (1997). Sexually aggressive children: Social demographics and psychological characteristics. In S. K. Araji (Ed.), *Sexually aggressive children: Coming to understand them* (pp. 50-54). Thousand Oaks, CA: Sage Publications.

Awad, G. A. & Saunders, E. B. (1991). Male adolescent sexual assaulters: Clinical observations. *Journal of Interpersonal Violence, 6*(4), 446-460.

Becker, J. V. (1988). The effects of child sexual abuse on adolescent sexual offenders. In G. Wyatt & G. Powell (Eds.), *Lasting Effects of Child Sexual Abuse* (pp. 193-207). Newbury Park: Sage Publications.

Becker, J. V. & Hunter Jr., J. A. (1997). Understanding and treating child and adolescent sexual offenders. In T. H. Ollendick & R. J. Prinz (Eds.), *Advances in clinical child psychology* (Vol. 19, pp. 177-197). New York: Plenum Press.

Becker, J. V., Kaplan, M. S., Cunningham-Rathner, J., & Kavoussi, R. J. (1986). Characteristics of adolescent incest sexual perpetrators: Preliminary findings. *Journal of Family Violence, 1*(1), 85-97.

Becker, J. V. & Stein, R. M. (1991). Is sexual erotica associated with sexual deviance in adolescent males? *International Journal of Law and Psychiatry, 14*(1/2), 85-95.

Beckett, R. (1999). Evaluation of adolescent sexual abusers. In M. Erooga & H. Masson (Eds.), *Children and young people who sexually abuse others: Challenges and responses* (pp. 204-224). London, United Kingdom: Routledge.

Blaske, D. M., Borduin, C. M., Henggeler, S. W., & Mann, B. J. (1989). Individual, family, and peer characteristics of adolescent sex offenders and assaultive offenders. *Developmental Psychology, 25*(5), 846-855.

Burnham, J., Moss, J., deBelle, J., & Jamieson, R. (1999). Working with families of young sexual abusers: Assessment and intervention issues. In M. Erooga & H. Masson (Eds.), *Children and young people who sexually abuse others: Challenges and responses* (pp. 146-167). London, United Kingdom: Routledge.

Burton, D. L. & Meezan, W. (2004). Revisiting recent research on social learning theory as in etiological proposition for sexually abusive male adolescents. *Journal of Evidence-Based Social Work, 1*(1), 41-80.

Cellini, H. R. (1995). Assessment and treatment of the adolescent sexual offender. In B. K. Schwartz & H. R. Cellini (Eds.), *The sex offender* (Vol. 1, pp. 6-1–6-12). Kingston, NJ: Civic Research Institute.

Corcoran, C., Miranda, A., Tenukas-Steblea, K., & Taylor, B. (1999). Inclusion of the family in the treatment of juvenile sexual abuse perpetrators. In B. K.

Schwartz (Ed.), *The sex offender* (Vol. 3, pp. 17-9–17-10). Kingston, NJ: Civic Research Institute.

Davis, G. E. & Leitenberg, H. (1987). Adolescent sex offenders. *Psychological Bulletin, 101*(3), 417-427.

Ertl, M. A. & McNamara, J. R. (1997). Treatment of juvenile sex offenders: A review of the literature. *Child and Adolescent Social Work, 14*(3), 199-221.

Fago, D. (1999). Comorbidity of attention-deficit/hyperactivity disorder in sexually aggressive children and adolescents. In B. K. Schwartz (Ed.), *The sex offender* (Vol. 3, pp. 16-1–16-7). Kingston, NJ: Civic Research Institute.

Federal Bureau of Investigation. (2002). *Crime in the United States: Persons arrested 2002*. Washington, DC: Author.

Fehrenbach, P. A., Smith, W., Monastersky, C., & Deisher, R. (1986). Adolescent sexual offenders: Offender and offense characteristics. *American Journal of Orthopsychiatry, 56*(2), 225-233.

Gray, A. S. & Pithers, W. D. (1993). Relapse prevention with sexually aggressive adolescents and children: Expanding treatment and supervision. In H. E. Barbaree, W. L. Marshall, & S. M. Hudson (Eds.), *The juvenile sex offender* (pp. 289-320). New York: The Guilford Press.

Greenfeld, L. (1997). *Sex offenses and offenders*. United States Department of Justice, Bureau of Justice Statistics. Washington, DC: USGPO.

Groth, A. N. & Birnbaum, J. (1979). *Men who rape: The psychology of the offender*. New York: Plenum.

Hagan, M. P. & Gust-Brey, K. L. (2000). A ten-year longitudinal study of adolescent perpetrators of sexual assault against children. *Journal of Offender Rehabilitation, 31*(1/2), 117-126.

Hall, G. C. (1995). Sexual offender recidivism revisited: A meta-analysis of recent treatment studies. *Journal of Consulting and Clinical Psychology, 63*(5), 802-809.

Hawkes, C., Jenkins, J., & Vizard, E. (1997). Roots of sexual violence in children and adolescents. In V. Varma (Ed.), *Violence in children and adolescents* (pp. 84-102). Bristol, PA: Jessica Kingsley Publishers.

Hunter Jr., J. A., Becker, J. V., & Kaplan, M. S. (1995). The adolescent sexual interest card sort: Test-Retest reliability and concurrent validity in relation to phallometric assessment. *Archives of Sexual Behavior, 24*(5), 555-561.

Hunter Jr., J. A., Figueredo, A. J., Malamuth, N. M., & Becker, J. V. (2003). Juvenile sex offenders: Towards the development of a typology. *Sexual Abuse: A Journal of Research and Treatment, 15*(1), 27-48.

Kahn, T. J. & Chambers, H. J. (1991). Assessing reoffense risk with juvenile sexual offenders. *Child Welfare, 70*(3), 333-345.

Katz, R. (1990). Psychological adjustment in adolescent child molesters. *Child Welfare & Neglect, 14*, 567-575.

Kavoussi, R. J., Kaplan, M. S., & Becker, J. V. (1988). Psychiatric diagnoses in adolescent sex offenders. *Journal of the American Academy of Child and Adolescent Psychiatry, 27*(2), 241-243.

Lab, S. P., Shields, G., & Schondel, C. (1993). Research note: An evaluation of juvenile sexual offender treatment. *Crime & Delinquency, 39*(4), 543-553.

Lane, S. (1997). Assessment of sexually abusive youth. In G. Ryan & S. Lane (Eds.), *Juvenile sexual offending: Causes, consequences, and correction* (pp. 219-263). San Francisco, CA: Jossey-Bass Publishers.

Lanyon, R. I. (2001). Psychological assessment procedures in sex offending. *Professional Psychology: Research and Practice, 32*(3), 253-260.

Lightfoot, L. O. & Barbaree, H. E. (1993). The relationship between substance use and abuse and sexual offending in adolescents. In H. E. Barbaree, W. L. Marshall, & S. M. Hudson (Eds.), *The juvenile sex offender* (pp. 203-224). New York: The Guilford Press.

Masson, H. (1995). Children and adolescents who sexually abuse other children: Responses to an emerging problem. *Journal of Social Welfare and Family Law, 17*(3), 325-336.

Messerschmidt, J. M. (1999). *Nine lives: Adolescent masculinities, the body and violence*. Boulder, CO: Westview Press.

Miner, M. & Crimmins, C. (1997). Adolescent sex offenders—Issues of etiology and risk factors. In B. K. Schwartz & H. R. Cellini (Eds.), *The sex offender* (Vol. 2, pp. 9-1–9-15). Kingston, NJ: Civic Research Institute.

National Adolescent Perpetrator Network. (1993). The revised report from the National Task Force on Juvenile Sexual Offending. *Juvenile & Family Court Journal, 44*, 1-120.

Perry, G. P. & Orchard, J. (1992). *Assessment and treatment of adolescent sex offenders*. Sarasota, FL: Professional Resource Press.

Pithers, W. D., Gray, A., Busconi, A., & Houchens, P. (1998). Caregivers of children with sexual behavior problems: psychological and familial functioning. *Child Abuse & Neglect, 22*(2), 129-141.

Ray, J. A. & English, D. J. (1995). Comparison of female and male children with sexual behavior problems. *Journal of Youth and Adolescence, 24*(4), 439-451.

Rich, P. (2003). *Juvenile sexual offenders: Understanding, assessing, and rehabilitating*. Hoboken, NJ: John Wiley & Sons, Inc.

Righthand, S. & Welch, C. (2001). *Juveniles who have sexually offended: A review of the professional literature*. Office of Juvenile Justice and Delinquency Prevention. Washington, DC: USGPO.

Rutter, M., Giller, H., & Hagell, A. (1998). *Antisocial behavior by young people*. Cambridge, United Kingdom: Cambridge University Press.

Ryan, G., Miyoshi, T. J., Metzner, J. L., Krugman, R. D., & Fryer, G. E. (1996). Trends in a national sample of sexually abusive youths. *Journal of the American Academy of Child and Adolescent Psychiatry, 35*(1), 17-25.

Schwartz, B. K. (1995). Characteristics and typologies of sex offenders. In B. K. Schwartz & H. R. Cellini (Eds.), *The sex offender* (Vol. 1, pp. 3-1–3-36). Kingston, NJ: Civic Research Institute.

Shaw, J. A., Campo-Bowen, A. E., Applegate, B., Perez, D., Antoine, L. B., Hart, E. L., Lahey, B. B., Testa, R. J., & Devaney, A. (1993). Young boys who commit serious sexual offenses: Demographics, psychometrics, and phenomenology. *Bulletin of the American Academy of Psychiatry and the Law, 21*(4), 399-408.

Smith, W. R. & Monastersky, C. (1986). Assessing juvenile sexual offenders' risk for reoffending. *Criminal Justice and Behavior, 13*(2), 115-140.

Travin, S., Cullen, K., & Protter, B. (1990). Female sex offenders: Severe victims and victimizers. *Journal of Forensic Sciences, 35,* 140-150.

Trzepacz, P. T. & Baker, R. W. (1993). *The psychiatric mental status examination.* London, United Kingdom: Oxford University Press.

Weinrott, M. R., Riggan, M., & Frothingham, S. (1997). Reducing deviant arousal in juvenile sex offenders using vicarious sensitization. *Journal of Interpersonal Violence, 12*(5), 704-728.

Will, D. (1999). Assessment issues. In M. Erooga & H. Masson (Eds.), *Children and young people who sexually abuse others: Challenges and responses* (pp. 86-103). London, United Kingdom: Routledge.

Worling, J. R. & Curwen, T. (2000). Adolescent sexual offender recidivism: Success of specialized treatment and implications for risk prediction. *Child Abuse & Neglect, 24*(7), 965-982.

Yokley, J. (1999). Using therapeutic community learning experiences with youth sex offenders. In B. K. Schwartz & H. R. Cellini (Eds.), *The sex offender* (Vol. 3, pp. 19-2–19-5). Kingston, NJ: Civic Research Institute.

Chapter 3

Adult Male Sex Offenders

Carolyn Hilarski
Carl W. Christensen

INTRODUCTION

Criminal offense is frightening. Sexual assault is especially terrifying. To appease increasing national concern, sexual aggression mandates have been implemented by the states (La Fond, 2003). Mental health and criminal justice systems have been charged with enforcing these directives. The remedy is difficult and depends upon continuous and accurate risk assessment related to the likelihood of reoffense (recidivism) since sexual offenders reoffend frequently and with multiple victims (R. K. Hanson, 1998). If community and offender well-being is the overall goal, then it is vital to identify the distinct complexities of the individual offender's multiple systems. In other words, how do family and work issues, biological, psychological, and social interactional issues synergistically influence each other to result in sexually aggressive behavior (Carich & Stone, 2001)? The information gleaned from such an in-depth risk assessment benefits community supervision officers and treatment providers in identifying specific triggers and risk factors associated with potential reoffending (R. K. Hanson & Bussiere, 1998).

This chapter provides the reader with pertinent and empirical information regarding individual and family assessment and treatment that includes relapse prevention and a case example with a comprehensive treatment plan pertaining to the adult male sex offender.

PREVALENCE

The consequences of sexual assault are often long-term and adverse. Males are most often the perpetrators of such aggression (Templeman & Stinnett, 1991). To illustrate, Templeman and Stinnett (1991) found that 65 percent of a sample of male college students self-reported a history of sexually aggressive behavior and a greater percentage fantasized about such aggression. Another study found that 120 men (6 percent), from a larger community sample of 1,882 males (ages 18 to 71), reported an average of 5.8 or greater than 1,000 severe incidences of sexually aggressive behavior. According to their self-report, these men were undetected repeat rapists. This particular study supports the proposal that sexually aggressive behavior is highly underreported (Lisak & Miller, 2002).

Recent estimates suggest that one third of the male prison population are sex offenders (Greenfeld, 1997). More than 60 percent of these individuals assault youth under the age of eighteen, and one third under the age of eleven (Flora, 2001). Indeed, the average male sexual molester of children will victimize hundreds of children in his career (Crolley, Thyer, & Bordnick, 1998).

Sexual assault is not decreasing. The U.S. Department of Justice Crime Reports revealed a 4 percent increase in sexual attacks from 2002 to 2003 (FBI, 2003).

Recidivism is high as well. A meta-analysis, meant to understand the extent of sexual reoffending, showed that more than one third of sex offenders would reoffend within a five year time span (R. K. Hanson & Bussiere, 1998).

PERSONAL CHARACTERISTICS

Those who sexually abuse are a heterogeneous group, presenting with diverse personal and offense characteristics (Shealy, Kalichman, Henderson, Szymanowski, & McKee, 1991). Personal characteristics might include some or all of the following issues: mental illness, personality disorders, sexual deviance, and prior legal issues (R. K. Hanson & Bussiere, 1998). Offense preferences range from the kind of victim chosen to the type of force used in the attack. Sexual aggression has three differentiating aspects: the victim's gender, the measure of force or threat used, and the age of the victim. Generally, sex offenders are male, highly respected, and known by their victim(s) (Hall, 1996). They often choose members of their own family as prey (Groth, 1982).

ETIOLOGY

Physical or sexual pleasure may not be the driving force behind sexual offending. Rather, sex offending may be the expression of such psychosocial issues as power and aggression. Rage, poor self-esteem, depression, or feeling inadequate may be mediating factors (Scheff & Retzinger, 2003). Nonetheless, sexually aggressive behavior is meant to manage the overwhelming thoughts and feelings of the offender (Hall & Barongan, 1997). Sexual assault is also thought to be a learned behavior. Adult male sex offenders commonly describe childhood experiences of primary caretaker instability and substance abuse, in addition to experiencing physical and/or sexual abuse (Burton, Nesmith, & Badten, 1997). Beginning research infers a significant relationship between pedophilia and a history of childhood sexual abuse (Lee, Jackson, Pattison, & Ward, 2002), and rape with a history of childhood physical abuse (Simons, Wurtele, & Heil, 2002). The adult with high levels of maltreatment in his childhood interprets this abuse as a "normal" way to achieve goals. Especially when the abuser is the "loved" primary caretaker (Cruise, Jacobs, & Lyons, 1994). This learned behavior or cycle of abuse put into practice leads to impaired relationships with others, generalized anger, and impulsive behavior (Knight & Prentky, 1990).

Social ineptness is another explanation for sex offending. Offenders frequently express self-depreciating thoughts resulting from feelings of loneliness and isolation (Hudson & Ward, 2000). Disorganized and/or anxious attachment with the primary caregiver is related to negative self-talk and social interaction difficulty (Marshall & Marshall, 2000). Inconsistent or avoiding caregiver response can create long-lasting insecurity (Marshall, Serran, & Cortoni, 2000). The individual feels unlovable and vulnerable to rejection. Choosing intimate and social interactions that he can control enhances his sense of safety (Smallbone & Dadds, 2000). The inability to initiate or maintain mutually satisfying intimate or social relationships can cause emotional pain. The offender perceives sexual offending as a solution to this problem (Marshall et al., 2000).

No single model is sufficient for explaining sexual offending. A combination of factors influence sexually aggressive behavior (Dube et al., 2001; Rind, Tromovitch, & Bauserman, 1998). One factor that is relevant to prevention is the primary caregiver and child attachment issue. Children with insecure attachments possess belief systems that love must be earned through "pleasing." These youth appear more vulnerable to grooming techniques (Marshall & Marshall, 2000) and experience greater consequences from perceived trauma (Smallbone & McCabe, 2003). Thus, services with missions of strengthening the caregiver and child relationship are necessary universal and selected prevention efforts.

THE CONSEQUENCES OF SEXUAL OFFENDING

Victims

Sexually assaulted individuals experience serious physical, cognitive, and affective harms (Briere & Elliott, 2003). Families of the victim also suffer from guilt and shame (Koverola & Proulx, 1996). Victims and their families live with the stigma associated with the sex offending circumstance (Stroud, 1999).

Sexual Abuser

Incarceration or legal intercession is a common consequence of *detected* sex offending. On average, 250,000 sex offenders experience some form of correctional supervision each year (Greenfeld, 1997). Moreover, in thirty-nine of fifty states, the sex offender is either legally mandated or strongly encouraged by parole boards to engage in therapy (Janus, 2000). Mandated therapy laws are the result of current research suggesting that without treatment, sex offenders become more violent and increase their level of offending (Marshall, Hudson, & Ward, 1992). Estimates propose that roughly one third of untreated sex offenders will reoffend in comparison to 19 percent of those treated (Hall, 1995). Offender resistance to the legal mandates results in jail time, longer prison terms, or a return to prison (Flora, 2001). The cost of offending continues after prison and/or treatment with regulations that require public notification of the sex offending crime.

RISK FACTORS

Any discussion of sex offending risk factors is suspect, as most offenders go unnoticed (Koss, 1996). Keeping this in mind, known sex offenders continue to offer useful information regarding assessment, intervention, and prediction.

Two types of risk factors delineate sex offending and reoffending: *static risk factors* and *dynamic risk factors*. Static risk factors are not subject to change and include the age (often young) or race (disproportionately a minority) of the offender, in addition to the number of prior offenses (R. K. Hanson & Bussiere, 1998).

Dynamic risk factors are changeable elements (e.g., deviant sexual interest and fantasy, identifying as a victim, denial, and negative beliefs about women) (R. F. Hanson et al., 2001). Skill deficits relating to anger, problem solving, and social issues are also included (Craig, Browne, & Stringer, 2003). In addition, suggested static and dynamic risk factors are an extensive history of sexual offenses and victimization, in addition to nonsexual criminal behavior, substance abuse, noncompliance with treatment, cultural socialization, and the presence of a personality disorder or other comorbid mental health issue (Carich & Mussack, 2001).

ASSESSMENT

Sexual aggressors share a number of common characteristics that vary in intensity according to the individual. These similarities relate to motivation, behavior, psychological, and historical issues (Nunes, Firestone, Bradford, Greenberg, & Broom, 2002). However, as offenders are overall a heterogeneous group, each treatment plan must be individualized to incorporate specific triggers and personality difficulties (Nunes et al., 2002). Any particular sex offense is likely the result of multiple factors that must be considered in treatment planning.

To evaluate the multidimensional nature of sex offending, Finkelhor's Four Preconditions of Sexual Abuse (1984, p. 58) is a clear and useful template.

1. *Motivation.* Assessment must identify what motivated the offender to sexually abuse. What are his or her sexual attractions (age,

gender, presence of pain or bondage) (Abel, Huffman, Warberg, & Holland, 1998)? What are the strengths of his or her sexual urges (Berlin, 1983)? What are his or her maladaptive beliefs (Blumenthal, Gudjonsson, & Burns, 1999; Ward, Hudson, Johnston, & Marshall, 1997)?

Paper and pencil tests, such as the Multiphasic Sex Inventory (MSI) (Nichols & Molinder, 1984), are designed to identify cognitive distortions regarding deviant sexual behavior, paraphilia, sexual propensity (e.g., voyeurism, pornography, bondage), social/sexual inadequacy, emotional neediness, and social and victimization history in adolescents and adults (Ward et al., 1997). The MSI is also useful for measuring treatment progress (Schlank, 1995).

The Abel Assessment for Sexual Interest (AASI) (Abel, Jordan, Hand, Holland, & Phipps, 2001) is a valid and reliable measure for adolescents and adults, of sexual attraction to children, sexual violence against adult men and women, and sadism. This ninety-minute assessment does not incorporate nude pictures or physiological measures.

The Sex Offender Needs Assessment Rating (SONAR) (Hanson, 2001) was developed to evaluate such dynamic factors as intimacy deficits, social interactions, attitudes regarding sex offending, self-regulation, substance abuse, mood, anger, and victim access. Research shows adequate internal consistency and ability to predict reoffending with this instrument (Hanson, 2001).

The comprehensive assessment will answer the following questions: What emotions motivated the sexually aggressive behavior (anger, rejection, need for control, lack of appropriate emotional, sexual and social outlets)? How do these issues effect motivation? What events and thoughts preceded the sexual abuse? How much is controlling others and evading responsibility a feature of the offender's life? What tasks of normal development have been missed or distorted in the offender's journey to abusing others?

2. *Overcoming internal barriers.* What role did pornography play in supporting deviant sexual interests? How did they overcome the fear of being caught and knowing the abuse was wrong? What awareness did the offender have of hurting the victim? What rationalizations and cognitive distortions are present? These factors are divulged in the objective measures previously cited.

Often offenders are embedded in family and peer systems that support their distorted thinking and abusive behavior. Issues to explore regarding family and peer codependence might include: How are *others* contributing to any thinking errors (Palmer, 1997)?

Exploring each family member's understanding of the family dynamics and issues relating to the abuse is vital. Family member assessment will examine the family structure, mother/child attachment, in addition to family member belief systems regarding: boundaries, rules, and roles. Encouraging the family to complete the Hanson Sex Attitude Questionnaire (R. K. Hanson, Gizzarelli, & Scott, 1994) can reveal family member attitudes associated with sexual abuse.

Substance use, concurrent health conditions, or stressors can reduce internal barriers. Feeling sorry for the self, self-medicating, and interpreting others attempts to stop the deviant behavior as victimizing the offender all lower internal barriers to self-control and facilitate abusing (Valliere, 1997). The MSI, SONAR, and AASI demonstrate utility in identifying cognitive distortions and other factors that contribute to ineffective internal controls (Schlank, 1995).

3. *Overcoming external barriers.* Assessing how the offender gained access to the victim without arousing suspicion will build an understanding of the offender's predatory behavior. How was privacy achieved and maintained? How was the usual supervision and caring of the child circumvented in order to offend? How did the offender respond to others' suspicions? What was the offender's response when the abuse was disclosed?

4. *Overcoming victim resistance.* Were threats or force used? How did the offender bribe or entice the victim's participation? Did the offender have available resources to attract the victim (e.g., drugs/alcohol, attractive cars, money, special privileges)? Manipulation and deception are vital for maintaining secrecy while outwardly presenting a charming and likeable persona. Many hours of interviewing may be necessary before this veneer is pierced.

How did the offender try to keep the victim from telling about the abuse? Children, even very young, usually know that sexual interaction with an adult is wrong. How the offender overcomes this is diagnostic of his or her manipulation of victims. Often bribes are used to create in the victim a false sense of obligation. Guilt for using drugs or alcohol supplied by the offender or engaging in other illicit behavior can keep the victim quiet. In young children, mystification by normalizing the sexual behavior or demanding obedience to the adult keeps the victim from telling.

Offenders often select victims who are limited in their ability or circumstances to report offensive behavior. Emotionally vulnerable children, members of troubled families, or children with developmental disabilities may be reluctant or unable to report abuse. Especially in offenders with multiple victims, assess for what characteristics the victims share. Are there particular features of physical appearance, age, or demeanor that the offender is targeting? Crime reports and collateral police interviews are often very useful in gaining a view of these factors.

A semistructured interview examining intimacy deficits, social influences, attitudes, sexual and general self-regulation, substance abuse, negative mood, anger/hostility, opportunities for victim access, and family issues generates empirical information essential for assessing risk, developing a treatment plan, and tracking treatment goals (R. K. Hanson, 1998).

The following treatment activities addressing each of Finkelhor's (1984) categories can become the basis for a well-structured, empirically based treatment plan.

INTERVENTIONS

The initial task in treatment, as in assessment, is to examine and explore the sexual abuse. Expecting, encouraging, and requiring the offender to describe the abuse emphasizes the importance of honesty and accepting responsibility for the abuse. Repeated discussion of the abuse, as the therapeutic relationship builds, should progressively reveal more details and often other abusing incidents. Treatment should also target attitudes, beliefs, and cognitive distortions that are linked to the story of the abuse (Ward et al., 1997). Progress in treatment should demonstrate a decrease of the psychological distortions that precipitate and support the sexually abusive behavior (English, Patten, & Jones, 1996).

Talking about the abuse is both difficult and embarrassing for offenders. Initially they often avoid trying to relate exactly what happened, preferring to argue the court case, the discrepancies in victim's statements, or negative thoughts about the investigation. Stopping these diversions and supporting honest and open communication is a crucial early treatment task. In order to handle this effectively, the clinician must learn to become receptive and nonreactive to the events in these stories. Often new clinicians experience feelings of shock, anger, and other negative emotions. Sound training, supervision, and experience, coupled with a commitment to the importance of having these details exposed, help the clinician maintain a therapeutic stance with the client and avoid having the treatment become focused on dealing with the worker's reactions (Rich, 1994). Family and group therapy can be useful settings for clients to experience the negative reactions of others to their behavior (Skibinski, 1994).

THERAPY GROUPS

A second activity proven important in supporting disclosure and therapeutic processing of the details of sexual abuse is group therapy (Jennings & Sawyer, 2003). Sex offender therapy groups are perhaps the only context in which an offender can share experiences with others who understand committing sexual abuse and the strategies used to avoid being held responsible. Effective therapy groups are made up of offenders representing various stages of treatment. This permits new entrants to see examples of how the denial, avoidance, and manipulation used in abusive behavior is altered and reduced and a healthy and safe lifestyle is built (Levenson & Macgowan, 2004). Effective groups confront maladaptive thoughts and behaviors, model new attitudes and beliefs about sexual abuse, and support openness, by sharing the experiences of telling others (family, employers, landlords) about the abuse, in addition to revealing their recovery process (Lothstein, 2001).

TREATMENT

Treatment objectives through individual, family, and group methods include the following:

Motivation

For offenders, learning to reduce their motivation for deviant sexual arousal is accomplished through such cognitive-behavioral techniques as: increasing self-awareness of sexually arousing circumstances, practicing thought-stopping, problem solving of how to avoid activating circumstances for sexually deviant thoughts and behaviors, and redirective thinking to nondeviant thoughts (Dougher, 1995).

For many offenders, redirecting themselves to finding age-appropriate and consensual sexual relationships is essential for strengthening internal barriers. Indeed, research suggests that promiscuity is related to sexual abuse and that men in committed relationships are less likely to engage in sexually aggressive behavior (Malamuth, Linz, Heavey, Barnes, & Acker, 1995). A satisfying and appropriate relationship that includes honest communication, clear boundaries, and acceptance increases the level of psychic energy meant for reaching therapeutic goals (Scheff & Retzinger, 2003).

An additional note is that sexually aggressive men regard themselves as possessing no feminine qualities. Thus, encouraging a male to appreciate feminine attributes decreases the likelihood of aggressive acts toward women (Lisak & Ivan, 1995).

Internal Barriers

Acknowledging the abuse openly to others often triggers feelings of guilt, humiliation, and embarrassment for the sexual offender. Attempts to avoid these feelings maintains the cycle of offending (Lane, 1997). Supporting the offender in tolerating negative feelings, rather than avoiding them, is an important therapeutic goal for developing and strengthening internal controls (Tierney & McCabe, 2001). Moreover, by addressing feelings and thoughts directly, the individual is able to use the cognitive-behavioral techniques of *reframing* and *problem solving* to actively participate in maintaining a sense of serenity. Integrating these behaviors in a lifestyle of nonoffending are important elements of risk reduction and rehabilitation (Launay, 2001).

External Barriers

Regulating the offender's movements through specialized supervision is the first goal of effective community management. Treatment can encourage and monitor offenders to avoid high-risk situations and require offenders to disclose to family, landlords, and employers their sexual abusing history. Ending the secrecy and denial in treatment, and in the community, challenges offenders to be accountable for their thoughts, behaviors, and circumstances. Although offenders are often initially fearful of the repercussions of such disclosing, research does not support this scheme (Quinn, Forsyth, & Mullen-Quinn, 2004).

Managing external barriers is also an important link between community supervision and treatment. Probation and parole officers can monitor the offender to ensure the avoidance of high-risk situations, behaviors, and attitudes. Using specialized conditions of probation/parole has become an important tool for community management. Encouraging compliance by routine polygraph examinations and monitoring movement with electronic bracelets can also strengthen community safety and discourage offenders from believing they can manipulate others to continue their deviant behavior (English et al., 1996).

Family therapy is an additional important intervention in rebuilding effective external barriers. Family members are often misdirected in their support of the offender, and, in more serious cases, collaborative with the offender's deviant behavior. Interventions that address family avoidance, denial, and distortions of the abuse begin with supporting the offender in disclosing to the family the extent of the sexual abusing behavior. Family therapy sessions that support family members in practicing honest and open communication regarding feelings of guilt, humiliation, and shame encourage system change. The family can play a vital role in both supervising the offender collaboratively with probation/parole and supporting the offender's development of a healthy, well-adjusted social, emotional, and behavioral life (Eher et al., 1997). Families, especially in incest cases, can recognize that their safety and satisfaction is tied to the recovery of the offender and should be encouraged to support and participate in the recovery process (DiGiorgio-Miller, 1998).

Empathy

Sexual offenders often do not recognize or acknowledge that sexual abuse is traumatic to the victim. This ability to avoid, ignore, or evade an awareness of the victim's reactions is an essential condition to committing sexual aggression (Fernandez & Marshall, 2003). Feminine socialization must be increased (Ward et al., 1997). Treatment focused on psychoeducational activities addressing the long-lasting effects of the sexual abuse often use films or videos that tell the stories of victims (Auburn & Lea, 2003). Group therapy discussions of childhood abuse in the lives of the offenders also sensitizes them to how the disruption of normal development, through abuse, can distort emotions and behaviors long into adulthood (Scott, 1994).

Finally, recognizing how the offender managed the victim's participation is a critical element of taking responsibility for the abuse. Using bribes, emotional coercion, charm, and the role of an authority figure all contribute to keeping the victim quiet and engaged with the offender. Recognizing the pattern of these manipulative behaviors and their presence in other relationships (including the group) can confront the offender and provide feedback about recognizing and reducing manipulative maneuvers in relationships (Flora, 2001). This is also a theme explored in family therapy (Rich, 1994).

Relapse Prevention

Relapse prevention is a relatively new therapeutic model borrowed from the field of addiction (Laws, Hudson, & Ward, 2000). This treatment component uses a cognitive-behavioral approach to address the dynamic factors of empathy, anger, and social interaction deficits found to be prevalent in sex offender characteristics (Polascheck, 2003). The supporting theory proposes that sex offending is a learned behavior; consequently, it can be "unlearned," or at a minimum modified. The model's purpose is to circumvent "slips" and reduce reoffending by incorporating new behaviors such as honest introspection (i.e., exploring the "self" and the level of motivation for change) and self-monitoring (i.e., understanding personal physiological and emotional levels of functioning) (Laws et al., 2000). Goals encourage the life-long awareness of risk factors, stress management, and the maintenance of healthy relationships (R. K. Hanson, 2000). The periodic use of the SONAR is useful for flagging relapse issues (Hanson, 2001).

CASE EXAMPLE

Child Protective Services (CPS) referred the Olson family to agency X because Tom Olson sexually abused his daughter, Debra. The investigation report indicated that Debra, age thirteen, would enter the parent's bedroom at night and climb into the bed between Tom and his wife, Martha. As Martha slept, Tom fondled Debra. Debra also indicated that Tom would fondle her when they were alone in the living room on the couch. After several months, Debra reported to her mother that her dad was "bothering her." Martha stated that she told Tom to stop "bothering" Debra. Tom promised to stop and did so for several months. When the fondling began again, Debra reportedly asked Tom to stop bothering her. The molestation paused for several weeks—then began once more. Debra, in reported frustration, told her teacher, which instigated a report to CPS. When questioned by CPS and the police, Tom acknowledged the abuse, and was directed to move out of the family home. Along with a petition filed in family court, a criminal complaint was filed by the district attorney's office in criminal court.

Tom Olson, age fifty-one, and his wife of twenty-one years, Martha, age fifty-two, have two children: Sam, seventeen years, and Debra, age thirteen. Sam has impulse-control problems and learning disabilities. Debra has long-standing mood difficulties in addition to learning issues. Martha suffers from depression. Both children and Martha are under psychiatric care. Martha does not work outside of the home.

Agency X received the referral and an intake session was scheduled to include the family, the CPS worker, the school social worker, and the agency psychiatrist. The criminal case had not yet been prosecuted and no one from probation was assigned to the case. By initially meeting with all of the people involved, a more comprehensive assessment could be developed. Participants were asked about their perceptions of the problem, what goals they would like to see accomplished, and what concerns they had for treatment. The family was shaken and upset by the abuse, but frightened about the future without Tom, the sole wage earner. The psychiatrist and school worker were supportive of the family, trying to work toward having Tom remain a father figure and contributor to the family.

The agency X therapist agreed to continue evaluating Tom and the family with the possibility of working toward eventual reunification. The first steps would involve a thorough assessment of Tom followed by a family assessment and initiating services with the family to address any trauma consequences.

Assessment

Tom's motivation for the abuse was assessed in interview and through administration of the MSI (Nichols & Molinder, 1984), SONAR (R. K. Hanson & Harris, 2001), and the AASI (Abel et al., 1998). On the MSI, Tom was moderately open about his sexual interests in adults and adolescents. He presented an awareness of the steps taken to commit sexual abuse, including persistent thoughts about sex, grooming the victim, and the rationalizations he used to continue doing what he knew was wrong.

Tom's profile on the AASI was congruent with the MSI and showed a strong attraction to adolescent females and less but significant interest in adult females. No attraction to younger children of either gender was noted. Interviews revealed strong motivations for abusing by wanting to feel in control and powerful in a family atmosphere that he experienced as chaotic, conflict-ridden, and unsatisfying. Martha's and Debra's depression, his son's explosive and irrational anger, and his own dissatisfaction with his job and family life, in addition to the family's seeming inability to solve the challenges of everyday life left Tom feeling angry. He became demanding and dictatorial at home. Consequently, family members were afraid to interact with him, which fueled his anger. Tom's negative thoughts and resulting emotions contributed to his emotional withdrawal and motivation to sexually abuse.

Tom's emotional distress eroded his internal barriers about abusing. As his emotional and sexual dissatisfaction grew, he increasingly rationalized his anger as trying to bring order to the perceived chaos and his abuse as seeking some caring and emotional satisfaction. Tom increased his use of pornography to achieve sexual satisfaction, along with abusing his daughter. He avoided conflict with the family by not communicating, which triggered feelings of isolation, inadequacy, and powerlessness.

The poor functioning of the couple, with little communication, no sexual interaction, and feelings of powerlessness, reduced feelings of cohesion and safety for everyone in the family. Martha's depression and withdrawal reduced her availability to the family. The children's emotional problems gave their complaints and distress less credibility and the parents felt powerless to help them. When Debra initially disclosed the abuse to Martha, the nonspecific nature of the complaint and Martha's vague request to Tom illustrated the ineffective communication and problem-solving activity of the family. These factors enabled Tom to continue his rationalizing and avoidance of the impact of his behavior on his family.

Debra's depression and need for support in a chaotic and conflict-ridden family became a context for her to tolerate the abuse for several months without telling. When Debra was able to tell her mother, she expected the abuse to stop and when it did not, it confirmed further the powerlessness of the adults to manage the family. Her courage in telling school staff is a testament to her desire for change and insistence that the abuse was wrong.

Treatment Plan

First Year

Tom's acknowledgment of the abuse, low score on the SONAR, and willingness to live separate from the family suggested his risk was low and he was appropriate for community-based treatment. The evaluation to the court summarized these factors and a treatment plan was developed to address the identified problems. The plan outlined the following goals and treatment activities:

I. Establish well-coordinated treatment and case-management activities with the service providers to increase the likelihood of the offender reaching his goals.
   A. Initial planning session involved all service providers and the family.
   B. Ongoing contact among service providers to monitor activities and address misunderstandings in a timely manner.
   C. Include new service providers as they engage with the family (e.g., probation).
   D. Agree that major changes in restrictions on the offender are subject to agreement by all providers.
II. Offender will maintain a separate residence.
   A. Offender maintains employment to economically support the family.
III. Service providers will monitor Tom's contact with family members.
   A. Therapy for Tom and Debra to increase understanding of roles, boundaries, and communication.
   B. Conjoint therapy for Tom and Martha to increase intimacy.
IV. Offender will engage in individual and group therapy to reduce sexual deviance, the use of pornography and rationalization, and increase anger-management skills.

A. Individual and group therapy to:
    1. Explore sexual abuse cycle and mismanagement of anger.
    2. Identify triggers and develop a relapse prevention plan.
  B. Individual, group, and family therapy to improve Tom's empathy for his victim and provide opportunities to take responsibility for the sexual abuse and its effects.
V. Individual therapy and support for family members to help increase the emotional availability of each member for the family work.
  A. Encourage and monitor all family members regarding individual counseling to reduce reported depressive feelings, any trauma resulting from the sexual abuse, and any problem issues related to the family work.
  B. Refer both children for remedial and academic counseling services to encourage their success in school.
VI. Family therapy to develop and practice effective family problem solving and communication skills.
VII. Increase Tom's contact with family members.
  A. Initial contact managed in family therapy sessions, initiated with an apology by Tom to Debra and the family.
  B. With Tom's placement on probation, probation officer supervises Tom's movement in community to ensure compliance with condition of no unsupervised contact with family.
  C. Involvement of Tom's sister, with whom he lives, in family sessions and her supervision of visits with wife, son, and later daughter.
  D. Tom's unsupervised contact with family based on progress in treatment and agreement of all service providers and the family.

During the first year Tom was involved in weekly offender group, intense family therapy, and treatment sessions with Debra. Frequent case conferences with the other service providers occurred as conflicts erupted within the family and within the helping system. The emphasis on addressing conflicts and managing disagreements openly contributed to the family's experiencing a reduction in feeling out of control. Cooperation improved and as the family atmosphere calmed the couple reported increased confidence in family management. In return, the children became more trusting and communicative.

Treatment shifted to the couple as Martha's mood improved and she became assertive in communicating her feelings and needs. Tom experienced this as threatening and it provoked feelings of anger, fear, and the desire to be in control. He had many opportunities in couple sessions to resist his impulse to explode and talk in a calm and reasoned way with Martha.

As the first year of treatment concluded, Tom successfully completed the offender's group. Debra and Sam's grades improved. In addition, Debra and Martha's mood improved and Sam's "acting out" lessened. Finally, the continued supervision regulating Tom's contact with the family by probation permitted CPS to close the case with family court.

Second Year

During the second year of treatment, Debra's individual treatment was concluded successfully. The family treatment reduced in frequency, with increasing demonstrations of effective communication and problem solving and few emotional outbursts. The family visits increased in frequency and the couple decided to have Sam move in with his father. The couple continued to explore their marriage and Martha increasingly felt ambivalent about continuing their relationship. However, their parenting was well-coordinated. Tom handled his displeasure with calm words rather than outbursts, and Martha was strong in her support of the children's needs. Tom was permitted unsupervised visits with Debra and these went well in everyone's perception.

One problem emerged when probation officers, during a routine home visit, checked Tom's computer history file and discovered visits to pornography sites. Tom denied doing this and Sam acknowledged visiting the sites. Probation officers continued to be concerned and requested an evaluation by another sex offender program. When the new evaluation was completed, the agency Y therapist met with the family, Tom's probation officer, and the evaluating clinician to discuss probation's concerns and maintain a focused and well-coordinated service plan. The group decided to continue treatment as planned. No indicators of deviance or pornography use emerged in subsequent months.

Third Year

The Olson case moved toward conclusion with reduced frequency of treatment sessions and increased family contact during the third year of service. Virtually no angry outbursts by Tom or Sam occurred and everyone reported feeling safe. Family members reported having increased emotional satisfaction and family cohesion. Tom and Martha continued to be uncertain about their marriage and decided to remain in separate households, with the children moving comfortably between them. The treatment plan moved into aftercare, with checkup sessions scheduled every few months for one year.

This case illustrates the complex clinical features of sexual abuse. With multiple service providers having different mandates, conflicts could easily have developed that would mirror the family's chaotic interaction and thus disrupt treatment and potentially increase the risk to the community. Ongoing assessment of the offender and his environment, which addresses the motivation, internal and exterior boundaries, and individual family member issues, coupled with a willingness to collaborate with other service providers offers the maximum opportunity for a successful outcome.

REFERENCES

Abel, G., Huffman, J., Warberg, B., & Holland, C. (1998). Visual reaction time and plethysmography as measures of sexual interest in child molesters. *Sexual Abuse: A Journal of Research and Treatment, 10*(2), 81-95.

Abel, G. G., Jordan, A., Hand, C. G., Holland, C. G., & Phipps, A. (2001). Classification models of child molesters utilizing the Abel Assessment for child sexual abuse interest. *Child Abuse and Neglect, 25*(5), 703-718.

Auburn, T. & Lea, S. (2003). Doing cognitive distortions: A discursive psychology analysis of sex offender treatment talk. *British Journal of Social Psychology, 42*(2), 281-298.

Berlin, F. (1983). Sex offenders: A biomedical perspective. In J. Greer & J. Stuart (Eds.), *The sexual aggressor: Current perspectives on treatment* (pp. 83-123). New York: Van Nostrand Reinhold.

Blumenthal, S., Gudjonsson, G., & Burns, J. (1999). Cognitive distortions and blame attribution in sex offenders against adults and children. *Child Abuse and Neglect, 23*(2), 129-143.

Briere, J. & Elliott, D. M. (2003). Prevalence and psychological sequelae of self-reported childhood physical and sexual abuse in a general population sample of men and women. *Child Abuse and Neglect, 27*(10), 1205-1222.

Burton, D. L., Nesmith, A. A., & Badten, L. (1997). Clinician's views on sexually aggressive children and their families: A theoretical explanation. *Child Abuse and Neglect, 21*(2), 157-170.

Carich, M. S. & Mussack, S. E. (2001). *Handbook for sexual abuser assessment and treatment.* Brandon, VT: The Safer Society Press.

Carich, M. S. & Stone, M. H. (2001). Aftercare for medium and hardcore sexual offenders. *Journal of Individual Psychology, 57*(1), 60-66.

Craig, L. A., Browne, K. D., & Stringer, I. (2003). Risk scales and factors predictive of sexual offence recidivism. *Trauma, Violence, & Abuse, 4*(1), 45-69.

Crolley, J. D. R., Thyer, B. A., & Bordnick, P. S. (1998). Evaluating outpatient behavior therapy of sex offenders: A pretest-posttest study. *Behavior Modification, 22*(4), 485-501.

Cruise, K. R., Jacobs, J. E., & Lyons, P. M. (1994). Definitions of physical abuse: A preliminary inquiry into children's perspectives. *Behavioral Science and the Law, 12*, 35-48.

DiGiorgio-Miller, J. (1998). Sibling incest: Treatment of the family and the offender. *Child Welfare, 77*(3), 335-346.

Dougher, M. (1995). Behavior techniques to alter sexual arousal. In B. Schwartz & H. Cellini (Eds.), *The sex offender: Correction, treatment and legal practice* (Vol. I, pp. 15-11–15-16). Kingston, NJ: Civic Research Institute.

Dube, S. R., Anda, R. F., Felitti, V. J., Chapman, D. P., Williamson, D. F., & Giles, W. H. (2001). Childhood abuse, household dysfunction, and the risk of attempted suicide throughout the life span: Findings from the Adverse Childhood Experiences Study. *Journal of the American Medical Association, 286*(24), 3089-3096.

Eher, R., Dwyer, M., Prinoth, S., Wagner, E., Fruhwald, S., & Gutierrez, K. (1997). Sex offenders in legal treatment and their relatives: Results of family therapy sessions. *Psychiatrische Praxis, 24*(4), 190-195.

English, K., Patten, S., & Jones, L. (1996). *Managing adult sex offenders on probation and parole: A containment approach.* Lexington, KY: American Probation Parole Association.

FBI. (2003). *Uniform crime reports for the United States.* Washington, DC: U.S. Government Printing Office.

Fernandez, Y. M. & Marshall, W. L. (2003). Victim empathy, social self-esteem, and psychopathy in rapists. *Sexual Abuse: A Journal of Research and Treatment, 15*, 11-26.

Finkelhor, D. (1984). *Child sexual abuse: New theory and research.* New York: Free Press.

Flora, R. (2001). *How to work with sex offenders: A handbook for criminal justice, human services, and mental health professionals.* Binghamton, NY: The Haworth Press.

Greenfeld, L. A. (1997). *Sex offenses and offenders: An analysis of data on rape and sexual assault.* Washington, DC: Department of Justice, Bureau of Justice Statistics.

Groth, A. N. (1982). The incest offender. In S. M. Sgroi (Ed.), *Handbook of clinical intervention in child sexual abuse* (pp. 215-239). Lexington, MA: Heath and Co.

Hall, G. C. N. (1995). Sexual offender recidivism revisited: A meta-analysis of recent treatment studies. *Journal of Consulting and Clinical Psychology, 63,* 802-809.

Hall, G. C. N. (1996). *Theory-based assessment, treatment, and prevention of sexual aggression.* New York: Oxford University Press.

Hall, G. C. N. & Barongan, C. (1997). Prevention of sexual aggression: Sociocultural risk and protective factors. *American Psychologist, 52*(1), 5-14.

Hanson, R. F., Saunders, B., Kilpatrick, D., Resnick, H., Crouch, J. A., & Duncan, R. (2001). Impact of childhood rape and aggravated assault on adult mental health. *American Journal of Orthopsychiatry, 71*(1), 108-119.

Hanson, R. K. (1998). What do we know about sex offender risk assessment? *Psychology, Public Policy, and Law, 14*(1-2), 50-72.

Hanson, R. K. (2000). What is so special about relapse prevention? In D. R. Laws, S. M. Hudson, & T. Ward (Eds.), *Remaking relapse prevention: A sourcebook* (pp. 27-38). Thousand Oaks, CA: Sage.

Hanson, R. K. & Bussiere, M. T. (1998). Predicting relapse: A meta-analysis of sexual offender recidivism studies. *Journal of Consulting and Clinical Psychology, 66,* 348-362.

Hanson, R. K., Gizzarelli, R., & Scott, H. (1994). The attitudes of incest offenders: Sexual entitlement and acceptance of sex with children. *Criminal Justice & Behavior, 21*(2), 187-202.

Hanson, R. K. & Harris, A. J. (2001). A structured approach to evaluating change among sexual offenders. *Sexual Abuse: A Journal of Research and Treatment, 13*(2), 105-122.

Hudson, S. M. & Ward, T. (2000). Relapse prevention: Assessment and treatment implications. In D. R. Laws, S. M. Hudson, & T. Ward (Eds.), *Remaking relapse prevention with sex offenders: A sourcebook* (pp. 102-122). Newbury Park, CA: Sage.

Janus, E. S. (2000). Sex predator commitment laws: Constitutional but unwise. *Psychiatric Annals, 30*(6), 411-420.

Jennings, J. L. & Sawyer, S. (2003). Principles and techniques for maximizing the effectiveness of group therapy with sex offenders. *Sexual Abuse: A Journal of Research and Treatment, 15*(4), 251-267.

Knight, R. A. & Prentky, R. A. (1990). Classifying sexual offenders: The development and corroboration of taxonomic models. In W. L. Marshall, D. R. Laws, & H. E. Barbaree (Eds.), *Handbook of sexual assault: Issues, theories, and treatment of the offender* (pp. 23-52). New York: Plenum.

Koss, M. P. (1996). The measurement of rape victimization in crime surveys. *Criminal Justice & Behavior, 23*, 55-69.

Koverola, C. & Proulx, J. (1996). Family functioning as predictors of distress in revictimized sexual abuse survivors. *Journal of Interpersonal Violence, 11*(2), 263-281.

La Fond, J. Q. (2003). Outpatient commitment's next frontier: Sexual predators. *Psychology, Public Policy, and Law, 9*(1/2), 159.

Lane, S. (1997). The sexual abuse cycle. In G. Ryan & S. Lane (Eds.), *Juvenile sexual offending: Causes, consequences, and correction* (pp. 77-121). CA: Jossey-Bass.

Launay, G. (2001). Relapse prevention with sex offenders: Practice, theory, and research. *Criminal Behavior & Mental Health, 11*(1), 38-54.

Laws, D. R., Hudson, S. M., & Ward, T. (2000). The original model of relapse prevention with sex offenders: Promises unfulfilled. In D. R. Laws, S. M. Hudson, & T. Ward (Eds.), *Remaking relapse prevention with sex offenders: A sourcebook* (pp. 3-26). Newbury Park, CA: Sage.

Lee, J. K., Jackson, H. J., Pattison, P., & Ward, T. (2002). Developmental risk factors for sexual offending. *Child Abuse and Neglect, 26*(1), 73-92.

Levenson, J. S. & Macgowan, M. J. (2004). Engagement, denial, and treatment progress among sex offenders in group therapy. *Sexual Abuse: A Journal of Research and Treatment, 16*(1), 49-63.

Lisak, D. & Ivan, C. (1995). Deficits in intimacy and empathy in sexually aggressive men. *Journal of Interpersonal Violence, 10*, 296-308.

Lisak, D. & Miller, P. M. (2002). Repeat rape and multiple offending among undetected rapists. *Violence and Victims, 17*(1), 73-84.

Lothstein, L. M. (2001). Treatment of non-incarcerated sexually compulsive/addictive offenders in an integrated, multimodal, and psychodynamic group therapy model. *International Journal of Group Psychotherapy, 51*(4), 553-570.

Malamuth, N. M., Linz, D., Heavey, C. L., Barnes, G. E., & Acker, M. (1995). Using the confluence model of sexual aggression to predict men's conflict with women: A 10-year year follow up study. *Journal of Personality and Social Psychology, 69*, 353-369.

Marshall, W. L., Hudson, S. M., & Ward, T. (1992). Sexual deviance. In P. H. Wilson (Ed.), *Principles and practices of relapse prevention* (pp. 235-254). New York: Guilford Press.

Marshall, W. L. & Marshall, L. E. (2000). The origins of sexual offending. *Trauma, Violence, & Abuse, 1*, 250-263.

Marshall, W. L., Serran, G. A., & Cortoni, F. A. (2000). Childhood attachments, sexual abuse, and their relationship to adult coping in child molesters. *Sexual Abuse: A Journal of Research and Treatment, 12*(1), 17-26.

Nichols, H. & Molinder, I. (1984). *Manual for the Multiphasic Sex Inventory.* Tacoma, WA: Criminal and Victim Psychology Specialists.

Nunes, K., Firestone, P., Bradford, J. M., Greenberg, D. M., & Broom, I. A. (2002). A comparison of the static-99 and the sex offender risk appraisal guide (SORAG). *Sexual Abuse: A Journal of Research and Treatment, 14*(3), 249-265.

Palmer, R. (1997). Assessment and treatment of incest families. In B. Schwartz & H. Cellini (Eds.), *The sex offender: New insights, treatment innovations, and legal developments* (Vol. II, pp. 18-1–18-12). New Jersey: Civic Research Institute.

Polascheck, D. L. L. (2003). Relapse prevention, offense process models, and the treatment of sexual offenders. *Professional Psychology—Research & Practice, 34*(4), 361-367.

Quinn, J. F., Forsyth, C. J., & Mullen-Quinn, C. (2004). Societal reaction to sex offenders: A review of the origins and results of the myths surrounding their crimes and treatment amenability. *Deviant Behavior, 25*(3), 215-232.

Rich, K. D. (1994). Outpatient group therapy with adult male sex offenders: Clinical issues and concerns. *Journal for Specialists in Group Work, 19*(2), 120-128.

Rind, B., Tromovitch, P., & Bauserman, R. (1998). A meta-analytic examination of assumed properties of child sexual abuse using college samples. *Psychological Bulletin, 124,* 22-53.

Scheff, T. J. & Retzinger, S. M. (2003). Shame, anger, and the social bond: A theory of sexual offenders and treatment. In M. Silberman (Ed.), *Violence and society: A reader* (pp. 301-311). Upper Saddle River, NJ: Prentice Hall.

Schlank, A. M. (1995). The utility of the MMPI and the MSI for identifying a sexual offender typology. *Sexual Abuse: A Journal of Research and Treatment, 7*(3), 185-194.

Scott, W. (1994). Group therapy for male sex offenders: Strategic interventions. *Journal of Family Psychotherapy, 5*(2), 1-20.

Shealy, L., Kalichman, S. C., Henderson, M. C., Szymanowski, D., & McKee, G. (1991). MMPI profile subtypes of incarcerated sex offenders against children. *Violence and Victimization, 6*(3), 201-212.

Simons, D., Wurtele, S. K., & Heil, P. (2002). Childhood victimization and lack of empathy as predictors of sexual offending against women and children. *Journal of Interpersonal Violence, 17,* 1291-1305.

Skibinski, G. J. (1994). Intrafamilial child sexual abuse: Intervention programs for first time offenders and their families. *Child Abuse and Neglect, 18*(4), 367-375.

Smallbone, S. W., & Dadds, M. R. (2000). Attachment and coercive sexual behavior. *Sexual Abuse: A Journal of Research and Treatment, 12,* 3-15.

Smallbone, S. W. & McCabe, B. A. (2003). Childhood attachment, childhood sexual abuse, and onset of masturbation among adult sexual offenders. *Sexual Abuse: A Journal of Research and Treatment, 15*(1), 1-9.

Stroud, D. D. (1999). Familial support as perceived by adult victims of childhood sexual abuse. *Sexual Abuse: A Journal of Research and Treatment, 11*(2), 159-175.

Templeman, T. L. & Stinnett, R. D. (1991). Patterns of sexual arousal and history in a "normal" sample of young men. *Archives of Sexual Behavior, 20*(2), 137-150.

Tierney, D. W. & McCabe, M. P. (2001). An evaluation of self-report measures of cognitive distortions and empathy among Australian sex offenders. *Archives of Sexual Behavior, 30*(5), 495-519.

Valliere, V. (1997). Relationship between alcohol use, alcohol expectancies, and sexual offenses in convicted offenders. In B. Schwartz & H. Cellini (Eds.), *The sex offender: New insights, treatment innovations, and legal developments* (Vol. II, pp. 3-1–3-14). New Jersey: Civic Research Institute.

Ward, T., Hudson, S. M., Johnston, L., & Marshall, W. L. (1997). Cognitive distortions in sex offenders: An integrative review. *Clinical Psychology Review, 17*(5), 479-507.

Chapter 4

Women Who Sexually Abuse Children

Myriam S. Denov
Franca Cortoni

INTRODUCTION

Interest in the issue of child sexual abuse has surged. However, almost all the empirical studies in this area have focused on female victims of male perpetrators and sexual offending has been construed in both the popular and professional domain as an exclusively male domain. Although little doubt exists that males commit the vast majority of sexual offences reported to police (Snyder, 2000), the notion of male abusers has become definitive within the field of child sexual abuse. This has obscured the recognition that females can perpetrate acts of sexual violence as well.

A significant impediment to the recognition of female sex offending has been idealized beliefs that females, and particularly mothers, are incapable of sexually abusing children. For example, Mathis (1972) dismissed the possibility that females could sexually abuse because it was "unthinkable" that a woman "might seduce a helpless child into sex play." Even if she did, "What harm could be done without a penis?" (p. 54). To perceive a woman as sexually aggressive, or worse, as a sexual offender, is contrary to traditional "sexual scripts" that are heterosexual and gendered (Byers, 1996). Specific sex roles are assigned to men and others are assigned to women. Traditional sexual scripts exclude the image of women as sexual aggressors, as initiating sex with men, as indicating their sexual interest and, at times, coercing their reluctant partners to engage in unwanted sexual activities (Byers & O'Sullivan, 1998). To be considered "feminine" means to be nurturing, protecting, and to be nonaggressive and nonsexual. As such, to accept that women sexually abuse children requires challenging powerful stereotypes about motherhood and female-child relationships (Denov, 2003a).

Although the evidence that women sexually abuse children has been available for many years, society has only recently begun to accept that it occurs and to explore it. Some effort has been made to study female perpetrators in the United Kingdom, the United States, and Canada from both a psychological/psychodynamic perspective (Cooper, Swaminath, Baxter, & Poulin, 1990; Rowan, Rowan, & Langelier, 1990; McCarty, 1986), and a sociological perspective (Mathews, Matthews, & Speltz, 1989; Saradjian, 1996), but our understanding of these women remains limited.

This chapter explores the complex issue of women who sexually abuse children. The first part of the chapter traces the aetiology of female sex offending, the debate concerning the prevalence of the phenomenon, and the consequences of female sex offending on both male and female victims. The second part of the chapter addresses assessment and treatment issues concerning female sex offenders and concludes with a case example and treatment plan, incorporating both short- and long-term objectives.

ETIOLOGY

Given the lack of research in the area, few well-formulated theories of female sex offending have been developed and a clear understanding of its etiology has not been reached. Much of the research that has been conducted in the area is based on very small sample sizes, mostly in the form of case studies. Researchers develop typologies of female sex offenders based on observable characteristics of the offenders and their offenses. Research to date has indicated that the life histories of abusers, their relationships, and social circumstances are related to their sexually abusive behavior (Saradjian, 1996).

According to Matthews (1993), female child molesters typically share the following traits: shame, low self-esteem, impaired empathy, and anger, which is said to be comprised of underlying pain and fear. Other authors have suggested that factors such as troubled childhoods (McCarty, 1986; Mathews et al., 1989), being sexually abused as a child (Rowan et al., 1990; Allen, 1991), severe psychological disturbance (McCarty, 1986; Rowan et al., 1990), substance abuse (Chasnoff et al., 1986), and a history of compulsive sexual activity (Mathews et al., 1989; Allen, 1991) may contribute to the aetiology of child sexual abuse by women.

One of the seminal studies in the area was conducted by Mathews et al. (1989), who carried out in-depth interviews over a one-year period with a sample of sixteen female sex offenders who were part of the Genesis II Female Sex Offenders Program. From their research, Mathews et al. (1989) generated three typologies of female sex offenders: teacher/lover, male-coerced/male-accompanied, and predisposed based on the offender's motivation to commit sexual offenses.*

Teacher/Lover

This type of offender is an adult woman who acts as the initiator of the sexual abuse of an adolescent, usually a male. The offender tends to act in a position of power through her age and role in the victim's life and has a difficult time accepting that her behavior is criminal given that she has no malice or hostility for the victim. Rather than criminal, the offender views her sexual interactions with the victim as an act of kindness and an overall expression of her love, thus minimizing and denying the harm inflicted on her victim. According to Mathews et al. (1989), the teacher/lover comes from a dysfunctional family, is usually a victim of severe emotional and verbal abuse as a child, particularly from an emotionally distant father, and may have a history of unsuccessful and abusive relationships as an adult.

Male-Coerced/Male-Accompanied

The women in this category endorse a traditional lifestyle with the husband as breadwinner and the wife as homemaker. Male-coerced offenders may be dependent on men, feel generally powerless in interpersonal relationships, and fear their partner's anger. These offenders are influenced by a male to participate in sexual abuse, often under the threat of physical punishment. The women are likely to join in the sexual abuse, which their partner has previously committed independently. Mathews et al. (1989) characterized these female of-

---

*Although several other authors have created similar typologies for female sex offenders and their offenses, Mathews' (1987) typology remains the most widely recognized.

fenders as passive, angry, having low self-esteem, problems with substance abuse, and low to average intellectual functioning. In an earlier classification of female sex offenders, Mathews (1987) made a distinction between male-coerced and male-accompanied offenders. Unlike male-coerced offenders who are reluctant to participate in abuse but do so because of a fear of punishment, the male-accompanied offenders usually participate more actively in abuse.

Predisposed

Unlike those in the male-coerced category, predisposed offenders initiate the sexual abuse independently. These have a long history of sexual abuse and are involved in unhealthy and abusive intimate relationships as adults. Mathews et al. (1989) note that predisposed offenders have "low self-esteem, passivity, extreme anger and acting out behavior, accompanied by . . . psychopathology (i.e., extreme distrust, anguish, nervousness, distorted thinking, feelings of persecution, and dependence on drugs, alcohol, food or dependent relationships with men)" (p. 39). For the most part, the victims of predisposed offender's are family members, often their own children, and their offenses involve violence. In addition to being sexually abused, victims of predisposed offenders are often physically abused or neglected by the offender.

Despite the growing research in the field, our current understanding of the aetiology of female sex offending is inconclusive at best. Larger and more representative samples are required to gain a deeper understanding of the genesis of the problem.

PREVALENCE

When authors speak of prevalence rates in relation to female sexual offending, they often speak of uncertainty and controversy (Denov, 2003b). In the 1970s and early 1980s, literature on sexual offenders suggested that sexual offending among females was so rare that it was "of little significance" (Mathis, 1972, p. 54). Similarly, Freund, Heasman, Racansky, & Glancy (1984, p. 193) declared that "pedophilia . . . does not exist at all in women." However, recent studies emerging from the United States, Canada, and the United Kingdom have begun to acknowledge the existence of female sexual offenders (Cooper et al., 1990; Fromuth & Conn, 1997; Saradjian, 1996). Nonetheless, prevalence of the phenomenon is still debated. Some authors and clinicians continue to assert that female sex offending is a rare phenomenon (American Psychiatric Association, 1994; O'Hagan, 1989). For example, in its discussion of *paraphilias*—a diagnostic category that includes acts of exhibitionism, fetishism, frotteurism, pedophilia, sexual masochism, sexual sadism, transvestism, and voyeurism—the *Diagnostic and Statistical Manual,* fourth edition (1994), indicates that "except for sexual masochism . . . paraphilias are almost never diagnosed in females" (p. 524). Similarly, O'Hagan (1989) declares that sexual abuse by females can be considered an "aberration" that has little or no significance for professionals working with sexual abuse.

In contrast, Mendel (1995) maintains that child sexual abuse by females is underrecognized and the lack of recognition is, in part, a result of traditional sexual scripts that depict women as incapable of committing sexual offenses (Denov, 2004). The following section provides an overview of the available data concerning the prevalence of female sex offending and addresses the debate as to whether the problem is rare or underrecognized.

Data from official sources on offender populations in the United States, the United Kingdom, and Canada lend support to the conclusion that female sex offending is indeed a rare phenomenon. According to the U.S. Department of Justice (2002), in the United States in 2001, 1.2 percent of those charged with forcible rape and 8 percent charged with sexual offenses were female. In the United Kingdom, Home Office figures show that 2 percent of adults convicted of a sexual offense were female (Home Office, 2001). Recent statistics from the Canadian Centre for Justice Statistics (2001) reveal that in Canada in 2000, 1.5 percent of adults convicted of sexual assault were female.

Case report literature on populations of male and female victims also reveals very small numbers of female perpetrators. Pierce and Pierce (1985) reviewed 205 cases of substantiated sexual abuse reported to a child abuse hotline between 1976 and 1979. One hundred and eighty victims were female and twenty-five were male. The authors found that only 1 percent of female victims and 4 percent of male victims were abused by a female perpetrator. Reinhart (1987) analyzed case reports between 1983 and 1985 of 189 sexually abused boys and 189 sexually abused girls who had been identified, evaluated, and referred to a center for child sexual abuse. Reinhart reported that 4.2 percent of the perpetrators of sexual abuse against the boys and 2.1 percent of the perpetrators against girls were female. Roane (1992) reviewed seventy-seven cases of sexually abused boys referred to a multidisciplinary child protection team. Six of the boys (7.8 percent) reported abuse by a female offender.

Overall, the case report literature points to the rarity of female sex offending. What is problematic about this assertion, however, is that it has not only assumed that the literature accurately reflects the true incidence of female sexual offending, but it has also failed to consider that case-report studies and self-report studies too often provide conflicting portraits of the prevalence of the phenomenon.

Upon examining the available self-report data on the issue of female sex offending, one might conclude that it is not rare, but under-recognized. With regard to studies that have explored male and female victim populations, Fritz, Stoll, & Wagner (1981) administered a questionnaire to 412 male and 540 female college students, and found that 4.8 percent of the men and 7.8 percent of the women reported having been molested as a child. Interestingly, 60 percent of the abused men and 10 percent of the abused women reported having been molested by a female. In their research involving college men, Fromuth and Burkhart (1989) discovered that 15 percent of 253 men in the first sample and 13 percent of 329 men in the second sample reported childhood sexual abuse. The majority of perpetrators were female: 78 percent of respondents in the first sample and 72 percent in the second sample reported having experienced sexual abuse by a female.

Allen (1991) surveyed seventy-five males and sixty-five females convicted of sexual offenses against children. Thirty-six percent of the male offenders and 72 percent of the female offenders reported they had been sexually abused as children. Of those who reported being sexually abused, 45 percent of the males and 6 percent of the females reported that their sexual abuser had been female. Mendel (1995) examined 124 sexually abused males undergoing therapy in private and community mental health clinics. He found that 60 percent of his sample reported childhood sexual activity with females, 14 percent indicated sexual interactions with females only, and 46 percent reported sexual activity with both males and females. Groth (1979) conducted a study of 348 convicted male rapists and child molesters and found that 106 offenders reported childhood sexual trauma. Of those reporting sexual trauma, 51 percent reported abuse by a male perpetrator and 42 percent reported abuse by a female perpetrator. Data was unavailable for 7 percent of the sample of offenders.

This review of the literature on female sex offending demonstrates that self-report studies yield notably higher rates of female sex offending than case-report studies, particularly for male victim populations. This suggests that female sexual offending may be under-reported to official agencies, and throws into question the accuracy of case-report data. In part, the discrepancy in case and self-report data may reflect the nature of these types of data collection. Case-report data reflects only those who are exposed to the criminal justice or social service systems. This data may be fraught with inconsistencies given that societal taboos may deter many victims from reporting female sex offending to the police and child welfare agencies (Denov, 2003b). Aside from victim underreporting, which may stem from the taboo nature of female sexual abuse, and that males are unlikely to report such abuse (Mendel, 1995), research has also suggested that dismissive professional responses may contribute to an underrecognition of the problem (Denov, 2001, 2003a). Professionals may minimize the seriousness of sexual abuse by females and not retain, investigate, and/or prosecute such cases. Ultimately, these cases may elude inclusion in official data.

Although the prevalence of the phenomenon continues to be difficult to determine, the problem may be greater than is revealed in official data. Nonetheless, cause for panic in searching out the "new" and previously undetected female sex offender is unwarranted. This is one of the dangers associated with providing attention to an under-recognized issue. What is essential is that mental health and child protection professionals who play a crucial role in the official recognition of the problem consider the possibility of female sexual abuse.

LONG-TERM CONSEQUENCES OF CHILD SEXUAL ABUSE BY FEMALES

Although ample literature addresses the long-term effects of sexual abuse by males, few studies have specifically examined the long-term effects of sexual abuse by females. Emerging studies reveal that both the public and professionals working in the area of child welfare perceive sexual abuse by females as relatively harmless when compared to sexual abuse by males (Broussard, Wagner, & Kazelskis, 1991; Hetherton & Beardsall, 1998; Denov, 2001). In contrast, research on male and female victims reveals that female-perpetrated sexual abuse may be harmful and debilitating to victims (Rosencrans, 1997). In Denov's (2004) study, all respondents who had been abused by both males and females reported that the sexual abuse by females was more harmful and detrimental than the sexual abuse they had experienced by males. The recent literature addressing the impact of sexual abuse by females has underscored victims' long-term difficulties with substance abuse, self-injury, suicidal ideation, depression, and rage. Other effects include problematic relationships with women, difficulties with sexuality, and identity issues.

Substance Abuse

Substance abuse is said to be a coping strategy among victims of child sexual abuse to help repress memories of the abuse, and to cope with emotions such as a sense of powerlessness, lower self-esteem, and the inability to trust others (Rohsenow, Corbett, & Devine, 1988). Several authors have documented substance abuse among their samples of victims of sexual abuse by females (Rosencrans, 1997; Krug, 1989). As this male victim explains, alcohol and drugs were efficient means to silence their rage and numb the pain that came from being sexually abused,

> I started drinking and taking drugs when I was twelve. That helped the pain go away. . . . No one would believe me about all of the . . . sexual abuse, so when I took the drugs and alcohol, I didn't even have to believe it myself. (Denov, 2004a, p. 1145)

Self-Injury

Self-injury has been described as tattooing one's rage on one's skin—or a means by which some individuals speak about social, political, and personal experiences, and cope with distress (Babiker & Arnold, 1997). Self-injurious behavior, whether in the form of slashing, cutting, or burning oneself, has been documented as a response to childhood sexual abuse, and has been reported in studies on victims of female sex offenders (Mitchell & Morse, 1998; Denov, 2004). As this female victim notes,

> When I talk about the sexual abuse by my mother . . . I often want to turn on myself. . . . I harm myself sexually. . . . I used to stick things up inside me. . . . My mother used to stick things inside me. I'm sure it's related to that. (Denov, 2004a, p. 1146)

Suicide

Suicidal tendencies have been found more frequently in sexual abuse victims than the general population. Brown and Anderson (1991) found that 88 percent of males sexually abused as children were suicidal in comparison to 57 percent of nonvictims of sexual abuse. Suicidal tendencies have been found among victims of female sexual abuse (Rosencrans, 1997). This female victim explains, "It's connected to all of the abuse. It left me with . . . suicidal wishes." (Denov, 2004b, p. 152)

Depression

Depression has been linked with child sexual abuse (Mendel, 1995). Hunter (1991) found that adults sexually abused as children to be more depressed than nonvictims. Depression as an aftereffect of sexual abuse has also been noted in the literature on female perpetration (Krug, 1989; Denov, 2004a). This female victim explains,

> It was terrible having these memories [of sexual abuse]. . . . I've been hospitalized three times for depression. Sometimes the memories of all this stuff would become so overwhelming that I just wasn't able to function. (Denov, 2004b, p. 153)

Rage

Dhaliwal, Gauzas, Antonowicz, & Ross (1996) assert that anger is a coping strategy to deal with sexual abuse. Briere, Evans, Runtz, & Wall (1988) found both sexually abused men and women manifested greater anger than their nonabused controls. Studies on survivors of female sexual abuse have noted rage among their participants (Krug,

1989; Denov, 2004a). For many survivors, the rage was directed toward the women who sexually abused them.

> I was in such a rage . . . The worst fantasy that I had was to . . . beat the hell out of [my perpetrator], rape, sodomize her and then say to her "Now *you* live with what I did, because that's what *you* did." (Denov, 2004b, p. 154)

Relationships with Women

Uncontrolled clinical reports with male and female victims of sexual abuse agree that maintaining sustained and meaningful relationships following a sexually abusive experience is difficult (Krug, 1989). Denov (2004a) suggests that sexual abuse by women may later result in mistrust and strained relationships with women. One female survivor reports,

> The sexual abuse affected my relationships with women all of my life. I could not trust women. I trusted men even though men [sexually] abused me as well. What was done to me by my mother and grandmother was so insidious that I just couldn't feel comfortable with a woman. (Denov, 2004a, p. 1147)

Several participants in Denov's study reported wanting to retaliate against female strangers in order to regain a sense of power and control because of the sexual abuse experience. These feelings often manifested in violent sexual fantasies.

> I [had sexual] fantasies and they were an angry way of gaining control and taking revenge on women. Because I was abused by a woman, I get these feelings where I want to fuck all the women that I can. . . . I'll be in control this time. (Denov, 2004a, p. 1148)

Fear of Sexuality and Sexually Abusing Children

Researchers have found that men and women who have been sexually abused by females may experience later difficulties with sexuality and intimacy (Rosencrans, 1997). Moreover, survivors report a fear of sexually abusing children. Denov's (2004a) study reveals that the fear of abusing children was so strong that several participants reported spending less time with their children or avoided being alone with them.

> I know that my sexual stuff has really warped my ability to parent my daughter. I'm afraid to be alone with my daughter. It's probably one of the most troubling components of my adult life. ... I'm afraid [of sexually abusing her]. (Denov, 4002a, p. 1150)

Self-Concept and Identity

The majority of the male and female participants in Denov's (2004a) study struggled with their sense of identity and self-concept. Female survivors reported negating their female identity as children and feared growing into women.

> Probably the first thing that really becomes clear to me when I'm able to look back on the experience, is that I did not want to grow to be a woman. I wanted desperately to be a boy. ... I think my motivation was ... that I did not want to grow up to assume the form of my abuser. (Denov, 2004b, p. 156)

Several female participants in this study continued to deny their femininity in adulthood. One respondent explained that to her, females are dangerous and potential sexual abusers and she would be safest to others and to herself, if she were not female.

> I don't even want to have a distinguishably female form. ... I just want to lose it all in fat. ... I wear bulky clothing, I dress in men's clothes ... I would be safest and be safe for other people if I'm not female. ... Being a woman is a large part of my identity and it's my biggest struggle. (Denov, 2004b, p. 156)

Male survivors in this study also reported difficulties with their identity and self-concept. In particular, many claimed that following the sexual abuse they felt as though they had "failed" as men. Being sexually victimized by a woman, a "weaker" gender, caused much humiliation and appeared to throw into question their sense of masculinity.

I felt like I was a victim, and for a man to be a victim is an embarrassment. . . . I was not only a victim, but a victim of a woman—a weaker gender. . . . It makes you a much lesser man. . . . I didn't feel very comfortable with my manliness. (Denov, 2004b, p. 157)

Victims of female sex offenders appear to experience similar aftereffects to those that have been identified among victims of sexual abuse by males. These comparable aftereffects include problems with substance abuse, self-injury, depression, suicide, and sexual difficulties. The long-term effects that appear unique to those sexually abused by females are the confusion surrounding their self-concept and identity, the intense rage that is often directed at women, and the ongoing struggle with daily relationships with women.

ASSESSMENT

Despite the increasing attention devoted to female sexual offenders, very little empirical work has clearly established the assessment and treatment needs of this unique population of offenders. In their review of the existing literature on women sexual offenders, Grayston and De Luca (1999) note that only sparse data exist on the topic, and that clinicians have developed highly tentative theories and clinical responses to female perpetrators based on inadequate samples. Similarly, in their review of twelve cases of female sexual offenders, Nathan and Ward (2002) comment that any comprehensive theory of female sexual offending should delineate distinct pathways to offending that will help to establish greater direction for assessment and treatment. Based on the limited available research, this section outlines the assessment and treatment needs of female sex offenders. Although cultural issues would normally be important components to consider within this context, the limited available research makes it currently impossible to make any clear statements or recommendations in that respect. The discussion of assessment focuses specifically on risk assessments and on establishing effective ways to assess an offender's unique treatment needs. The segment on treatment highlights the importance of the therapeutic context in addressing issues concerning relationship needs, emotional regulation, coping strategies, thinking patterns, deviant fantasies and arousal, and self-management. The section ends with a case study of a thirty-five-year-old woman sexual offender, and based on her family history and offense characteristics and motivations, discusses her unique treatment needs.

The goals of a specialized assessment of sexual offenders are to determine the likelihood of sexual reoffending and to ascertain areas for therapeutic intervention that will reduce that risk and provide offenders with alternatives models of thinking and behavior. The assessment of risk should be based on a thorough analysis of the offending behavior, including the presence of a co-offender, and an analysis of the elements that contributed to the offense. The assessment of treatment needs should be guided by the current, albeit limited, empirical knowledge of the factors that appear related to sexual offending in female offenders. This section first reviews issues related to risk assessment, and then draws tentative conclusions on the factors that appear related to sexual recidivism in women. It then details the content of the assessment for treatment needs.

Risk of Recidivism

Criminal justice systems are primarily concerned with risk of reoffending and the type of interventions required to effectively manage that risk (Andrews & Bonta, 2003). Women who come to the attention to the criminal justice system as a result of their sexual offending behavior will therefore typically require an assessment of risk of recidivism and of treatment need. Normally, a risk assessment focuses on the static and dynamic risk factors that predict sexual recidivism. Static factors, by their very nature, are unchangeable. Examples of static factors related to sexual recidivism in male offenders include a past history of sexual offending, male victims, stranger victims, and the presence of sexually deviant interest (Hanson & Thornton, 2000). Dynamic risk factors are those factors that are related to sexual recidivism but are changeable. Some examples of dynamic risk factors in male sexual offenders include intimacy deficits, attitudes supportive of sexual abuse, and sexual preoccupation (Hanson & Harris, 2001).

Unfortunately, very little is known about the static and dynamic risk factors of female sexual offenders. The low rates of reported cases of sexual abuse by women and the low rates of sexual recidivism of these offenders make it very difficult to conduct research in the area. For example, in a follow-up of 115 U.S. female sexual offenders for an average of five-and-a-half years (ranging from two months to ten years), Peterson, Colebank, and Motta (2002) found a zero rate of sexual recidivism. In this study, all the women had been or continued to be in treatment for their sexually offending behavior. In a follow-up of seventy-two female sexual offenders incarcerated in Canada between 1972 and 1998, Williams and Nicholaichuk (2001) found a sexual recidivism rate of 3.3 percent (two cases). These two recidivists were women who had exclusively engaged in solo offending. Based on their research, Williams and Nicholaichuk (2001) suggest that a history of sexual reoffending, nonincest offending, and solo offending are static factors related to sexual recidivism in female offenders. In women offenders in general, dynamic risk factors related to general recidivism include antisocial attitudes and associates, substance abuse as precursor to offending, problematic relationships, and emotional dyscontrol (Blanchette, 2001). As discussed in the following, these factors are also commonly found in female sexual offenders. It is reasonable at this time to also consider these factors in an assessment of risk of sexual recidivism.

Treatment Needs

To date, research indicates that female sexual offenders have a few aspects in common with male sexual offenders. On the basis of available evidence, common to both male and female sexual offenders are denial or minimization of the offending behavior, distorted cognitions about the sexual offending, attitudes that condone sexual abuse, intimacy deficits, and the use of sex to regulate emotional states or fulfill intimacy needs (Grayston & De Luca, 1999; Nathan & Ward, 2002). In addition, for at least some of these offenders, a desire for sexual gratification is directly related to the abuse.

An element that appears unique to female sexual offenders is the frequent presence of a co-offender (Grayston & De Luca, 1999). Of the women who co-offended, a subgroup is clearly identified as having been coerced into the offending while another subgroup of offenders co-offends willingly. Some of these women even initiate the offending behavior. Some female offenders engage in both solo and co-offending (Grayston & De Luca, 1999). From these findings, the role of the co-offender in the offending behavior needs to be carefully assessed to determine the full extent of the woman's willingness to participate in the abuse. Different treatment needs are likely to emerge if the woman was coerced into the abuse, as opposed to being a willing participant or an initiator. A coerced offender may demonstrate significant deficits in assertiveness and an exaggerated dependence on her co-offender. Deviant arousal and fantasizing, and attitudes that condone sexual abuse may appear more frequently in initiators or willing participants. An in-depth examination of the elements that motivated the abuser and her current views of the offending behavior will be enlightening in that respect.

An examination of the developmental and family history of the offender is often a good starting point for the assessment. It helps the woman open up and become more comfortable during the evaluation before the focus turns to the offending behavior itself. Obtaining this history also sets the stage for examining her current functioning, including her marital and parental status, her coping patterns, and her general social functioning, including the use of substances. This information provides clues to the elements that have likely contributed to the development of the offending behavior, and sets the context from which realistic goals for the future can be established. For example, a woman who intends on reuniting with her children, whom she abused, may need to reset her goals.

The background information also helps establish how a history of physical, emotional, or sexual victimization may be linked to her current behavior. If sexual victimization is present, do not let it obscure the woman's responsibility in her current offending behavior. Although sexual victimization is likely related to her pattern of relating to others, as well as her pattern of coping, it is highly unlikely that it is the main reason why the woman chose to engage in the abuse herself. Empirical evidence clearly shows that only a proportion of women who sexually abuse were sexually victimized themselves (Wiegel, Abel, & Jordan, 2003). Paying undue attention to the victimization history could cloud other issues that are related to the offending behavior such as relationships and attitudes supportive of sexual abuse. Such a focus may also inadvertently reinforce distorted beliefs about the woman's lack of responsibility for the offending behavior and for making the necessary changes to her life (Eldridge & Saradjian, 2000).

The development and history of sexual behavior is another important area to assess. Tied to this area is the meaning and role of sex in the woman's life. Her beliefs about sexual activity, and by extension sexual abuse, may be linked to her beliefs about gender roles, sense of entitlement, or refusal to acknowledge the harm caused by the abuse. In this context, the role that sex and sexuality play in the woman's life needs to be determined to help establish its potential motivational role in the offending behavior. In addition, a careful examination of the coping patterns of women is required to determine the role sexual activity in general and sexual abuse in particular may play in alleviating negative emotional states. The presence and extent of deviant sexual fantasies and arousal will needs to be considered within this context.

The link between pro-offending attitudes and criminal behavior for all types of offenders of both genders is firmly established (Andrews & Bonta, 2003; Blanchette, 2001). In male sexual offenders, pro-abuse attitudes are a major dynamic risk factor (Hanson & Harris, 2001). Female sexual offenders also have distorted beliefs about themselves and about children as well as deny or minimize their involvement in the abuse (Grayston & De Luca, 1999; Saradjian, 1996). Any assessment would therefore need to elucidate the presence of denial and minimization, pro-offending attitudes and other distorted beliefs and to determine their likely contribution to the offending behavior. Core beliefs about relationships, children, and gender roles also require examination as they are likely intertwined with pro-offending attitudes (Eldridge & Saradjian, 2000; Mann & Beech, 2003).

TREATMENT

Women who sexually abuse children must identify and effectively deal with the factors that contributed to their offense (Eldridge & Saradjian, 2000). The main goals of treatment are therefore to identify such factors, to understand the needs the sexually abusive behavior fulfills, and to develop alternate positive ways to meet those needs. A need for power, love, or intimacy characterize women who sexually offend (Saradjian, 1996). These needs are related to poor attachment and patterns of dysfunctional relationships resulting from emotional, physical, and/or sexual abuse experienced during childhood. These abusive experiences are predominant in the developmental experiences of women who sexually offend (Grayston & De Luca, 1999; Saradjian, 1996), as they are in the experiences of women offenders in general (Task Force on Federally Sentenced Women, 1990).

Ward and Stewart (2003) argue that one way to reduce sexual reoffending is to provide offenders with the ability to lead "good lives." These authors based their argument on the underlying theoretical basis of well-being and personal identity, which states that humans are goal-directed and inclined to obtain "goods" that will improve their well being. "Good lives" refer to ways of living that are healthy for the individual, and "goods" refer to valued outcomes (Ward & Stewart, 2003). Primary "goods" or valued outcomes, without which the "good life" cannot be achieved, include life, knowledge, excellence at play and work, autonomy and self-directness, meaning and purpose in life, freedom from emotional turmoil, happiness, relationships, and community. In the case of women who sexually abuse, their sense of well-being is distorted and they have learned to fulfill their needs in dysfunctional ways (Eldridge & Saradjian, 2000). Treatment needs to focus on those areas not only to help prevent a return to previous dysfunctional patterns, but also to provide an improvement in the general well-being of these women. In this manner, the prevention of further sexual offending behavior is likely to be improved (Ward & Stewart, 2003).

Relationships Needs

According to Saradjian (1996), a fundamental need identified in female sexual offenders involves the giving and receiving of human care, and a need for a degree of control and power in their lives. Too frequently, these women have enmeshed relationships and a limited sense of autonomy. Treatment would need to focus on identifying the various issues that are preventing the woman from leading a fulfilling life, and on equipping her with the skills, values, beliefs, and supports required to help her establish satisfying relationships.

Emotional Regulation

An inherent aspect of relationships and of positive coping is emotional regulation. Female sexual offenders, as with many male sexual offenders, often do not understand their emotional states, mislabel them, or simply react to them in extreme ways (Eldridge & Sarajdian, 2000). Treatment would need to help the woman learn strategies to first accurately identify these feelings, and develop strategies to effectively manage them. For example, learning to identify the physiological states associated with various feelings, and learning to label those feelings appropriately, allows for the use of appropriate coping that directly address those emotional states. These include learning to tolerate negative emotional states, and learning to let them go in safe ways. For some women, these emotional states may be overwhelming. In such cases, the woman would need help in learning to tolerate and express her feelings without feeling overwhelmed.

Coping Strategies and Coping Patterns

Lazarus and Folkman (1984) define coping as "constantly changing cognitive and behavioral efforts to manage specific external and/or internal demands that are appraised as taxing or exceeding the resources of the person" (p. 141). The coping literature outlines two major approaches to coping: *intraindividual* and *interindividual*. The intraindividual approach is based on a contextual approach to coping and is concerned with how people cope in a given situation (Parker & Endler, 1996). The interindividual approach is based on a trait or dispositional model of coping. It identifies basic coping patterns, also called coping styles, used by individuals across situations. The premise of the interindividual approach is that individuals have a preference or a prototypical manner of attempting to cope with problematic situations when a variety of coping responses is feasible (Endler & Parker, 1999). Consequently, people will exhibit consistency in the nature of their coping strategies across situations. Eldridge and Saradjian (2000) posit that for female sexual offenders, sexual abuse becomes a coping mechanism used to avoid feelings such as fear, anger, and loneliness. The use of sex as a coping strategy is prevalent in male sexual offenders (Cortoni & Marshall, 2001), and a deficit in coping strategies is viewed as a fundamental problem with sexual offenders, leading to an increased risk of relapse (Miner, 2000; Miner, Day, Nafpaktitis, 1989).

In treatment with female offenders, the intraindividual approach to coping is typically utilized. In other words, the tendency is to examine the coping responses of the woman in the context of specific situations and to work at changing the woman's response to those situations. Although identifying specific skill deficits is important, the general coping pattern in response to all kinds of stressors should also be addressed. For example, if the woman consistently evades or denies all kinds of problematic situations or life problems, simply teaching her to be proactive in a given situation will not address this overall tendency. Treatment should focus on helping the woman develop a coping pattern that will be useful to address all kinds of stressors, and not just those directly related to her offending behavior. In this way, she will be better equipped to deal with the inevitable problems that life brings. As well, if the woman engages in much more productive problem-solving modes in general, she would be more likely to be effective in problem solving particular situations directly related to her risk of recidivism.

Thinking Patterns

As previously discussed, attitudes and beliefs supportive of sexual offending is an important aspect of treatment. These attitudes and beliefs are typically formed by early childhood experiences and are either confirmed or modified by further experiences in life. They become schemas that follow a similar theme or pattern (Mann & Beech, 2003). In treatment, cognitive restructure techniques are helpful to address the specific cognitive distortions related to the offending behavior (Marshall, Anderson, & Fernandez, 1999). In addition, treatment should address the core beliefs that facilitate abusive behavior (Mann & Beech, 2003). These core beliefs may be related to gender roles, or a sense of entitlement to one's needs above others.

Using her life history, the woman can identify her habitual patterns of thinking and examine their impact not only on her offending behavior, but also on other problematic areas of her life such as relationship problems or emotional regulation. Enduring maladaptive themes that influence several aspects of the woman's life beyond the offending behavior are important areas to address in treatment. These themes should be analyzed, and their accuracy and utility questioned (Langton & Marshall, 2000). Evidence disconfirming dysfunctional beliefs are useful within this context. For example, providing psychoeducational material about the effects of all kinds of abuse can counteract the belief that abuse is a normal part of growing up. The goals are to help the woman identify her maladaptive thinking patterns, understand the role they played in creating an unhealthy life, and develop alternative schemas to help set the foundation for healthier living.

Deviant Fantasies and Arousal

As with a segment of male sexual offenders, deviant arousal and fantasies are part of the dynamics of the offending behavior in cases of female sexual offenders (Eldridge & Saradjian, 2000; Grayston & De Luca, 1999; Mathews et al., 1989; Nathan & Ward, 2002). Little is known about the role these fantasies and arousal may play in the etiology of sexual offending in females. Eldridge and Saradjian (2000) consider that the fantasies are a stage between negative emotions and offending. Further, they posit that deviant fantasies, mental rehearsal or daydreaming may actually play a role in helping the woman make sense of her own victimization. Although this position clearly awaits empirical verification, they suggest traditional behavioral techniques such as covert sensitization to help the woman control her deviant arousal.*

Marshall et al. (1999) discuss how addressing factors related to sexual offending such as intimacy deficits and attitudes supportive of sexual abuse may reduce deviant arousal. For male offenders, deviant arousal is connected to negative emotional states (Looman, 1995; McKibben, Proulx, & Lusignan, 1994; Proulx, McKibben, & Lusignan, 1996). To date, it appears that, at least for a number of female sexual offenders, the deviancy is tied to factors such as a need for power or the regulation of emotions (Saradjian, 1996). Similar to male offenders, addressing these needs in female offenders may concurrently eliminate the presence of deviant arousal. Although this position also awaits empirical verification, viewing deviant sexual arousal in women as simply masking other needs allows for therapeutic exploration and resolution of these other needs, an approach that is consistent with the good lives model presented by Ward and Stewart (2003).

---

*The application of behavioral techniques to modify deviant arousal requires specialized knowledge and the reader is referred to Marshall et al. (1999) for their excellent review of this area.

Self-Management

The concept of relapse prevention has undergone considerable changes in recent years (Laws, Hudson, & Ward, 2000). These changes were brought about by an increased understanding of the underpinning of sexually offending behavior, as well as the need for more effective treatment modalities (Laws et al., 2000). Conceptually, relapse prevention is the self-management of behavior, leading to long-lasting behavioral changes. The traditional relapse prevention model focuses on the identification of high-risk situations and identification of strategies to avoid those situations. In contrast, the self-management model focuses on the development of a realistic and meaningful approach to managing and leading one's life in a manner that eliminates the need for the behavior one is attempting to change. This approach is more consistent with the literature on the psychology of goal setting and helps reduce resistance in treatment by ensuring the work is meaningful for the offender (Mann, 2000).

The development of the self-management plan is ongoing throughout the therapeutic process. For women who sexually offend, using the self-management approach requires an understanding of the goals met by the offending behavior. Only then can treatment offer the possibility of meeting those goals in more appropriate ways. Using the "New Me" model, Eldridge and Saradjian (2000) discuss how to help the woman establish a "New Life" plan. An inherent component of this plan is the understanding of what motivated the woman to initially offend and/or continue to offend. A detailed life and offense pattern analysis provides an understanding of the needs, however dysfunctional, that were met via the abusive behavior. Further, this analysis identifies the factors that directly contributed to the offending behavior such as distorted beliefs, relationship needs, and deviant arousal. Ward and Stewart (2003) conceptualized these factors as obstacles associated with a distortion of the needs fulfilled by the offending behavior. Although the overall goal of treatment is to help the woman remove these obstacles from her life, the self-management plan aims to provide a "map" from which the woman will develop her new "good life" that will ensure her needs are realistically and appropriately met. The following case will illustrate this process.

CASE EXAMPLE

Jane is a thirty-five-year-old woman convicted of sexually abusing two boys, ages three and five, who were in her care while their mother worked. The abuse started with fondling, and eventually involved Jane performing fellatio on the boys, sometimes up to four times per week. The abuse lasted approximately six months. The abuse was discovered when the boys were playing and started to reenact some of the offending behavior at home. During the assessment, Jane was reluctant to discuss the details of the offenses. She stated that her actions never seemed to bother the boys and that they never cried. She also felt that the boys benefited from the closeness inherent in the abuse. She also believed it did not hurt them as she used to play sexual games as a child, and she had found them enjoyable. Jane did recognize that others would feel differently about her behavior. She was not able to explain her thought processes that led her to the offending behavior, nor could she identify her emotional states when the offending took place. Jane grew up in a foster home from the age of two until she was seventeen, when her foster mother became ill and passed away. Her foster father was physically and emotionally abusive toward Jane and her foster siblings. Jane has had no contact with her foster siblings or father since she left the home at age seventeen. She also has no contact with her biological family. At the time of the offenses, Jane was separated from her abusive husband and living alone. He was not involved in the offending behavior. Since her separation, Jane received social assistance, and supplemented her income by providing child care. Jane is a high school graduate but has no marketable skills. Her work history is nonexistent as her husband supported her during their marriage.

When her life history was examined, it became evident that Jane was chronically lonely. She had no adult friends. Her only significant adult relationship was her marriage, which lasted from ages nineteen to thirty-three. Her ex-husband, whom she met in high school, became increasingly emotionally and physically abusive toward her, and prevented her from establishing a circle of friends outside of the marriage.

Jane reported that while growing up, she and her siblings engaged in sexual games, mostly in the context of "playing doctor." She spoke fondly of those memories, stating that those games were always enjoyable times during an otherwise stressful childhood. Her foster parents never found out about those games. Jane's first consensual experience with sexual intercourse was at age fourteen with a fifteen-year-old boy who lived in the same neighborhood. Jane reported engaging in regular intercourse from the age of fifteen with boys she was dating. She met her husband at age eighteen and they married when they graduated high school when they were both nineteen years old. Jane reported that during her marriage, as her husband's abuse increased, Jane would seek out opportunities to have sex with him as those were the only times she felt like he still cared for her.

Jane's goal for the future is to obtain a job so she can become self-supportive, and to eventually again marry.

Treatment Plan

Jane has a number of unmet needs in her life. These include a lack of healthy relationships, emotional loneliness, few external interests, and minimal marketable skills. A profound lack of intimacy, combined with childhood and adult experiences of positive feelings with sexual activity, appear to have contributed to the sexual abuse. Further, Jane developed a set of beliefs that facilitated the abusive behavior. In her mind, the boys enjoyed the sexual activity, and it was only a way for her to show them that she cared. Finally, Jane appeared to have developed a pattern of coping based on avoidance of issues. Instead, she relied on sex to meet her emotional needs, allowing her to remain in abusive relationships.

A number of treatment goals should be established to help Jane meet her needs in healthier ways and prevent a return to offending behavior. The most pressing treatment need is the restructuring of Jane's beliefs regarding sexual abuse and the belief that her actions were largely harmless and benign to the well-being of the boys. Jane would also need to understand the connection between the sexual abuse and her feelings of loneliness and lack of intimacy. By recognizing this connection, she may be better equipped to develop the necessary skills to achieve her goal of establishing and maintaining healthy adult relationships. This lack of intimacy would be considered an important dynamic risk factor in this case, and would need to be addressed rapidly in treatment. Given her history of abuse in her close relationships, Jane would concurrently need to explore dynamics of abuse and its detrimental effects, as well as its potential impact on her current situation. She would also need to address her avoidance of issues. Under such conditions, she would then be better equipped to select nonabusive partners in the future as well as becoming better equipped to deal with problems in general.

In the longer term, Jane would need to develop satisfying outside interests. These may take time to establish, and she likely will need ongoing coaching and support. Schooling or job training that does not put her in contact with children will also be required to help Jane establish a new life where she can continue to develop once therapy has concluded. Her self-management plan will include improved ways to effectively manage her emotions; concrete steps to develop and maintain a wide range of healthy relationships, not just a romantic relationship; steps to establish interests that will provide more balance in her life; and developing work skills to provide some satisfaction and a sense of accomplishment. With this plan, developed in accordance with her goals, Jane can continue to work toward life choices that are healthier, and offense-free.

CONCLUSION

The issue of women who sexually abuse children is one that forces us to challenge powerful stereotypes about motherhood and female-child relationships that are deeply held, even cherished by our society. Females are thought of as nurturers, those who provide care for others, not as people who harm or abuse them, particularly not sexually. Perhaps it is for this reason that the issue of women who sexually abuse children has garnered little attention until quite recently. Although there is little doubt that males make up the majority of sex offenders, women do commit sexual offenses against children. Despite a growing interest in the issue over the last fifteen years, our knowledge surrounding this population of offenders remains in its infancy. As this chapter has demonstrated, evidence concerning the prevalence of female sex offending is contradictory, we have a limited understanding of the causes and complexities that underlie the phenomenon, and the assessment and treatment needs of female sex offenders remain largely tentative and inconclusive. What has been established in much of the literature, is that although the general public views sexual abuse by females as relatively harmless and innocuous as compared to similar abuse by males (Broussard et al., 1991), female-perpetrated sexual abuse appears to have long-term and debilitating consequences for victims, both male and female (Mendel, 1995; Denov, 2004). All of these factors point to the need for the issue, and all of its complexities, to be thoughtfully and carefully explored. As the topic begins to gain greater attention and recognition among clinicians, policymakers, and professionals working in the area of child sexual abuse, the gaps in our understanding of the phenomenon may begin to be addressed.

REFERENCES

Allen, C.M. (1991). *Women and men who sexually abuse children: A comparative analysis.* Orwell, VT: The Safer Society Press.

American Psychiatric Association. (1994). *Diagnostic and statistical manual of mental disorders* (4th ed.). Washington, DC: Author.

Andrews, D.A. & Bonta, J. (2003). *The psychology of criminal conduct* (3rd ed.). Cincinnati, OH: Anderson.

Babiker, G. & Arnold, L. (1997). *The language of injury: Comprehending self-mutilation.* Leicester: BPS Books.

Blanchette, K. (2001). *Classifying female offenders for effective intervention: Application of the case-based principles of risk and need.* Unpublished manuscript, Carleton University.

Briere, J., Evans, D., Runtz, M., & Wall, T. (1988). Symptomatology in men who were abused as children: A comparison study. *American Journal of Orthopsychiatry, 58,* 457-461.

Broussard, S., Wagner, N. G., & Kazelskis, R. (1991). Undergraduate students' perceptions of child sexual abuse: The impact of victim sex, perpetrator sex, respondent sex, and victim response. *Journal of Family Violence, 6,* 267-278.

Brown, G.R. & Anderson, B. (1991). Psychiatric morbidity in adult inpatients with childhood histories of sexual and physical abuse. *American Journal of Psychiatry, 148,* 55-61.

Byers, E. (1996). How well does the traditional sexual script explain sexual coercion? Review of a program of research. *Journal of Psychology and Human Sexuality, 8,* 6-26.

Byers, E. & O'Sullivan, L. (1998). Similar but different: Men's and women's experiences of sexual coercion. In P. Anderson & C. Struckman-Johnson (Eds.), *Sexually aggressive women* (pp. 144-168). London: The Guildford Press.

Canadian Centre for Justice statistics. (2001). *Adult Criminal Court Data Tables 1999/00.* Ottawa, Ontario: Author.

Chasnoff, I., Burns, W., Schnoll, S., Burns, K., Chissum, G., & Kyle-Spore, L. (1986). Maternal-neonatal incest. *American Journal of Orthopsychiatry, 56*(4), 577-580.

Cooper, A., Swaminath, S., Baxter, D., & Poulin, C. (1990). A female sexual offender with multiple paraphilias: A psychologic, physiologic (laboratory sexual arousal) and endocrine study. *Canadian Journal of Psychiatry, 35,* 334-337.

Cortoni, F. & Marshall, W.L. (2001). Sex as a coping strategy and its relationship to juvenile sexual history and intimacy in sexual offenders. *Sexual Abuse: A Journal of Research and Treatment, 13,* 27-44.

Denov, M. (2001). A culture of denial: Exploring professional perspectives on female sex offending. *Canadian Journal of Criminology, 43,* 303-329.

Denov, M. (2003a). To a safer place? Victims of sexual abuse by females and their disclosures to professionals. *Child Abuse and Neglect, 27,* 47-61.

Denov, M. (2003b). The myth of innocence: Sexual scripts and the recognition of child sexual abuse by female perpetrators. *Journal of Sex Research, 40*(3), 1-12.

Denov, M. (2004a). The long-term effects of child sexual abuse by female perpetrators: A qualitative study of male and female victims. *Journal of Interpersonal Violence, 19*(10), 1137-1156.

Denov, M. (2004b). *Perspectives on female sex offending: A culture of denial.* Aldershot, UK: Ashgate Publishing.

Dhaliwal, G., Gauzas, L., Antonowicz, D., & Ross, R. (1996). Adult male survivors of childhood sexual abuse: Prevalence, sexual abuse characteristics, and long-term effects. *Clinical Psychological Review, 16,* 619-639.

Eldridge, H. & Saradjian, J. (2000). Replacing the function of abusive behaviors for the offender: Remaking relapse prevention in working with women who sexually abuse children. In D. R. Laws, S. M. Hudson, & T. Ward (Eds.), *Remaking relapse prevention with sex offenders: A sourcebook* (pp. 402-426). Thousand Oaks, CA: Sage Publications.

Endler, N.S. & Parker, J.D.A. (1999). *Coping Inventory for Stressful Situations: Manual* (2nd ed.). Toronto: Multi-Health Systems, Inc.

Freund, K., Heasman, G., Racansky, I.G., & Glancy, G. (1984). Pedophilia and heterosexuality vs. homosexuality. *Journal of Sex and Marital Therapy, 10,* 193-200.

Fritz, G.S., Stoll, K., & Wagner, N.N. (1981). A comparison of males and females who were sexually molested as children. *Journal of Sex and Marital Therapy, 7,* 54-59.

Fromuth, M. & Burkhart, B. (1989). Long-term psychological correlates of childhood sexual abuse in two samples of college men. *Child Abuse and Neglect, 13,* 533-542.

Fromuth, M. & Conn, V. (1997). Hidden perpetrators: Sexual molestation in a nonclinical sample of college women. *Journal of Interpersonal Violence, 12,* 456-465.

Grayston, A.D. & De Luca, R.V. (1999). Female perpetrators of child sexual abuse: A review of the clinical and empirical literature. *Aggression and Violent Behavior, 4,* 93-106.

Groth, N. (1979). Sexual trauma in the life histories of rapists and child molesters. *Victimology, 4,* 10-16.

Hanson, R.K. & Harris, A.J.R. (2001). A structured approach to evaluating change among sexual offenders. *Sexual Abuse: A Journal of Research and Treatment, 13,* 105-122.

Hanson, R.K. & Thornoton, D. (2000). Improving risk assessments for sexual offenders: A comparison of three actuarial scales. *Law and Human Behavior, 24,* 119-136.

Hetherton, J. & Beardsall, L. (1998). Decisions and attitudes concerning child sexual abuse: Does the gender of the perpetrator make a difference to child protection professionals? *Child Abuse and Neglect, 22,* 1265-1283.

Home Office. (2001). *Statistics on women and the criminal justice system.* London: Her Majesty's Stationery Office (HMSO).

Hunter, J.A. (1991). A comparison of the psychosocial maladjustment of adult males and females sexually molested as children. *Journal of Interpersonal Violence, 6,* 205-217.

Krug, R.S. (1989). Adult males report of childhood sexual abuse by mothers: Case descriptions, motivation and long-term consequences. *Child Abuse and Neglect, 13,* 111-119.

Langton, C.M. & Marshall, W.L. (2000). The role of cognitive distortions in relapse prevention programs. In D. R. Laws, S. M. Hudson, & T. Ward (Eds.), *Remaking relapse prevention with sex offenders: A sourcebook* (pp. 167-186). Thousand Oaks, CA: Sage Publications.

Laws, D.R., Hudson, S.M., & Ward, T. (Eds.) (2000). *Remaking relapse prevention with sex offenders: A sourcebook.* Thousand Oaks, CA: Sage Publications.

Lazarus, R.S. & Folkman, S. (1984). *Stress, appraisal, and coping.* New York: Springer Publishing Company.

Looman, J. (1995). Sexual fantasies of child molesters. *Canadian Journal of Behavioural Science, 27,* 321-332.

Mann, R.E. (2000). Managing resistance and rebellion in relapse prevention intervention. In D. R. Laws, S. M. Hudson, & T. Ward (Eds.), *Remaking relapse prevention with sex offenders: A sourcebook* (pp. 187-200). Thousand Oaks, CA: Sage Publications.

Mann, R.E. & Beech, A.R. (2003). Cognitive distortions, schemas, and implicit theories. In T. Ward, D.R. Laws, & S.M. Hudson (Eds.), *Sexual deviance: Issues and controversies* (pp. 135-153). Thousand Oaks, CA: Sage Publications.

Marshall, W.L., Anderson, D., & Fernandez, Y. (1999). *Cognitive behavioral treatment of sexual offenders.* London: Wiley.

Mathews, R., Matthews, J., & Speltz, K. (1989). *Female sexual offenders: An exploratory study.* Orwell, VT: Safer Society Press.

Mathis, J.L. (1972). *Clear thinking about sexual deviation.* Chicago: Nelson Hall.

Matthews, J.K. (1993). Working with female sexual abusers. In M. Elliot (Ed.), *Female sexual abuse of children* (pp. 57-73). New York: The Guilford Press.

Matthews, R. (1987). *Preliminary typology of female sex offenders.* MN: PHASE and Genesis II for Women.

McCarty, L. (1986). Mother-child incest: Characteristics of the offender. *Child Welfare, 65,* 447-458.

McKibben, A., Proulx, J., & Lusignan, R. (1994). Relationships between conflict, affect and deviant sexual behaviors in rapists and pedophiles. *Behaviour Research and Therapy, 13,* 571-575.

Mendel, M.P. (1995). *The male survivor: The impact of sexual abuse.* London: Sage Publications.

Miner, M.H. (2000). Competency-based assessment. In D. R. Laws, S. M. Hudson, & T. Ward (Eds.), *Remaking relapse prevention with sex offenders: A sourcebook* (pp. 213-224). Thousand Oaks, CA: Sage Publications.

Miner, M.H., Day, D.M., & Nafpaktitis, M.K. (1989). Assessment of coping skills: Development of a Situational Competency Test. In D. R. Laws (Ed.), *Relapse prevention with sex offenders* (pp. 127-136). New York: Guilford.

Mitchell, J. & Morse, J. (1998). *From victims to survivors: Reclaimed voices of women sexually abused in childhood by females.* New York: Accelerated Development.

Nathan, P. & Ward, T. (2002). Female sex offenders: Clinical and demographic features. *The Journal of Sexual Aggression, 8,* 5-21.

O'Hagan, K. (1989). *Working with child sexual abuse.* Milton Keynes, UK: Open University Press.

Parker, J.D.A. & Endler, N.S. (1996). Coping and defense: A historical overview. In M. Zeidner & N. S. Endler (Eds.), *Handbook of coping: Theory, research, applications* (pp. 3-23). New York: John Wiley & Sons.

Peterson, K.D., Colebank, K.D., & Motta, L.L. (2002, November). *Female sexual offender recidivism.* Paper presented at the 20th Research and Treatment Conference, Association for the Treatment of Sexual Abusers, San Antonio, Texas.

Pierce, R. & Pierce, L. (1985). The sexually abused child: A comparison of male and female victims. *Child Abuse and Neglect, 9,* 191-199.

Proulx, J., McKibben, A., & Lusignan, R. (1996). Relationships between affective components and sexual behaviors in sexual aggressors. *Sexual Abuse: A Journal of Research and Treatment, 8,* 279-289.

Reinhart, M. (1987). Sexually abused boys. *Child Abuse and Neglect, 11,* 229-235.

Roane, T. (1992). Male victims of sexual abuse: A case review within a child protection team. *Child Welfare, 3,* 231-239.

Rohsenow, D., Corbett, R., & Devine, D. (1988). Molested as children: A hidden contribution to substance abuse? *Journal of Substance Abuse Treatment, 5,* 13-18.

Rosencrans, B. (1997). *The last secret: Daughters sexually abused by mothers.* Brandon, VT: Safer Society Press.

Rowan, E.L., Rowan, J.B., & Langelier, P. (1990). Women who molest children. *Bulletin of the American Academy of Psychiatry and the Law, 18,* 79-83.

Saradjian, J. (1996). *Women who sexually abuse children: From research to clinical practice.* London: Wiley.

Snyder, H. (2000). *Sexual assault of young children as reported to law enforcement: Victim, incident and offender characteristics.* U.S. Department of Justice, Washington, DC: Bureau of Justice Statistics.

Task Force on Federally Sentenced Women. (1990). *Report of the task force on federally sentenced women: Creating choices.* Ottawa, Ontario: Ministry of the Solicitor General.

United States Department of Justice. (2002). *Crime in the United States 2001.* Washington, DC: Federal Bureau of Investigation.

Ward, T. & Stewart, C.A. (2003). Good lives and the rehabilitation of sexual offenders. In T. Ward, D.R. Laws, & S.M. Hudson (Eds.), *Sexual deviance: Issues and controversies* (pp. 21-44). Thousand Oaks, CA: Sage Publications.

Wiegel, M., Abel, G.G., & Jordan, A. (2003, October). *The self-reported behaviors of adult female child abusers.* Paper presented at the 22nd Annual Research and Treatment Conference, Association for the Treatment of Sexual Abusers, St. Louis, Missouri.

Williams, S.M. & Nicholaichuk, T. (2001, November). *Assessing static risk factors in adult female sex offenders under federal jurisdiction.* Paper presented at the 20th Research and Treatment Conference, Association for the Treatment of Sexual Abusers, San Antonio, Texas.

Chapter 5

Perpetrators Within Professions

Joe Sullivan
Anthony Beech

INTRODUCTION

Any organization or institution, whether statutory or voluntary, where children are cared for is vulnerable to infiltration by members of various professions who wish to abuse (Sullivan & Beech, 2002). Historically, child care institutions created environments within which individuals in positions of authority were able to misuse and abuse their positions (Bottoms, Shaver, Goodman, & Qin, 1995; Isley & Isley, 1990). In terms of general characteristics, the following observations can be made. Haywood (1994), Haywood et al. (1996), Langevin, Curnoe, & Bain (2000), Plante, Manuel, and Bryant (1996), and Sullivan and Beech (2004) report that the perpetrators in their studies of clerics who sexually abused children were significantly different from other child molesters in age, education, and IQ. Here it was found that the perpetrators, as might be expected, were generally older and better educated than other sexual offenders were. Hence, they may well have the personal resources to effectively manipulate the environment and both potential and actual victims. Studies focusing on the characteristics of perpetrators within professions have found that they adapt to their surroundings and often have more than one type of offense. Brannan, Jones, & Murch (1993) report that perpetrators used the special features of the institutional environment to facilitate the abuse and prevent disclosure of the abuse by the children and other professionals. Faller (1988) found that the majority of offenders in an institutional setting were deliberately seeking situations in which they might abuse.

Sullivan and Beech (2004) found that in a sample of abusers within a profession, over one-third had never been convicted of a sexual offense. The reasons for this were either victims did not want to make a formal complaint to the police, or they had reported the matter to the professional's superiors, where it had gone no further, or that the abuse was reported to the police who investigated the matters but the case was not considered strong enough to be prosecuted. Of those convicted, a significant number had more than one conviction for a sexual offense. All of these participants had previously offended within a teaching capacity and reoffended in a different teaching, tutoring, or coaching capacity. In the Sullivan and Beech (1994) study, perpetrators in specific professions were also asked whether gaining access to children in order to sexually abuse them formed a part of their decision to choose their career paths. More than half said abuse was part of their motivation for choosing their jobs or that they had chosen their work specifically for the opportunity to sexually abuse children.

OVERVIEW OF THE TYPICAL PERPETRATOR WITHIN PROFESSIONS

Prevalence

Many methodological difficulties are associated with determining the incidence and the prevalence of child sexual abuse (Mandeville-Norden & Beech, 2004). Differences in the samples studied, the definitions of abuse, the age differentiation of abuser to victim, and the method of administration can all contribute to compromising the accuracy of these estimates (Leventhal, 1998). Holmes and Slap (1998) conducted a meta-analysis of 166 studies that looked at the prevalence of sexual abuse of boys. Due to the methodological difficulties, in particular the researchers' definitions of abuse, the prevalence figures varied substantially from 4 to 76 percent. Using the legal criterion may seem sensible, however, this is likely to artificially inflate the figures, given that many individuals report consensual sexual experiences before the age of sixteen (Ghate & Spencer, 1995).

A recent study by the National Society for the Prevention of Cruelty to Children into the prevalence of child abuse (Cawson, Wattam, Brooker, & Kelly, 2000) examined the respondents' experience of sexual behavior in detail. Respondents were asked about any sexual activities that had taken place against their wishes, before their reaching the age of sixteen. In addition, the results differentiated between cases in which the perpetrator of the sexual act was more than five years older than the victim, in order to illustrate the difference between sexual abuse and peer sexual exploitation. Furthermore, the study examined the results in relation to sexual acts perpetrated by family members and nonfamily members. The results showed that 1 percent of the respondents had been sexually abused by parents or caregivers, and 3 percent by other relatives. Eleven percent had been abused by other known people, with 8 percent of the abuse involving physical contact. Only 4 percent of the respondents stated that they had been abused either by a stranger or by someone that they had just met.

Finkelhor, Williams, & Burns (1988) reported that 17 percent of sexual abuse cases occur in child care institutions. Nunno (1992) notes that when compared with other sexual offenders, professionals who sexually abuse children with whom they work are considered a small but significant problem. Organizations such as faith communities, schools, and child care services have long been targeted by offenders who have either generated or made use of existing environments of pervasive secrecy (Green, 1999). Whether public or private, voluntary or statutory, institutions and organizations have provided abusers with almost limitless opportunities for the manipulation and abuse of children (Nolan, 2001; Utting, 1998; Waterhouse, 2000). Agencies and organizations who work with children are increasingly becoming aware not only of the need to create cultures of safety, not just to protect children, but also to ensure that the staff responsible for the care of children feel secure.

The literature available on the abuse of children in care institutions suggests that the complaints appear to be of a sexual nature and that the majority have not been reported (Gallagher 1999a, 1999b). A study by Rindfleisch and Rabb (1984) found that 31 of every 1,000 children reported allegations. Nunno (1992) found that 158 in every 1,000 children reported sexual abuse. Public inquiries, local investigations, and reviews have resulted from the disclosure or discovery of institutional sexual abuse. Groze (1990) highlighted the differences in the process of investigating allegations of abuse within institutions compared with allegations within the family. Abuse within residential children's homes may well mean that hundreds of children and staff need to be interviewed and large numbers of alleged perpetrators arrested, interviewed, and charged.

The perception that institutional child sexual abuse is a great evil (Nolan, 2001) and that such offenders are "sexual terrorists" (Utting, 1998) supports the public's mind that sexual offenders have characteristics that set them apart. The dangerous inference of this perception is that, by implication, professionals who would seek to sexually abuse children should therefore be immediately identifiable to the outside world. Clearly, the suggestion that professional perpetrators are easy to identify is at odds with the reality.

ABUSE SETTINGS

Child Care Institutions

Studies considering the nature of abuse within institutions have shown that children are differentially at risk (Gallagher, 1999b). McFadden and Ryan (1992) found that girls and older children were more at risk of being abused in foster placements than boys or younger children. The type of institution also seems to have a correlation with the children most likely to be abused. Westcott and Clement (1992) reported that boys were more at risk in residential schools while girls were more at risk in children's homes. This may have something to do with the nature of all-male institutions such as residential schools, in which men are more likely to be in primary care roles or some abusive behaviors are institutionally perpetuated, making the environment more facilitative of sexual abuse.

Churches

Numerous high profile cases relating to faith community leaders who were accused and convicted of child sexual abuse have been in the media. Kelly (1998) suggests that there is a prevalence of approximately 2 to 3 percent of child abusers within the Catholic Church in the United States (Kelly, 1998). In terms of actual numbers of pedophilic priests, Berry (1992) stated that between 1983 and 1987, more than 200 Roman Catholic priests or religious brothers were reported to the Vatican Embassy for sexually abusing children. Most of the cases related to the sexual abuse of teenage boys. This averaged out to nearly one accusation a week in those four years alone and by 1992 was estimated to have cost the church $400 million in settlements to victims and treatment of the perpetrators. One of the most comprehensive surveys in the United Kingdom (Nolan, 2001), found that allegations had been made against 112 out of 5,600 Catholic priests with twenty-one cases ending in a conviction. In the United States, Jenkins (1986) noted that there are more than 400 documented cases of child sexual abuse by Catholic clergy. To give some idea of the scale of the problem over the years, in the archdiocese of Chicago between 1963 and 1991, allegations were made against fifty-nine of the serving priests at the time. Forty-one were found to be credible under civil law standards of proof (Saradjian & Nobus, 2003). The combination of the underreporting of child abuse, and the Church's policy of keeping matters hidden, means that these figures are highly likely to be an underestimate of the level of the problem. Historically, the Church's response has been to initiate surreptitious parish changes for offending priests (Blanchard, 1991; Lasser, 1991). This has only served to exacerbate the problem by giving the priest access to more unsuspecting victims and their families.

The Nolan review (Nolan, 2001) was set up in response to a seemingly endless stream of allegations and convictions of Roman Catholic priests for child sexual abuse during the 1980s and 1990s in the United Kingdom. The review has sought to make radical changes in the organization of the Roman Catholic Church and its perspective on child protection. The first report of the Nolan review "Child Protection in the Catholic Church in England and Wales" was published in 2001 and made some radical recommendations for changes in how allegations of abuse with the Church were managed. Among the recommendations were the establishment of a U.K. child protection unit to screen all clergy, laystaff, and volunteers, and the establishment of a national database of applicants for ordination. The report also suggested that all cautioned or convicted clergy should be prevented from future contact through the Church with children.

The problem is not restricted to the Roman Catholic Church however, and professional perpetrators have been identified within all Christian churches and all the major faith communities. In general, church organizations were lax in recognizing the extent of sexual abuse by faith community leaders and some churches have been accused of conspiring to keep allegations quiet or too readily accepting the denial of the alleged perpetrator (Francis & Turner, 1995). Most of the faith communities in the United Kingdom have subsequently devised and published child protection policies, often following allegations against their religious leaders or workers. Findlater (2000) suggests that non–Christian faith communities have been slower to react, perhaps because of fewer scandals to date.

Voluntary Settings

Voluntary organizations working with children also make an attractive setting for those who wish to create opportunities to sexually abuse children. Over the years, these organizations have also been subject to allegations of sexual abuse. Guidelines arising from the inquiries into abuse within child care establishments recommended greater accountability in the voluntary sector, and uniformity of procedures for dealing with allegations of misconduct regarding staff (Social Services Inspectorate, 1995). This may be because the organizations are smaller than the statutory sector child care facilities, or that because of their voluntary status, they are not perceived as being accountable in the same way (Stanley, 1999). In a Social Services Inspectorate report, further concerns were raised about the selection procedures and safeguards undertaken by independent organizations that in some cases supplied 45 percent of staff to residential homes (Social Services Inspectorate, 1995).

Foster Care

Children are not just at risk within organizations and institutions. Although foster care placements are a preferred method of caring for children, they can also be used by those intent upon sexually abusing children (Waterhouse, 2000). Browne and Lynch (1999) report that many children had abusive experiences in foster placements before entering residential care. As opportunities to abuse children within institutions and organizations are restricted, perpetrators adapt to gain access to children in other settings.

Sports Settings

Sports clubs and teams provide another arena within which professional perpetrators can exploit the hopes, aspirations, and vulnerabilities of children. The exclusivity of the relationships and the regular contact through training or competing can be used to facilitate sexual manipulation. Brackenridge (2004) notes that passion for sport, in North America and Europe, has acted a political shield and prevented scrutiny of its practices until recently. The concerns of national and international sporting organizations have been heightened by sexual abuse allegations, which have extended throughout their entire structure from local administrators to elite coaches. Studies in Canada (Kirby, Greaves, & Hankivsky, 2000), Norway (Fasting, Brackenridge, & Sundgot-Borgen, 2000), and Australia (Leahy, Pretty, & Tenenbaum, 2002) indicate that such abuse is a serious issue in sports. Research focuses on the identification of specific risk factors for the perpetrators, the potential victims, and the sporting bodies (Brackenridge, 2001; Bringer, Brackenridge, & Johnston, 2002), in an attempt to develop safer environments for children and adult athletes. A Child Protection in Sport unit (www.thecpsu.org.uk) now operates in the United Kingdom.

ETIOLOGY OF ABUSE

Offenders who commit sexual offences against children are by no means a homogenous group. Indeed, sex offenders will show differing psychological characteristics and distortions that may have a bearing on the nature of their offense and on their choice of victim. Nonetheless, a number of widely accepted psychological profiles exist to a greater or lesser degree in most child sex offenders (Fisher, Beech, & Browne, 1999). For example, most will show some degree of cognitive distortions (distorted attitudes) about children (Saradjian & Nobus, 2003; Sullivan & Beech, 2004). Thompson, Marolla, & Bromley (1998) identified two broad types of distortions in clergy sex offenders, which they labeled "justifications" and "excuses." Thompson et al. (1998) define an excuse as an admission that the act in question was bad, wrong, coupled with a denial of responsibility; while a justification is defined as an admission of full responsibility for the act in question, coupled with a denial that it was wrongful. The idea of justifications is particularly significant in offenders who are identified as being highly deviant (Beech, 1998), where children are viewed as being sexually aware as well as being likely to coerce adults into sexual acts. Because of such justifications/distortions, these offenders will not perceive any harm caused as a result of their actions (Ward & Keenan, 1999). Further, Saradjian and Nobus (2003) found that the accused clergy used their religious role and relationship with God within their distorted beliefs. These beliefs were predominantly concentrated in the areas of giving themselves permission to offend, reduction in guilt after offending, and maintaining a positive sense of self.

Ward and Keenan (1999) outline a number of deviant schemas, which they claim will account for the cognitive distortions/justifications held by individuals who sexually abuse children. These described the offender as viewing the child as a sexual being, feeling entitled to abuse children, that the abuse will not cause real harm to the victim, that children are most likely to fulfill the offenders' needs than others, and that the offender has no control over his or her actions. Such highly deviant child sex abusers exhibit high levels of social inadequacy, which may explain the offenders' need and desire to interact with children. Other differences have been highlighted, which are particularly pertinent to the group being reported on here.

Evidence suggests a correlation between the levels of these psychological distortions/inadequacies and the offenders' offence history. Indeed, Beech (1998) found that the more pronounced the difficulties (i.e., those falling into the highly deviant range) the greater the number of victims of the highly deviant perpetrators. These victims are more likely to be extrafamilial, and more likely to be male. Hence, many professional perpetrators fit this profile, in that they are highly likely to have a number of victims and will have predominantly offended against males. This finding is consistent with other research in this area (Haywood et al., 1996; Loftus & Camargo, 1993; Sullivan & Beech, 2004).

Sullivan and Beech (2004) investigated when their sample of professional abusers first became aware of their sexual interest in children. Just over half said they were ten to sixteen years, around a third (32 percent) said they were between seventeen and twenty-one years, 10 percent said they were in their twenties, while 7 percent said they were less than ten years old. The group was also asked how old they were when they committed their first sexual offense against a child. Fifty-two percent admitted that they sexually abused as a child before the age of twenty-two, while 27 percent admitted having sexually abused a child before the age of sixteen. Sullivan and Beech (2004) found in their study that even though the majority (71 percent) of the participants had sexually abused prepubescent children, 24 percent of the sample reported that they had exclusive sexual interest in children. This propensity for a more diverse sexual interest has not been reported in other research. When the sample were asked about their primary sexual interest regarding gender, 56 percent admitted an exclusive sexual interest in males, 22 percent in females, and 22 percent in both males and females.

BEHAVIORAL CONSEQUENCES

The exploration of the different types of behavior used by perpetrators suggests that there is no one type of institutional or professional perpetrator. Sloan (1988) suggested that authoritarian and controlling characteristics were most typical of professional perpetrators, whilst Gallagher (2000) found that although some were authoritarian or charismatic others were found to be quiet, unassuming, or inadequate. Colton and Vanstone (1996) report that victims of professional offenders in their sample typically perceived the perpetrator as a peer, father figure or a rescuer.

Abel, Osborn, & Warberg (1998) note that sexual aggressors who work with children establish a relationship in which physical touching turns to more sexualized touching (e.g., grooming). Gallagher (1998; 1999a) looked at the methods of manipulation used by perpetrators and suggested the term *entrapment* better explained the nature of their behavior than the more generalized term of grooming. Gallagher found that perpetrators used a variety of emotional inducements and materials to draw the child into the abuse. He also suggested that perpetrators were careful to select vulnerable groups of children such as those with learning disabilities or special needs. Langevin et al. (2000) report that a significantly greater number of professional perpetrators (clerics) in their study group used physical force as part of their grooming of victims when compared with a control group of non-professional perpetrators. This included physical force such as punching, slapping, strapping, kicking, and generally demeaning the victims.

Sullivan and Beech (2004) investigated what grooming techniques that their sample of professional abusers used and found that 76 percent said that they used emotionally coercive techniques rather than physical force. One participant said he exclusively used physical force and 22 percent said they had used a combination of both persuasive techniques and physical force. Grooming techniques commonly used by professional perpetrators involved taking children away from the normal work environment. Seventy-eight percent of the Sullivan and Beech (2004) sample admitted doing this. This typically involves arranging to take children away overnight, which provided perpetrators with extended periods with the children, often away from adequate supervision structures. Two-thirds of the sample reported that they had taken children away overnight in order to facilitate sexually abusing them. Typically, these trips were described as being educational or recreational, and involved other professionals accompanying the children, although some were private arrangements with parents. One participant spoke of abusing children at a summer camp. He was also responsible for the camp infirmary where he would sexually abuse children who became ill, upset, or homesick. A number of the sample in the Sullivan and Beech (2004) study admitted using the Internet either to access pornography or to attempt to contact children for potential sexual contact. Twenty-nine percent admitted using the Internet to collect pornography, while 10 percent admitted to also attempting to contact children to sexually abuse through chat rooms on the Internet.

Over half of Sullivan and Beech's (2004) sample (53 percent) reported sexually abusing children abroad. Seventy-five percent of this group reported that they traveled with the specific intention of sexually abusing children. Of these, 37 percent abused local children, 44 percent brought children with them to abuse in a foreign country, and 19 percent abused both local children and those they had brought with them. Some men spoke of organizing trips abroad, where until recent legislative changes, they could not be prosecuted for abusing children. One participant spoke of taking twelve different children separately on trips to Euro Disney in Paris, France. These visits obviously required overnight stops. To cover the eventuality that he would be challenged about traveling and sharing a room with a child who was not related to him, the perpetrator had obtained a letter from the children's parents giving him full parental responsibility for the child during the trip. This suggests that professional perpetrators, who abuse children abroad, are more likely to abuse children they have brought with them to a foreign country.

Another aspect of abuse by professionals who work with children is that the abuse may involve more than one abuser (Gallagher, 1999b; White & Hart, 1995; Gallagher, Hughes, & Parker, 1996). Finkelhor et al. (1988) report that 17 percent of the sexual abuse cases in their study had multiple perpetrators. The sharing and passing of victims between numbers of different abusers was also discovered in the Waterhouse inquiry into abuse in children's home in North Wales (Waterhouse, 2000). This suggests that one of the key differences between professional perpetrators and other extrafamilial sex offenders is the level of sophistication of the techniques used by the professionals to manipulate the victims and those who might protect them.

To avoid detection, professional perpetrators need to be more focused on disguising their behavior and/or ensuring that their position is so unassailable that they will not be challenged. However, when the participants in the Sullivan and Beech (2004) study were asked if they were aware of having a reputation for sexual inappropriateness among the children with whom they worked, just over 40 percent said yes. This suggests that their behavior was not completely disguised from the outside world and if children were aware, then perhaps adults will also have been or certainly should have been more aware of such a reputation.

Westcott (1991) suggests four barriers to reporting of abuse within institutions: lack of procedures/policies for reporting and investigating a complaint of institutional abuse, institutional abuse viewed as the problem of the individual member of staff, not the institution, the closed nature of institutions, and the belief system surrounding institutions.

Utting (1998) proposed a protective strategy consisting of the following main points: a threshold of entry to paid and voluntary work with children which is high enough to deter committed abusers, management which pursues overall excellence and is vigilant in protecting children and exposing abuse, disciplinary and criminal procedures which deal effectively with offenders, and an approved system of communicating information about known abusers between agencies.

CURRENT EMPIRICAL ASSESSMENT

The clinical assessment of a professional perpetrator, as with any child sex offender, must take place over a twenty-eight-day residential period and include sixty hours of group therapy and eight hours of individual therapy. Before beginning the assessment, an offender completes a series of psychometric questionnaires to assist in creating a psychological profile of his or her needs (Beech, Fisher, & Thornton, 2003). These psychometric tests (e.g., STEP, Sex Offender Treatment Programme Battery) are used in Europe and certainly could be used in North America (Beech, Fisher, & Beckett, 1999). (See Exhibit 5.1.)

Beech (1998) divides abusers into two main groups: high deviancy and low deviancy, because of their deviation on psychometric measures from nonoffending norms. The STEP scales measure socioaffective problems (scales 1 to 6), pro-offending attitudes (scales 7-10), deviant sexual interest (scale 11), and relapse-prevention strategies (scale 12).

High-deviancy abusers, according to this system, have high levels of cognitive distortions about children, high levels of distorted attitudes about their victims, high levels of deviant sexual interest/sexual obsessions, and high levels of self-reported sexual deviance patterns (Beech, 1998). They also report difficulty in forming intimate attachments with adults, while at the same time perceive that their emotional needs can be met by children. High-deviancy abusers were also found to have other socioaffective difficulties.

Low-deviancy abusers, according to the STEP system, do not have generalized cognitive distortions about children (Fisher et al., 1999). Nor do they evidence the high levels of emotional identification with children observed in high-deviancy abusers. On the contrary, emotional identification with children in this group was found to be significantly lower than nonoffender controls (Fisher et al., 1999). These authors also found that low-deviancy individuals showed significantly higher levels of social adequacy problems than nonoffenders, but this was not as marked as that found in high-deviancy abusers. Low-deviancy abusers were found to have poor empathy for their victims (Fisher

EXHIBIT 5.1. STEP Measures

Short Self-Esteem Scale
(Thornton, 1989)

This scale measures the level of self-esteem in child abusers, which is typically lower than nonoffenders. Thornton reported the internal consistency of this eight-item scale as .80 (Cronbach's alpha). Beech (1998) reported the test-retest reliability of this scale to be .75 in a group of forty untreated child molesters. Child sexual offenders have been found to have significantly lower levels of self-esteem than nonoffenders as measured by this scale (Fisher et al., 1999). Thornton, Beech, and Marshall (2004) report that lower levels of self-esteem, as measured by this scale, were associated with higher sexual recidivism rates.

UCLA Emotional Loneliness Scale
(Russell, Peplau, & Cutrona, 1980)

This scale measures the ability to be appropriately intimate with other adults, which is typically poorer in high-deviancy child abusers. Russell et al. reported an internal consistency of .91 (Cronbach's alpha). Beech (1998) reported the test-retest reliability of this scale to be .70 over a seven-month period in a group of forty-four treated child molesters. Fisher et al. (1999) found that child sexual offenders reported significantly higher levels of emotional loneliness, as measured by this scale than nonoffenders did.

Underassertiveness Scale
(from the Social Response Inventory,
Keltner, Marshall, & Marshall 1981)

This scale is a self-report measure of underassertiveness, which is typically higher in high-deviancy child abusers (Beech, 1998). Beech (1998) reported the test-retest reliability of this scale to be .80 (Cronbach's alpha) over a seven-month period in a group of 44 treated child molesters. Fisher et al. (1999) found that child sexual offenders reported significantly higher levels of underassertiveness, as measured by this scale, than nonoffenders did.

Personal Distress Scale
(from the Interpersonal Reactivity Index,
Davis, 1983)

This scale measures the ability to cope with negative feelings (Salter, 1988). High-deviancy child abusers typically report a marked inability

(continued)

(continued)

to deal with negative feelings (Fisher et al., 1999). Davis reported a coefficient of .78 and a test-retest reliability of .68 in fifty-six males over a two-and-a-half-month period. Child sexual offenders report significantly higher levels of personal distress than nonoffenders as measured by this scale (Fisher et al., 1999).

Nowicki-Strickland Locus of Control Scale
(Nowicki, 1976)

This scale measures the extent to which individuals feel that events are contingent upon their own behavior and the extent to which they feel that events are outside of their control. High-deviancy child abusers typically report this (Fisher et al., 1999). Nowicki and Duke (1974) reported test-retest reliability of .83 in 158 subjects over a six-week period. Nowicki and Duke (1982) reported the internal consistency of this scale as .69. Child abusers typically report an internal locus of control if successfully treated (Fisher et al., 1998).

Multiphasic Sex Inventory (MSI): Cognitive Distortions and Immaturity Scale
(Nichols & Molinder, 1984)

Although called a cognitive distortions scale, the MSI measures the level of accountability accepted for offending behaviors (Beech et al., 1999). Gillis (1991) reported the internal consistency of the scale as .73. Simkins, Ward, Bowman, & Rinck (1989) reported the test-retest reliability of this scale to be .84 over a three-month period. After treatment, Beech et al. (1999) found a significant reduction in the level of denial of accountability for offending, as measured by this scale, in seventy-seven child sexual abusers.

Victim Empathy Distortions Scale
(Beckett & Fisher, 1994)

This questionnaire measures an offender's understanding of the effect that his or her abuses has had on his or her own victim(s) and how the victim(s) felt about such sexual contact. High-deviancy child abusers typically report high levels of victim empathy distortions. Beech (1998) reported the internal reliability of this scale to be high (Cronbach's = .89) in 140 untreated child molesters and the test-retest reliability to be .95 in forty-six untreated child molesters. Child sexual offenders report significantly higher levels of victim empathy distortions, than nonoffenders, as measured by this scale (Fisher et al., 1999).

Cognitive Distortions Scale
(from the Children and Sex Questionnaire, Beckett, 1987)

This scale was designed to measure the extent to which abusers portray their victims as in some way responsible for encouraging or initiating sexual contact. High-deviancy child abusers have significantly higher levels of cognitive distortions than nonoffenders as measured by this scale (Fisher et al., 1999). Thornton (personal communication, November 1993) reported the internal consistency to be .90 in a sample of 270 child molesters. Beech (1998) found the test-retest reliability to be .77 in forty-five untreated child molesters over a seven-month period.

Emotional Identification with Children Scale
(from the Children and Sex Questionnaire, Beckett, 1987)

This scale measures the emotional significance of children to the offender. High-deviancy child abusers typically report significantly higher levels of emotional overidentification/emotional congruence with children than nonoffenders (Fisher et al., 1999). Thornton (personal communication, November, 1993) reported the internal reliability to be .90 in a sample of 270 child molesters. Beech (1998) reported the test-retest reliability to be .63 in forty-five untreated child molesters over a over a seven-month period.

MSI: Justifications Scale
(Nichols & Molinder, 1984)

This scale addresses the various justifications/cognitive distortions sexual offenders may use to explain their offenses. Simkins et al. (1989) reported the test-retest reliability to be 0.78 over a three-month period. Nichols and Molinder (1984) do not report the internal consistency of this scale. Beech et al. (1999) found a significant reduction in the level of justifications reported by seventy-seven child abusers who had undergone cognitive-behavioral therapy (CBT) treatment for their sexual offending.

MSI: Sexual Obsessions
(Nichols & Molinder, 1984)

This scale measures sexual obsessions and any tendency to exaggerate problems. Nichols and Molinder reported an internal consistency of .65 (KR20). Simkins et al. (1989) reported the test-retest reliability to be .80 over a three-month period. Beech et al. (1999) found a significant reduction in the level of sexual obsessions reported by seventy-seven child abusers, on this scale, who had undergone CBT for their sexual offending.

(continued)

> *(continued)*
>
> ### Relapse Prevention Questionnaire
> ### (Beckett, Fisher, Mann, & Thornton, 1998)
>
> This measure assesses three areas. The first covers the subject's awareness of thoughts and feelings which lead to offending, their willingness to admit to planning, recognition of where an offence is most likely to occur, and the characteristics of the victims they are most likely to offend against. They were also asked about how other people might know that they were at risk of reoffending and their motivation for offending. The second examines the strategies the offender would use to cope with risk situations and deviant thoughts and feelings. A third section consists of a question about the offender's own perception of level of risk of reoffending. The interrater reliability of this measure has found to be high (Fisher, personal communication, November, 1993). Treated child abusers typically have high scores on this measure, after treatment (Fisher, Beech, & Browne, 2000).

et al., 1999). This psychological profile shows that professional perpetrators are more likely to fit the high-deviancy profile.

An offender would also complete the STEP assessment at the end of treatment in order to ascertain whether change had taken place. Treatment impact was evaluated by looking at whether offenders had shifted significantly in their attitudes following treatment on the measures described in Exhibit 5.1. The methodology used here is termed clinically significant change (Hansen & Lambert, 1996). Responses were examined at an individual level to ascertain whether someone had moved from a score more likely to be found in a dysfunctional distribution of scores (i.e., child abuser attitudes) to a score more likely to be found in a functional distribution of responding (i.e., non–child abuser attitudes).

A clinical assessment would consist of a detailed functional analysis to determine the underlying motives and functions for the offending behavior. Functional analysis typically involves obtaining detailed information about the *antecedents, behaviors,* and *consequences* of offending (the ABC model). This should include the actual behaviors carried out along with the accompanying thoughts and emotions. Unfortunately this is not always a straightforward task with sex offenders due to them frequently being at some level of denial about aspects of the offence and therefore not willing to be completely truthful about the areas that the assessor needs to obtain information about. Indeed, even in those offenders who are open about the level of their offending behaviors there is often a reluctance to disclose their thoughts and feelings around their offending. In order to assist in gaining the information for the functional analysis it can be helpful to provide the offender with a framework to understand the process of offending.

Currently, the most useful framework is called a *decision chain* (Ward, Louden, Hudson, & Marshall, 1995). This model supersedes earlier frameworks such as Finkelhor's (1984) preconditions to abuse or the Wolf (1984) offense cycle. A decision chain is a sequence of choices leading to an offense. Each choice is characterized in terms of the situation it took place in, the thoughts that made sense of and responded to the situation, and the emotions and actions that arose from these thoughts. Thus, in any analysis of offense behaviors the diversity in offending must be taken into account. This accommodates individuals whose firmly entrenched beliefs about the legitimacy of sexual contact with children or forced sex with adults leads them to experience positive emotions during the offense process. Decision chains can represent with equal facility offenses that spring from negative emotional states and poor coping strategies (as in the Wolf cycle) and those where these negative factors are not involved (Eldridge, 1998; Laws, 1999; Ward & Hudson, 1996). An exploration of victim awareness, empathy, and the role of fantasy in sexual offending would also be part of such a clinical assessment. Kelly (1998) notes that special consideration must be given to spiritual assessment for clergy offenders.

EMPIRICAL INTERVENTIONS FOR PERPETRATORS WITHIN PROFESSIONS

CBT is the method of treatment in the United States and the United Kingdom is (Beech & Fisher, 2002). For an overview of this approach, see Marshall, Anderson, & Fernandez (1999). To give a brief synopsis, the behavioral component addresses the overt and covert behavior of an individual and the principles of learning theory. Originally this was confined to the use of procedures to alter behavior (rewarding desired behaviors and punishing unwanted behaviors) but has since broadened to include modeling (demonstrating a desired behavior) and skills training (teaching specific skills through behavioral rehearsal). The cognitive component of the CBT approach addresses the thoughts or cognitions that individual's experience, which are known to affect mood state and hence have an influence upon subsequent behavior. Cognitive therapy aims to encourage an individual to think differently about events, thus giving rise to different affect and behavior. The use of self-instruction, self-monitoring, and the development of an awareness of how one thinks affects how one feels and behaves, are vital components in cognitive therapy. CBT provides a comprehensive approach to treating sex offenders, which now has research evidence to support its efficacy (Alexander, 1999; Friendship, Mann, & Beech, 2003; Hanson et al., 2002).

The Wolvercote Clinic ran an intensive CBT program designed for offenders who were likely to benefit from an environment providing high levels of supervision and monitoring (Eldridge & Wyre, 1998), which was of particular benefit to high-risk professional perpetrators. The specific goals of the program were to challenge offenders' denial/minimization of their offenses by encouraging them to take full and active responsibility for their sexual behavior; to identify and challenge distorted perceptions and attitudes toward the appropriateness of sexual contact with children (cognitive distortions); increase awareness of the victim's perspective of sexual abuse; address identified social skills deficits that may hinder the development or maintenance of more appropriate adult intimate relationships; and help participants to recognize, avoid or cope with situations which could lead to further sexual assaults (relapse prevention).

Typically, an offender would undertake a four-week assessment (covering group and individual exercises and observation in formal and informal settings and the administration of psychological tests). Subsequently, an offender would undertake a two- to four-week preintervention phase (covering an in-depth identification of offending patterns, overcoming the blocks to effective intervention, and beginning to identify a relapse-prevention plan). The offender would then begin a six- to twelve-month work treatment program. A large part of the program was devoted to group work, which typically took place three hours a day, five days per week. The areas covered in this part of the program are outlined in Table 5.1.

TABLE 5.1. Description of the Group-Based Rolling Program at Wolvercote Clinic

Core element	Module	Length
Offending Pattern		
Victim awareness/empathy	1	8 days + 2 RP linked
Fantasy in offending	1	8 days + 2 RP linked
Sexuality and relationships	1	8 days + 2 RP linked
Assertiveness and self-efficacy	1	8 days + 2 RP linked
Offending Pattern Review		5 to 10 days
Victim awareness/empathy	2	8 days + 2 RP linked
Fantasy in offending	2	8 days + 2 RP linked
Sexuality and relationships	2	8 days + 2 RP linked
Assertiveness and self-efficacy	2	8 days + 2 RP linked
Offending Pattern Review 2		5 to 10 days
Victim awareness/empathy	3	8 days + 2 RP linked
Fantasy in offending	3	8 days + 2 RP linked
Sexuality and relationships	3	8 days + 2 RP linked
Assertiveness and self-efficacy	3	8 days + 2 RP linked
Offending Pattern Review 3		5 to 10 days
Victim awareness/empathy	4	8 days + 2 RP linked
Fantasy in offending	4	8 days + 2 RP linked
Sexuality and relationships	4	8 days + 2 RP linked
Assertiveness and self-efficacy	4	8 days + 2 RP linked

RP: Relapse prevention.

The treatment program also included supplementary groups such as enhanced thinking skills, learning from the past and personal childhood/adolescent experiences, and strategies for the future. Individual therapy and skills practice within the positive living environment of the clinic were also conducted. Review weeks were incorporated into the program when problems related to issues of group dynamics or self-awareness could not be contained within the normal modules. Family and cultural issues were addressed where appropriate.

The specific methods used by the treatment providers to tackle distorted thinking (both about children and generally about their own victims) were the standard approaches. The methods generally covered the following areas:

1. *Education:* The relationship between distorted thinking and offending behavior are addressed.
2. *Socratic questioning:* This form of questioning enables the individuals to achieve insights themselves rather than being told what is right by the therapist (Beck, 1976).
3. *Cognitive restructuring:* This approach involves challenging the way individuals think which can lead them to change their way of thinking. In the case of sex offenders, this involves identifying the pro-offending beliefs and then using Socratic questioning, discussion, and the provision of information to help the individuals challenge their thinking. The goal is for them to develop antioffending beliefs.

RELAPSE PREVENTION

This area of work concerns getting offenders to identify particular types of precursors (thoughts, moods, or situations) to their offending. Once these "warning signs" have been identified, the aim of therapy is to empower offenders to develop appropriate self-management skills to prevent relapse (Beech & Fisher, 2000; Laws, 1999; Pithers, Marques, Gibat, & Marlatt, 1983). Thus, offenders develop both an awareness of all their risk factors and appropriate strategies to cope safely with these factors. The latest treatment relapse-prevention programs highlight to offenders the idea that there are positives about not reoffending and new appealing life goals (e.g., old me/new me) (Mann, Webster, Schofield, & Marshall, 2004). However, a major criticism regarding the relapse-prevention model developed from work on addictions by Marlatt (1982) and applied to sexual offenders by Pithers et al. (1983) is that it only describes a single pathway to the commission of a sexual offense. Specifically, it suggests that individuals commit sexual offences largely because of skills deficits, with negative mood states and/or adverse life events being major precursors of relapse.

However, there is more than one route to the commission of a sexual offense. Sexual offenders, and here specifically child abusers, can be categorized as being either approach (acquisitional) or avoidant (inhibitory) goal offenders, regarding their desires to have further sexual contact with children (Eldridge, 1998; Hudson, Ward, & McCormack, 1999; Proulx, Perreault, & Ouimet, 1999; Ward & Hudson, 1998). Ward, Hudson, & Keenan (1998) note that approach goal abusers do not regard sexual contact between adults and children as wrong. Consequently, positive affective states, explicit planning, and the presence of cognitive distortions (e.g., viewing the victim as a consensual partner) typify the offense pathway of professional perpetrators. Avoidant goal offenders are less likely to hold such distorted views about the appropriateness of sexual contact with children. However, self-regulation deficiencies, inadequate coping skills (underregulation), or inappropriate strategies (misregulation), ultimately result in the commission of further offenses.

Bickley and Beech (2002) provide support for the approach/avoidance distinction by demonstrating that approach goal offenders endorse significantly more distorted attitudes and beliefs regarding the appropriateness of sexual contact with children (cognitive distortions) and have reduced empathy for their victims compared to avoidant goal individuals. Therefore, an important implication of this work is that approach and avoidant goal offenders have quite different treatment needs. It is too early to comment on the impact that this approach will have. Nevertheless, it can be seen as a step forward from considering that all offenders follow the same path to offense/relapse. By assessing the type of goal an individual possesses, the clinician should then tailor a treatment plan to suit the offender's need.

The identification of self-regulation deficiencies (e.g., undercontrol or misregulation), highlight markedly different treatment needs. These include work on impulse control, mood management, problem solving and strategy selection, and coping with unexpected high-risk situations. The aim of targeting these areas should be to aid offenders in taking greater responsibility for their actions, developing appropriate coping responses (e.g. assertiveness), and increasing self-efficacy beliefs about dealing with possible high-risk situations (Bickley & Beech, 2003).

CASE EXAMPLE

RO was a thirty-five-year-old physical education teacher arrested as part of a police investigation into child pornography on the Internet. He had no previous convictions and was regarded as a dedicated and caring professional. When arrested he admitted downloading the images and said he was relieved to have been finally caught as he was concerned his behavior was escalating and may have culminated in his committing contact sexual offenses against children. He said,

> By the end I had seen so much of the stuff that it had lost its uniqueness, it's enjoyment factor. I moved on from pictures to MPEGs [movie clips]. I was trying to download movies rather than still pictures, because that was even more real. Again, having seen quite a few of those, that [lessened] in terms of excitement; however, I still used them to masturbate. I was actually getting more from being around other offenders and pretending to be young myself, to live out a fantasy through cybersex. But it had become quite addictive.

Psychometric Assessment

The psychometric assessment showed that RO had problems in the following areas: underassertiveness, difficulty in forming appropriate adult relationships, a sexual preoccupation with children, cognitive distortions about children, justifications, and an emotional fixation on children (i.e. feeling that his emotional needs could be met by children). The psychometric assessment identified that he was highly motivated to engage in treatment and recognized his risk of reoffending. The conclusions of the clinical assessment supported the psychometric findings and suggested that RO was suitable for treatment. An analysis of his offense account suggested that he was not being honest about the extent of his sexually abusive behavior and raised questions about his sexually inappropriate behavior toward the children with whom he worked, before involvement with the Internet.

Treatment Plan

RO completed twelve months of residential treatment during which time he fulfilled 750 hours of group CBT. The treatment program also included supplementary groups such as enhanced thinking skills, learning from the past and personal childhood/adolescent experiences, and strategies for the future. Individual therapy also occurred and skills practice within the positive living environment of the clinic was conducted with RO. He completed a structured CBT workbook, which accompanied the treatment program that had the following core modules: victim awareness and empathy, fantasy in sexual offending, sexuality and relationships, assertiveness, self-efficacy, and offending pattern review. In addition, he completed an Enhanced Thinking Skills program. The ETS is a program based on the premise that much antisocial behavior stems from the offenders' inability to reach their goals in prosocial ways because they lack various cognitive skills. These deficiencies are not related to intelligence or educational attainment but are rather concerned with the styles of thinking and attitudes that lead to antisocial behavior. The program has been found to be useful for offenders, regardless of offense type, who have difficulties with problem solving, impulse control, perspective taking, lack of empathy, and other areas of critical reasoning (Ross & Fabiano, 1985).

During his therapeutic intervention, RO explored is motivation to sexually offend, commenting that,

> I am not sure why I became [interested in children]. I was aware that I was aroused to younger boys when I was just an adolescent around about thirteen or fourteen. I think that I probably would have had the arousal to children, anyway, but the abuse I suffered helped be to formulate a belief system in which abuse was not wrong, it was okay. That was based on how I romanticized the abuse with the PE teacher when I was eleven to thirteen. I saw that very much as a relationship, an equal relationship, and that kind of fuelled my belief system that when I was older that would still be okay as it was for him and me.

As was the case for the majority of other professional perpetrators in the study, RO said that he had been aware of his sexual interest in younger children before he was eighteen years old and that his choice of career was significantly influenced by his sexual interest in children.

Here RO commented that,

> I had started targeting children when I was fourteen, and one boy in particular. I had already thought of myself as a pedophile when I was thirteen. I'd seen that word used or heard the word used on news items and looked it up and thought oh that's me. So the decision to coach younger boys, seven or eight years old, was made when I was sixteen. As I got older, I was thinking what am I going to do workwise. Then I thought well teaching is the best opportunity to be around young boys.

RO had a belief system that strongly supported his desire to be sexual with children and in common with many of the professional perpetrators in our study. He had a sense of entitlement.

> At the time I was angry that it was illegal more that it was "wrong." [I] thought there was a feeling of being uncomfortable that no matter how I would kind of try to make it work in my head I could not square the circle, for example, there was always a nagging doubt that it was wrong but at the time, there was more frustration and anger attached to it. I was going down that line rather than the guilt line. I think guilt and fear were around and that was because I could recognize that if I was to progress and abuse a child then it would be unwelcome and damaging and I couldn't square that in my head. And then I would twist that around and then blame society because it would only be harmful because it was such a big no.

In exploring the nature of his manipulation of his colleagues to facilitate his sexual abuse of children, we asked RO how he disguised his behavior and hid his sexual interest in children from others at work. He said,

> I didn't. An issue came up with one boy that I had targeted. Staff became increasingly concerned about the fact that I was talking about him all of the time. I actually disclosed my sexual attraction to children to a few very close colleagues. They were a bit shocked and surprised and to their credit did try and help. They said, "What's wrong with men?" you know, "Why don't you try out the gay scene?" One of them, a lesbian, took me around the

gay scene. It was no good; I was arrested on suspicion in 1994. The mother of that targeted boy found some love letters I had written him. I was disciplined at work for that. I was put on a final written warning for a year. But there were quite a few individuals, I think there were about four or five people within the college, plus senior management who knew about the offense at least—well, the alleged offenses—who were aware of my sexual attraction to children. I think they trusted me that I would not do anything daft, but they were conscious that it was a very risky environment for me. She [the mother of the alleged victim] informed the cricket club and I was interviewed by them. I lied to the chairman and vice-chairman. I said I was gay and sort of went down that route. It's like hiding in the open, disclose a little but don't disclose everything. Make it a painful experience and they will think they have been told the whole truth. I think that's what I did with that. I lied.

RO also disclosed that he had been grooming his pupils and other children he met through coaching sports. He sexualized his interactions with them, wrote some of them love letters, and persistently brushed against them when the opportunity arose. He said that he wanted to take the sexual contact further but felt he lacked the courage to do so. In addition, RO said that he developed relationships with other sex offenders he met on the Internet in the hope of accessing children to have sex with through these contacts. He also disclosed a sadistic strand to his escalating fantasy. He said that he had been engaging in fantasy role-play with other people he met on the Internet who had a sexual interest in children, noting that,

> There was one guy I met in a chat room who claimed that he had been quite violent toward children. We used to chat about what we would do to a child if we ever got hold of one.

Analysis of RO's collection of indecent images of children supports his interest in sadistic sexual practices.

Postintervention Evaluation

The postassessment treatment evaluations showed that RO had made significant progress in the following areas: forming adult relationships; a sexual preoccupation with children; appropriate social norms concerning children; cognitive distortions and justifications regarding his sexually abusive behavior. In addition, there were improvements, although not clinically significant, in his levels of underassertiveness and an emotional fixation on children. Ultimately, RO completed treatment with sufficient clinically significant change to be regarded as treated.

Postscript: Use of the Internet

The Internet encourages the establishment of networks of people with a sexual interest in children. These groups provide a sense of community and validation of beliefs about children and sex. Participants in the Sullivan and Beech (2004) study report that this networking encourages the development of deviant sexual fantasy content as well as an escalation in the nature of their sexually abusive behavior.

Second, the levels of disclosed sadistic interest are higher among those who use the Internet as part of their pattern of sexual offending. This phenomenon is linked to the observation of the impact of networking, but may also be influenced by the accessibility of a wide range of sexually explicit and abusive material.

REFERENCES

Abel, G.G., Osborn, C.A., & Warberg, B.W. (1998). Professionals. In W.L. Marshall, Y. Fernandez, S.H. Hudson, & T. Ward (Eds.), *Sourcebook of treatment programs for sexual offenders* (pp. 319-335). NY: Plenum.

Alexander, M.A. (1999). Sexual offender treatment efficacy revisited. *Sexual Abuse: A Journal of Research and Treatment, 19,* 101-116.

Beck, A.T. (1976). *Cognitive therapy and the emotional disorders.* New York: International Universities Press.

Beckett, R.C. (1987). The children and sex questionnaire. Available from Richard Beckett, Room FF39, The Oxford Clinic, Littlemore Health Centre, Sanford Rd., Littlemore, Oxford.

Beckett, R.C. & Fisher, D. (1994, November). *Assessing victim empathy: A new measure.* Paper presented at the 13th Conference of the Association for the Treatment of Sexual Abusers (ATSA), San Francisco, USA.

Beckett, R.C., Fisher, D., Mann, R., & Thornton, D. (1998). The relapse prevention questionnaire and interview. In H. Eldridge, *Therapist guide for maintaining change* (pp. 138-150). London: Sage.

Beech, A.R. (1998). A psychometric typology of child abusers. *International Journal of Offender Therapy & Comparative Criminology, 42,* 319-339.

Beech, A.R. & Fisher, D.D. (2002). The rehabilitation of child sex offenders. *The Australian Psychologist, 37,* 206-214.

Beech, A.R., Fisher, D., & Beckett, R.C. (1999). STEP3: An evaluation of the prison sex offender treatment programme. U.K. Home Office Occasional Report. Home Office Publications Unit, 50, Queen Anne's Gate, London, SW1 9AT, England. Available electronically at www.homeoffice.gov.uk/rds/pdfs/occ-step3.pdf.

Beech, A.R., Fisher, D.D., & Thornton, D. (2003). Risk assessment of sex offenders. *Professional Psychology: Research and Practice, 34,* 339-352.

Berry, J. (1992). *Lead us not into temptation.* Doubleday: London.

Bickley, J.A., & Beech, A.R. (2002). An empirical investigation of the Ward and Hudson self-regulation model of the sexual offence process with child abusers. *Journal of Interpersonal Violence, 17,* 371-393.

Bickley, J. & Beech, A.R. (2003). Implications for treatment of sexual offenders of the Ward and Hudson model of relapse. *Sexual Abuse: A Journal of Research and Treatment, 15,* 121-134.

Blanchard, G.T. (1991). Sexually abusive clergymen: A conceptual framework for intervention and recovery. *Pastoral Psychology, 39,* 237-246.

Bottoms, B. L., Shaver, P. R., Goodman, G. S., & Qin, J. (1995). In the name of God: A profile of religion-related child abuse. *Journal of Social Issues, 51,* 85-111.

Brackenridge, C.H. (2001). *Spoilsports: Understanding and preventing sexual exploitation in sport.* London: Routledge.

Brackenridge, C.H. (2004). A whole new ball game? Sex offending in sport. *ATSA: the Forum,* XVI, 1-4. Available at http//:asta.com/theForum/VolumeXVI/Spring.

Brannan, C., Jones R., & Murch, J. (1993). *Castle Hill Report.* Shropshire County Council: Shrewsbury, UK.

Bringer, J.D., Brackenridge, C.H., & Johnston, L.H. (2002). Defining appropriateness in coaching-athlete sexual relationships: The voice of coaches. *Journal of Sexual Aggression, 8,* 83-98.

Browne, K. & Lynch, M.A. (1999). The experiences of children in public care. *Child Abuse Review, 8,* 353-356.

Cawson, P., Wattam, C., Brooker, S., and Kelly, G. (2000). *Child maltreatment in the United Kingdom: A study of the prevalence of child abuse and neglect.* London: NSPCC.

Colton, M. & Vanstone, M. (1996). *Betrayal of trust: Sexual abuse by men who work with children.* London: Free Association Books.

Davis, M.H. (1983). Measuring individual differences in empathy: Evidence for a multiple dimensional approach. *Journal of Personality and Social Psychology, 44,* 113-126.

Eldridge, H. (1998). *Maintaining change: A personal relapse prevention manual.* Thousand Oaks: Sage Publications.

Eldridge, H. & Wyre, R. (1998). The Lucy Faithful Foundation residential program for sexual offenders. In W.L. Marshall, Y. Fernandez, S.H. Hudson, & T. Ward (Eds.), *Sourcebook of treatment programs for sexual offenders* (pp. 79-92). New York: Plenum.

Faller, K.C. (1988). The spectrum of sexual abuse in daycare: An exploratory study. *Journal of Family Violence, 3,* 283-98.

Fasting, K., Brackenridge, C.H., & Sundgot-Borgen, J. (2000) *Sexual harassment in and outside sport.* Oslo: Norwegian Olympic Committee.

Findlater, D. (2000, February). *Sex offending in the church.* Unpublished paper to NOTA: Scotland.

Finkelhor, D. (1984). *Child sexual abuse: New theory and research.* London: Macmillan.

Finkelhor, D., Williams, L., & Burns N. (1988). *Nursery crimes: A study of sexual abuse in day care.* Newbury Park: Sage.

Fisher, D., Beech, A.R., & Browne, K.D. (1998). Locus of control and its relationship to treatment change in child molesters. *Legal and Criminological Psychology, 3,* 1-12.

Fisher, D., Beech, A.R., & Browne, K.D. (1999). Comparison of sex offenders to non-sex offenders on selected psychological measures. *International Journal of Offender Therapy and Comparative Criminology, 43,* 473-491.

Fisher, D., Beech, A.R., & Browne, K.D. (2000). The effectiveness of relapse prevention training in a group of incarcerated child molesters. *Crime, Psychology and Law, 6,* 181-195.

Francis, P. & Turner, N. (1995). Sexual misconduct within the Christian Church: Who are the perpetrators and those they abuse? *Counseling and Values, 39,* 218-227.

Friendship, C., Mann, R., & Beech, A. (2003). Evaluation of a national prison-based treatment program for sexual offenders in England and Wales. *Journal of Interpersonal Violence, 18,* 744-759.

Gallagher, B. (1998). *Grappling with smoke: Investigating and managing organised abuse—A good practice guide.* London: NSPCC Publications.

Gallagher, B. (1999a). The abuse of children in public care. *Child Abuse Review, 8,* 357-365.

Gallagher, B. (1999b). Institutional Abuse. In N. Parton, & C. Wattam (Eds.), *Child sexual abuse: Responding to the experiences of children* (pp. 197-210). Chichester: Wiley.

Gallagher B. (2000). The extent and nature of known cases of institutional child sexual abuse. *British Journal of Social Work, 30,* 795-817.

Gallagher, B., Hughes, B., & Parker, H. (1996). The nature and extent of know cases of organized child sexual abuse in England and Wales. In P. Bibby (Ed.), *Organised abuse: The current debate* (pp. 215-230). Aldershot, UK: Arena.

Ghate, D. & Spencer, L. (1995). *The prevalence of child sexual abuse in Britain.* London: HMSO.

Gillis, J.R. (1991). *The rapist as a sexually deviant offender.* Unpublished doctoral dissertation. Queens University, Kingston, Ontario, Canada.

Green, L. (1999). *Getting the balance right: A cross comparative analysis of the balance between legal interventions and therapeutic support systems in relation to responses to child sexual abuse in England, Belgium and the Netherlands.* Report prepared for the EC. University of Huddersfield, Centre for Applied Childhood Studies: Huddersfield.

Groze, V. (1990). An exploratory study into institutional maltreatment. *Children and Youth Services Review, 12,* 229-241.

Hansen, N. & Lambert, M. (1996). Clinical significance: An overview of methods. *Journal of Mental Health, 5,* 17-24.

Hanson, R.K., Gordon, A., Harris, A.J.R., Marques, J.K., Murphy, W., Quinsey, V.L., & Seto, M.C. (2002). First report of the collaborative outcome data project on the effectiveness of psychological treatment for sex offenders. *Sexual Abuse: A Journal of Research and Treatment, 14,* 169-194.

Haywood, T.W. (1994, October). *Cleric misconduct with minors: Minimization and self-reported functioning.* Paper presented to the 13th Annual Conference of the Association for the Treatment of Sexual Abuse, San Francisco.

Haywood, T.W., Kravitz, H.M., Grossman, L.S., Wasyliw, O.E., & Hardy, D.W. (1996). Psychological aspects of sexual functioning among cleric and non-cleric molesters of children and adolescents. *Child Abuse and Neglect, 20,* 527-536.

Holmes, W.C. & Slap, G.B.C. (1998). Sexual abuse of boys: Definition, prevalence, correlates, sequel, and management. *Journal of the American Medical Association, 280,* 1855-1862.

Hudson, S.M., Ward, T., & McCormack, (1999). Offense pathways in sexual offenders. *Journal of Interpersonal Violence, 14,* 779-798.

Isley, P.J. & Isley, P. (1990). The sexual abuse of male children by church personnel: Intervention and prevention. *Pastoral Psychology, 39,* 85-98.

Jenkins, P. (1986). *Pedophiles and priests: Anatomy of a contemporary crisis.* New York: Oxford University Press.

Kelly, A.F. (1998). Clergy offenders. In W.L. Marshall, Y. Fernandez, S.H. Hudson, & T. Ward (Eds.), *Sourcebook of treatment programs for sexual offenders* (pp. 303-318). New York: Plenum.

Keltner, A.A., Marshall, P.G., & Marshall, W.L. (1981). Measurement and correlation of assertiveness and social fear in a prison population. *Corrective and Social Psychiatry, 27,* 41-47.

Kirby, S., Greaves, L., & Hankivsky, O. (2000). *The dome of silence: Sexual harassment and abuse in sport.* London: Zed Books.

Langevin, R., Curnoe, S., & Bain, J. (2000). A study of clerics who commit sexual offenses: Are they different from other sex offenders? *Child Abuse and Neglect, 24,* 535-545.

Lasser, M.R. (1991). Sexual addiction and the clergy. *Pastoral Psychology, 39,* 213-235.

Laws, D.R. (1999). Relapse Prevention: The state of the art. *Journal of Interpersonal Violence, 14,* 285-302.

Leahy, T., Pretty, G., & Tenenbaum, G. (2002). Prevalence of sexual abuse in organised competitive sport in Australia. In C. Brackenridge and K. Fasting (Eds.), *Sexual harassment and abuse in sport: International research and policy perspectives* (pp. 19-46). London: Whiting and Birch.

Leventhal, J.M. (1998). Epidemiology of sexual abuse of children: Old problems, new directions. *Child Abuse and Neglect, 22,* 481-491.

Loftus, J.A. & Camargo, R.J. (1993). Treating the clergy. *Annals of Sex Research, 6,* 287-304.

Mandeville-Norden, R. & Beech. A.R. (2004). Community based treatment of sex offenders. *Journal of Sexual Aggression.*

Mann, R.E., Webster, S.D., Schofield, C., & Marshall, W.L. (2004). Approach versus avoidant goals in relapse prevention with sexual offenders. *Sexual Abuse: A Journal of Research and Treatment, 16,* 65-76.

Marlatt, G.A. (1982). Relapse prevention: A self-control program for the treatment of addictive behaviors. In R.B. Stuart (Ed.), *Adherence, compliance and generalization in behavioral medicine* (pp. 329-378). New York: Bruner/Mazel.

Marshall, W.L., Anderson, D., & Fernandez, Y. (1999*). Cognitive-behavioral treatment of sexual offenders.* Chichester: Wiley.

McFadden, E.J. & Ryan, P. (1992, August). *Preventing abuse in family foster care: Principles for practice.* Paper presented at the Ninth International Congress on Child Abuse and Neglect: Chicago.

Nichols, H.R. & Molinder, I. (1984). *Multiphasic sex inventory manual.* Available from authors, 437 Bowes Drive, Tacoma, WA, 98466.

Nolan, L. (2001). First report of the review on child protection in the Catholic Church in England and Wales. Available at www.nolanreview.org.uk.

Nowicki, S. (1976). *Adult Nowicki-Strickland internal-external locus of control scale: Test manual.* Available from S. Nowicki, Jr., Department of Psychology, Emory University, Atlanta, GA, 30322.

Nowicki, S. & Duke, M.P. (1974). A locus of control scale for college as well as non-college adults. *Journal of Personality Assessment, 38,* 136-137.

Nowicki, S. & Duke, M.P. (1982). A review of the Nowicki-Strickland locus of control scales. In H. Lefcourt (Ed.), *Research with the locus of control construct, Vol. 2: Methods and application* (pp. 9-39). New York: Academic Press.

Nunno, M.A. (1992). *Factors contributing to abuse and neglect in out-of-home settings*. Paper presented at NSPCC conference on The International Abuse of Children, May: London.

Pithers, W.D., Marques, J.K., Gibat, C.C., & Marlatt, G.A. (1983). Relapse prevention: A self-control model of treatment and maintenance of change for sexual aggressives. In J. Greer & I. R. Stuart (Eds.), *The sexual aggressor: Current perspective on treatment* (pp. 292-310). New York: Van Nostrand Reinhold.

Plante, T.G., Manuel, G., & Bryant, C. (1996) Personality and cognitive functioning among hospitalized sexual offending Roman Catholic priests. *Pastoral Psychology, 45*, 129-139.

Proulx, J., Perreault, C., & Ouimet, M. (1999). Pathways in the offending process of extrafamilial sexual child molesters. *Sexual Abuse: A Journal of Research and Treatment, 11*, 117-129.

Rindfleisch, N., & Rabb, J. (1984). Dilemmas in for planning for the protection of children and youths in residential facilities. *Child Welfare, 63*, 205-215.

Ross, R.R. & Fabiano, E.A. (1985). *Time to think: A cognitive model of delinquency prevention and offender rehabilitation*. Johnson City, TN: Institute of Social Sciences and Arts.

Russell, D., Peplau, L.A., & Cutrona, C.A. (1980). The revised UCLA loneliness scale: Concurrent and discriminant validity evidence. *Journal of Personality and Social Psychology, 39*, 472-480.

Salter, A. (1988). *Treating child sex offenders and their victims: A practical guide*. London: Sage.

Saradjian, A. & Nobus, D. (2003). Cognitive distortions of religious professionals who sexually abuse children. *Journal of Interpersonal Violence, 18*(8), 905-223.

Simkins, L., Ward, W., Bowman, S., & Rinck, C.M. (1989). The Multiphasic sex inventory as a predictor of treatment response in child abusers. *Annals of Sex Research, 2*, 205-226.

Sloan, J. (1988). Institutional abuse. *Child Abuse Review, 2*, 7-8.

Social Services Inspectorate. (1995). *Unregistered children's homes*. Department of Health, HMSO: London.

Stanley, N. (1999). *Institutional abuse*. London: Routledge.

Sullivan, J. & Beech A. (2002). Professional perpetrators: Sex offenders who use their employment to target and sexually abuse the children with whom they work, *Child Abuse Review, 11*, 153-167.

Sullivan, J. & Beech A. (2004). Are professional perpetrators different from other sex offenders? *Journal of Sexual Aggression, 10*, 39-50.

Thompson, J.G., Marolla, J.A., & Bromley, D.G. (1998). Disclaimers and accounts in cases of Catholic priests accused of pedophilia. In A. Shupe (Ed.), *Wolves within the fold* (pp. 175-190). New Brunswick: Rutgers University Press.

Thornton, D. (1989). *Self-esteem scale.* Unpublished manuscript. Available from David Thornton, the Sand Ridge Secure Treatment Center, Mauston, Wisconsin.

Thornton, D., Beech, A., & Marshall, W.L. (2004). Pre-treatment self-esteem and post-treatment sexual recidivism. *International Journal of Offender Therapy and Comparative Criminology, 48,* 587-599.

Utting, W. (1998). *People like us.* London: HMSO.

Ward, T. & Hudson, S.M. (1996). Relapse prevention: A critical analysis. *Sexual Abuse: A Journal of Research and Treatment, 8,* 177-200.

Ward, T. & Hudson, S.M. (1998). A model of the relapse process in sexual offenders. *Journal of Interpersonal Violence, 13,* 700-725.

Ward, T., Hudson, S.M., & Keenan, T. (1998). A self-regulating model of the sexual offense process. *Sexual Abuse: A Journal of Research and Treatment, 10,* 141-157.

Ward, T. & Keenan, T. (1999). Child molesters' implicit theories. *Journal of Interpersonal Violence, 14*(8), 821-838.

Ward, T., Louden, K., Hudson, S., & Marshall, W.L. (1995). A descriptive model of the offence chain in child molesters. *Journal of Interpersonal Violence, 10,* 453-473.

Waterhouse, R. (2000). *Lost in Care.* London: HMSO.

Westcott, H. (1991). *Institutional abuse of children—from research to policy: A Review.* London: NSPCC.

Westcott, H. & Clement, M. (1992). *Experience of child abuse in residential care and educational placements: Results of a survey.* London: HSPCC.

White, I.A. & Hart, K. (1995). *Report of the inquiry into the management of child care in the London Borough of Islington.* London Borough of Islington, London, UK.

Wolf, S.C. (1984, September). *A multifactorial model of deviant sexuality.* Paper presented at the Third International Conference of Victimology, Lisbon.

Chapter 6

Intellectually and Developmentally Challenged Sex Offenders

William R. Lindsay
Lesley Steptoe
Kathleen Quinn

INTRODUCTION

Research and clinical interest in sex offenders with intellectual disabilities (ID) has increased considerably over the past fifteen years. Although most of this work has been conducted in regard to the sex offenders themselves, more recently some research has extended to consideration of the wider family and community context for the development, assessment, and treatment of sex offenders with ID. The link between delinquency, upbringing, family characteristics, and community characteristics is being investigated (Farrington, 1995; Patterson & Yoerger, 1997), and this has recently been considered in offenders with ID (Lindsay, Sturmey, & Taylor, 2004). The extent to which these variables extend to sex offenders is complex and will be dealt with later in this chapter. The following pages will consider prevalence, characteristics, and typologies of sex offenders with ID; assessment issues; the relevance of family and cultural issues; and treatment issues, including relapse prevention.

PREVALENCE AND CHARACTERISTICS

The main problem with the body of studies that have investigated the prevalence of criminal behavior in the population of individuals with ID is the disparate nature of the methodologies. Studies have investigated prevalence in high-security hospitals (Walker & McCabe, 1973); prisons (MacEachron, 1979); criminal justice services (Mason & Murphy, 2002); appearance at court (Messinger & Apfelberg, 1961); and appearance at police stations (Lyall, Holland, Collins, & Styles 1995). These studies have found considerable variations in the incidence of offenders in these highly differing populations. Walker and McCabe (1973), in a study of individuals in special hospitals, found that 35 percent were diagnosed as having ID. Messinger and Apfelberg (1961), in their study of approximately 57,000 individuals assessed for the courts in New York, found that about 2.5 percent had ID. MacEachron (1974) reviewed the literature on prevalence rates for offenders with intellectual disabilities studied in prison. She found a range from 2.6 to 39.6 percent. In her own more carefully controlled study, employing recognized intelligence tests, she studied 436 adult male offenders in Maine and Massachusetts state penal institutions. She found prevalence rates of ID of about 0.6 to 2.3 percent.

Clearly, little relationship exists between these various populations, although they all are subsumed under the heading of studies on prevalence of people with ID in the criminal population. The importance of contextual factors is highlighted in the work of Lyall, Holland, & Collins (1995) and Lyall, Holland, Collins, & Styles (1995). In separate studies, they reviewed the incidence of people with ID in criminal populations. In one study they reviewed people arrested and screened by the police and found to have been in a special school for children for mild or severe ID. They found that none of the subjects had a measured IQ less than seventy. However, several reported having learning support at school and by this less exact assessment, might have been classified as falling within an ID range. In the second study, they reviewed adults living in residential placements for people with ID and investigated those who had been interviewed by police because of alleged offenses. In the latter study, they noted that none of those interviewed by police appeared in court despite the seriousness of many of the offenses. None of the sample received a prison sentence and none were diverted to the health services. These authors concluded that the various residential and support systems were extremely tolerant in relation to offending and challenging behavior in people with ID. They also noted a lack of established links between the criminal justice agencies and other services.

Two recent reports in Scotland have found consistent results with these studies. Meyer (2003), in a study of sixteen prison and detention facilities, found a prevalence of 0.3 percent of individuals with ID in Scottish prisons. A further report (Managed Forensic Care Network, IDDS Sub-Committee, Scottish Executive, 2004) calculated the prevalence of offenders with ID in a large community population. They based their figures on referrals to a mature service for offenders with ID. This service had comprehensive contacts with the criminal justice services, the courts, the health services, social services, and all relevant agencies dealing with people with ID and offender services. Based on an eleven-year study of referral patterns they calculated that around 2 percent of the theoretical intellectual disability population had been assessed by the service. This amounted to around 10 percent of the identified population of individuals with IQ less than 75. This figure is consistent with that found by Hayes (1991) in her study of offenders in New South Wales. Using intelligence tests and assessment of social and adaptive skills, she reported that around 13 percent of people known to the ID services had been convicted of offenses.

Hayes (1994) studied a population of individuals referred to an Australian court in a mixed rural and urban setting. She found that 14 percent had an IQ of less than 70. In a further study (Hayes, 1996), she reviewed incidence in a rural setting where there was a large Aboriginal population. Here she found an incidence of 36 percent of individuals with an IQ of less than 70. Clearly there are significant cultural factors operating in these kinds of studies.

In a comprehensive study in the United Kingdom, Bucke and Brown (1997) reviewed 3,950 detainees across thirteen police stations and reviewed 12,500 custody records. They concluded that around 2 percent of detainees were initially treated as mentally disordered or handicapped. Unfortunately, they did not differentiate between types of mental disorder and developmental disability, but the percentages are clearly low.

In their comprehensive review of epidemiological studies in United States prisons, Noble and Conley (1992) conclude that

> there is little point in trying to nail down to the nearest decimal point the percentage of people with mental retardation and other mental disabilities who reside in the nation's prisons. We know

that the number is significant and that many inmates with mental retardation are not receiving appropriate services. (p. 45)

This pragmatic conclusion is certainly relevant to all of the assessment settings already mentioned and is also relevant to the various different types of offending including sex offenders.

Prevalence of Sex Offenders with ID

Several researchers have reported an increasing incidence or a relatively high incidence of sex offending in this population. Gross (1985) reported that between 21 and 50 percent of offender with ID had committed sexual assault. In their study of patients committed under a hospital order, Walker and McCabe (1973) found that 28 percent of 331 men with ID had committed sexual offense. Day (1994) has little doubt that sex offenses are overrepresented amongst this client group. Lund (1990) reported a doubling of the incidence of sex offending when comparing sentencing in 1973 to 1983. He concluded that this rise might be the result of deinstitutionalization policies whereby people with ID are no longer detained in hospitals for indeterminate lengths of time. Therefore, those with propensities toward sexual offending would be more likely to be living in the community and as a result more likely to be subject to judicial processes should they engage in sexually abusive behavior.

Lindsay et al. (2004) reported an eleven-year review of sexual and nonsexual offenders with ID. In their sample of consecutive referrals, they noted 106 men who had committed sexual offenses or sexually abusive incidents and seventy-eight men who had committed other types of offenses and other serious incidents. In this sample, 57.6 percent of those referred had been referred for a sexually related incident. This figure is consistent with those reported by Gross (1985).

In this context, it should be noted that tolerance for any kind of sexual misdemeanor in contemporary society has reduced considerably. In our experience, tolerance for nonsexual incidents is much higher, and can even be astonishingly high compared to sexual misdemeanors. Case examples in the past year include an assault on two detective constables which was not prosecuted because the (competent) assailant had intellectual disabilities, yet a man received a one-year probation sentence for touching another client on the bottom (outside his clothes) and asking if he would like to have sex. Although we do not wish to excuse the latter incident, clear differences exist in societal tolerance of these incidents.

TYPOLOGIES OF OFFENDERS

Griffiths, Fedoroff, Richards, & Cos-Lindenbaum (in press) reviewed the applicability of DSM-IV diagnostic criteria to the diagnosis of paraphilia in persons with ID. They reviewed the evidence in relation to exhibitionism, fetishism, frotteurism, pedophilia, sexual masochism, sexual sadism, transvestic fetishism, and voyeurism. They note that lack of sexual knowledge and institutional learning are both major factors when considering whether these typologies are appropriate. Several authors (e.g., Lindsay, 2002), have commented that understanding is a crucial aspect in deciding whether a particular behavior is an offense. If one does not have the intellectual capacity to understand that public masturbation, for example, is not only a crime, but is also against the conventions of society, then it cannot be an offense to act in such a manner.

Holland (2004) writes "for an illegal act to result in conviction, it is not sufficient for it to have been demonstrated that an act has been committed *(actus reus)* but that there has been a guilty state of mind *(mens rea)* or recklessness on the part of the alleged perpetrator" (p. 28).

Griffiths et al. (2005) also note that institutional learning may be such that an individual believes a certain inappropriate sexual act to be normal through experiences of personal abuse, disinhibited lifestyles, and so on. They also make the point that certain sexual behaviors, which could be interpreted as fetishes, may be symptomatic of genetic syndromes. They present the example that object insertion in orifices (including genitalia) could be symptomatic of Smith-Magenis syndrome or that nonconsenting touching or rubbing (frotteurism) may be a result of Tourette's syndrome or Smith-Magenis syndrome. Nevertheless, they feel that these diagnostic criteria are broadly relevant for individuals with ID.

In an alternative approach to typology, Lindsay (2004) reviews the empirical evidence supporting various hypotheses that researchers have developed over the years to account for sex offenses in this population. The first and perhaps the most prevalent hypothesis was previously mentioned. Lack of sexual knowledge as a factor in inappropriate sexual advances and incidents has been considered under the term "counterfeit deviance" (Hingsburger, Griffiths, & Quinsey 1991; Luiselli, 2000). Counterfeit deviance refers to behavior that is undoubtedly deviant but may be precipitated by factors such as lack of sexual knowledge, poor social and heterosocial skills, limited opportunities to establish sexual relationships, and sexual naivety rather than any specific aspect of paraphilia. As a result, intervention should emphasize developmental maturation and educational input rather than focus on sexual deviance. Interestingly, although this hypothesis is widespread, relatively little empirical evidence exists for or against counterfeit deviance.

Two recent studies have cast some doubt on the hypothesis as a primary motivating factor. Griffiths (personal communication) compared sex offenders with ID with control subjects. Sexual knowledge was assessed using the SSKAAT-R (Socio-Sexual Knowledge and Attitudes Assessment Tool—Revised) (Griffiths & Lunsky, 2003). She found no differences between sex offenders with ID and control subjects. The lack of a significant difference between groups is itself an important finding. The counterfeit deviance hypothesis would suggest that sex offenders have a lower level of sexual knowledge, knowledge of appropriate behavior and inappropriate behavior, and so on, which might result in a higher incidence of sexually inappropriate behavior. Those individuals with a higher level of sexual knowledge would understand that such behavior was both inappropriate and illegal. The fact that no difference was found does not lend any support to this typology.

Lindsay, Michie, Martin, & Grieve (in press) compared a group of thirty-six sex offenders with thirty-six control subjects on their sexual knowledge. No differences were found between the groups on IQ and age. On most measured variables, sex offenders were significantly more knowledgeable than control subjects. However, Lindsay et al. also found that the knowledge of sex offenders was far from optimum, with significant gaps especially in the areas of sexually transmitted diseases and birth control.

Their conclusion was consistent with that of Baroff (1996) when he wrote in the context of his experience with a wide range of offenders with ID that although relatively few retarded offenders will be unaware of the illegality or "wrongfulness" of their acts . . . there is still the question of whether the defendant who is retarded should be held to the same standard of responsibility as those who are not. (p. 319)

By this statement, he was indicating that although sex offenders with ID will understand that their behavior is wrong, they cannot be expected to understand the extent of its illegality, inappropriateness, harm done to the victim, and so on, because of their intellectual limitations. Therefore, although counterfeit deviance may not be supported as a primary typology, lack of knowledge may feature in the assessment and treatment of sex offenders with ID.

A large group of aetiological factors that have been extensively researched fall under the heading of psychosocial and developmental factors. The most significant of those is childhood sexual abuse, which has been cited by several authors as a possible reason why individuals with ID commit sexual offenses. Thompson and Brown (1997) noted a high rate of sexual abuse experienced by individuals with ID and further noted that another individual from this client group had perpetrated the abuse. Furey (1994), in a study of 461 cases of sexual abuse of adults with ID, found that 42 percent of the abuse had been perpetrated by those who themselves had ID. The "abused to abuser" hypothesis is one that has gained prominence in the field. Unfortunately, few studies support this hypothesis (Sequeira & Hollins 2003). Beail and Warden (1995), in a study of thirty-five men who had committed sexual abuse, found a high incidence (82 percent) of abusive incidents in the participant's own childhood. However, lack of standardized assessment and appropriate control comparisons made such conclusions speculative.

Lindsay, Law, Quinn, Smart, & Smith (2001) compared forty-six sexual offenders and forty-eight nonsexual offenders in relation to their experience of sexual and physical abuse in childhood. Comprehensive assessments of abuse were taken over a period of one year and were conducted independently by a range of professionals involved with these cases. They found a higher rate of sexual abuse in the histories of sexual offenders when compared to the nonsexual offenders (38 versus 12.7 percent), and a higher rate of physical abuse in the histories of the nonsexual offenders when compared to the sexual offenders (33 versus 13 percent). They concluded that although sexual abuse was a significant variable in the history of sexual offenders with ID, it seemed neither a sufficient explanation nor an inevitable consequence in relation to sex offending. Most of the individuals who committed a sexual offense had not themselves been sexually abused in childhood. Therefore, sexual abuse was an insufficient aetiological explanation for sexual offending.

Mental illness has been indicated in relation to sexual offense typology. Day (1993) noted a high incidence of psychiatric illness in sex offenders with ID. In a report on sixty-four patients admitted to a treatment unit for severe challenging behavior including a large number of sexual offense cases, Xenitidis, Henry, Russell, Ward, & Murphy (1999) noted that psychiatric illness was recorded in 48.4 percent, nonpsychotic illness in 18.8 percent, autism in 17.2 percent, and epilepsy in 25 percent of the cohort. Part of the reason for referral for these individuals was mental illness and therefore the sample may have been considerably skewed. Nevertheless, it does indicate the importance of considering mental illness in this client group.

Diagnostic criteria are extremely important in relation to this variable. Lund (1990) reported on 274 offenders with an intellectual disability. Most were under care orders. This was a longitudinal study that was not confined to individuals admitted to a hospital and 91.77 percent of this cohort was diagnosed as having a mental illness. However, 87.5 percent of these diagnoses were categorized as behavior disorder. Clearly this gives rise to doubts concerning inclusion criteria and the classification of mental illness across studies.

Day (1994) reported that 32 percent of the sample of sex offenders with an intellectual disability had suffered psychiatric illness in adulthood. Lindsay et al. (2002) reported a study of sixty-two sex offenders and abusers with intellectual disability. They also found that 32 percent had a significant mental illness including psychotic disorders, bipolar disorders, and major depression. In these latter two studies, mental illness and behavior disorder were diagnosed separately.

These research reports lack control conditions, which are crucial in judging whether mental illness is differentially prevalent in this group when compared to others. Lindsay, Smith, et al. (2004) compared 106 sexual offenders with seventy-eight male nonsexual offenders. They found that 32 percent of the sexual offenders and 33 percent of the nonsexual offenders were diagnosed as having a major mental illness including psychosis, major depression, or bipolar mood disorder.

Sixty three percent of the sexual offenders and 58 percent of the nonsexual offenders received no medication. Therefore, there were no differences between the groups on either mental illness or medication categories. This finding suggests that mental illness is not a differential feature of sex offenders with ID. However, that is not to say that it will not feature prominently in individual cases by interacting with other variables such as sexual deviance or sexual preference.

Deviant sexual interest and tendencies toward sexual offending are the primary reasons cited for the commission of sexual offenses in mainstream offenders. Harris et al. (2003) reviewed a number of studies on risk prediction, psychopathy, and sexual deviance. This is an extensive review of previous studies and in addition, they replicate previous findings using the records of 369 sex offenders across a range of settings. They note that the two best predictive variables in relation to sex offense recidivism are sexual deviancy as measured by the penile plethysmograph and psychopathy as measured by the Hare Psychopathy Checklist (Hare, 1991). Therefore, sexual deviancy and sexual preference are clearly implicated in mainstream offenders.

Lindsay et al. (2002) found that for 62 percent of referred sex offenders with ID, there was either a previous conviction for a sexual offense or clear documented evidence of sexual abuse having been perpetrated by that individual. In their subsequent review of cases, Lindsay, Elliot, and Astell (2004) note that 72 percent of cases in a sex offender group had committed a previous incident of sexual abuse. Thirty five percent of those was a nonpenetrative sexual act with a minor, 16 percent was indecent exposure, 14 percent was sexual assault, 10 percent sexual harassment, 8 percent prostitution, and less than 5 percent each for unlawful sexual intercourse, rape, procurement, incest, gross indecency, bestiality, and attempted rape. This high incidence of previous inappropriate sexual behavior would indicate a degree of persistence to the sexual abuse (excluding prostitution). If one considers that any incidence of inappropriate sexual behavior in an individual with ID is generally followed by severe criticism, withdrawal of privileges, family censure, and so on, one realizes that these incidents continue in the face of disincentives. Therefore, drive toward inappropriate sexual behavior must be considered as a distinct possibility.

More persuasive evidence comes from the series of studies by Blanchard et al. (1999), who investigated patterns of sexual offending in 950 participants. They found that in comparison to other categories of sex offender, sexual offenders with ID were significantly more likely to commit sex offenses against younger children and male children. These authors concluded that "the results suggested that mentally retarded offenders choices of male or female victims were not primarily determined by accessibility (or other circumstantial factors) but rather by their relative sexual interest in male and female children" (p. 119). They go so far as to postulate that pedophilia or some types of pedophilia may be a developmental disorder. Given our current knowledge of developmental disorders and the fact that sexual preference has never featured as an issue in any of the writing on any of the developmental disorders, this seems highly unlikely. This hypothesis indicates the strength of the relationships found in their study and, coming as it does from a well-conducted series of studies, this information constitutes strong evidence that deviant sexual preference plays at least some role in this client group.

Evidence on the typologies for sexual offenders with ID is developing well. Griffiths et al. (2005) have written that with certain caveats, DSM-IV criteria for paraphilias may be appropriate to this client group. The concept of counterfeit deviance in relation to inappropriate sexual behavior has been clarified more recently. As has been previously noted, little evidence supports that sexual offenders with ID have a poorer sexual knowledge than appropriate control groups. However, it remains the case that their sexual knowledge is less comprehensive than those individuals without ID. Therefore, counterfeit deviance may play some part in the commission of sexual offenses. Sexual deviance and inappropriate sexual preference may play a more significant role. One study in particular (Blanchard et al., 1999) provides persuasive evidence that sexual preference rather than circumstantial or psychosocial variables is salient when considering this client group.

ASSESSMENT ISSUES

Assessment issues have been slower to develop than treatment or management procedures. However, a number of advances have occurred over the past few years in relation to a range of assessments. Lindsay (2002) notes four categories of assessment: investigating the characteristics of offenders, assessing competence and ability to consent in relation to criminal justice procedures, assessing individuals for treatment, and assessing risk for future recidivism. A great deal of work has been completed on the first aspect in relation to characteristics of offenders such as mental illness, previous sexual abuse, drug or alcohol use (Glaser & Deane, 1999; McGillivray & Moore, 2001), educational history, and age at first offense (Caparulo, 1991; Day, 1993).

Work has also been done on family disturbance in childhood. For example, Day (1993), Caparulo (1991), and Hayes (1991) all note a high level of family disturbance in childhood for sex offenders with ID. The difficulty with this work is that it does not have a control condition and therefore we do not know the extent to which all individuals with ID have experienced the same family disturbance. As we have seen, Day (1994) noted a high level of mental illness in this client group. However, Lindsay, Elliot, and Astell (2004), employing a suitable control group, have shown that the level of mental illness is no higher than other groups of offenders with ID.

Several advances have been made in the assessment technology for gaining self-reports from people with ID in general and sex offenders in particular. Finlay and Lyons (2001) and Dagnan and Lindsay (2004) outlined some of the developments in self-report measures for clients with ID and noted some of the difficulties in gaining self-report. The Beck Anxiety Inventory and the Beck Depression Inventory have both been adapted for this client group. Interestingly, Lindsay and Lees (2003), in a study of sixteen sex offenders and sixteen control subjects, found that the sex offending group scored significantly lower on both the Beck anxiety and depression inventories than control subjects. The absolute levels of anxiety and depression reported by both groups was relatively high, but the sex offender group reported less emotional disturbance than controls.

Parry and Lindsay (2003) adapted the Barratt Impulsiveness Scale (Barratt, 1994) for use with offenders with intellectual disability and administered the test to twenty-two sexual offenders and nineteen control subjects. Previously, Glaser and Deane (1999) had hypothesized that one of the major motivations for committing a sex offense for men with intellectual disability was impulsivity. In their study, they found so few differences between sex offenders and control subjects that they postulated that impulsivity may be the only defining factor in the commission of a sex offense. However, Parry and Lindsay (2003) found that the opposite was the case. The sexual offenders had an impulsivity score one-third less than nonsexual offenders. Nonoffenders with ID reported intermediate levels of impulsivity between sexual offenders and other types of offenders. Although these studies indicate sex offenders as a cohort to be lower in impulsivity and emotional ability, this does not discount the possibility of impulsivity and emotional disturbance being important in the commission of specific offenses. Indeed, for individuals who are less familiar with an emotional or impulsive episode, it might make them more at risk of losing a degree of self-restraint under these conditions. Similar developments have been made in the assessment of anger (Taylor, Thorne, & Slavkin, 2004), Novaco and Taylor (2004), and propensities toward fire setting (Taylor et al., 2004). Therefore, a number of developments have been reached in relation to assessing characteristics of offenders.

Developments have also been made in assessing competence and ability to consent. These include criminal justice procedures (Beail, 2002) and consent to clinical and research interventions (Arscott, Dagnan, & Stenfert, Kroese, 1999). In relation to competency to stand trial, it is now recognized that people with ID may be disadvantaged by the criminal justice process because of lack of understanding of the gravity of the situation, lack of support, and lack of appropriate representation from early stages in the process.

Gudjonsson and his colleagues (Gudjonsson, 1992; Gudjonsson, Clare, Rutter, & Pearse, 1993) conducted a series of studies showing that people with ID are more vulnerable to false confession during interrogative interview due to heightened propensity toward acquiescence and suggestibility. Gudjonsson and MacKeith (1994) presented a carefully analyzed case study to illustrate the way in which these psychological processes caused an individual to confess falsely to a double murder. He developed scales that assess the extent to which interviewees will yield to leading questions and change their responses as a result of interrogative pressure. Although they are not without their conceptual and practical difficulties (Beail, 2002), the Gudjonsson suggestibility scales (Gudjonsson, 1998) are used widely for assessment of suggestibility under conditions of interrogative pressure. The competency assessment to stand trial (CAST-MR, Everington & Luckasson, 1994; Everington & Fulero, 1999) has been developed specifically to assess the extent to which a client with

ID understands criminal justice processes in court. Therefore, a number of developments have been made in relation to competency and criminal investigation.

The final two areas of assessment, assessing specific issues related to sex offender treatment and risk of future recidivism, are of particular interest. Until the past few years, few innovations occurred in these areas. However, a few studies have been published indicating that clinicians and researchers are addressing these particular issues in relation to sex offenders with ID. Kolton, Boer, & Boer (2001) investigated the use of the Abel and Becker cognition scale (Abel, Becker, & Cunningham-Rathner, 1984), which assesses the extent to which sex offenders hold cognitive distortions that might justify or mitigate their sex offending against children.

Kolton et al. (2001) employed eighty-nine sex offenders with ID and found that the response options of the test needed to be changed from the four choice system (1 = agree, 4 = strongly disagree) to a dichotomous (agree/disagree) to reduce extremity bias in the sample. They found that the revised assessment provided reasonable psychometric properties and the study was the first to provide some evidence that cognitive distortions and attitudes in sex offenders with ID can be assessed with some reliability and validity.

Carson, Whitefield, & Lindsay (2002) described the development of a series of questionnaires dealing with attitudes consistent with rape, voyeurism, exhibitionism, dating abuse, homosexual assault, offenses against children, and stalking. Preliminary results indicated that the questionnaires may prove reliable, internally consistent, and valid, and would discriminate between sex offenders, other offenders, and nonoffenders.

Broxholme and Lindsay (2003) reported pilot work on this questionnaire and found that each section discriminated significantly between a group of seventeen male sex offenders, nineteen male non–sex offenders, all with ID, and thirty-six non–sex offenders without ID. This self-report questionnaire dealing with cognitive distortions has been used successfully as a treatment outcome measure (Lindsay & Smith, 1998; Rose, Jenkins, O'Connor, Jones, & Felce, 2002).

New developments have been made in the assessment of risk of recidivism in offenders with ID in general and sex offenders in particular. Harris (2003) notes that there has been a phenomenal explosion in the development and predictive accuracy of risk measures. Lambrick

(2003) found that these developments have not extended to the field of ID. Lambrick notes that some risk assessments include intellectual disability as a static risk factor. He also comments on the importance of separating those offenders with and without ID and assessing risk factors specifically relevant to each client group.

One of the most researched risk-assessment measures is the Violence Risk Appraisal Guide (VRAG) and its sister assessment the Sex Offender Risk Appraisal Guide (SORAG) (Quinsey, Harris, Rice, & Cromier, 1998). Not only has this assessment been found to be as good as or better than other risk assessments in relation to prediction of future recidivism (Harris et al., 2003; Barbaree, Seto, Langton, & Peacock, 2001), it has also been validated with a cohort of individuals with ID. Quinsey, Book, & Skilling (2004) employed the VRAG with fifty-eight clients with ID who had been transferred to community settings. All clients had histories of serious antisocial behaviors and were followed up for fifteen months to two years. Interrater agreement was excellent for VRAG scores and estimation of incident violence. Based on 500 reported incidents, the data indicated that the VRAG was a good predictor of future antisocial behavior in new settings to which the men had been transferred. In comparison to other predictive variables, the VRAG was the best predictor of new violent and sexual offending.

One of the twelve variables considered by the VRAG is "lives with both parents until the age of sixteen." If the individual being assessed has only lived with one parent, this is a risk factor. It should be emphasized that the Quinsey assessment is not a judgmental assessment. It is strictly data-based and the fact that this is judged as a risk factor is a purely empirical finding. If an individual has not lived with both parents (i.e., if parents have been separated at some point during these years), his or her risk for future recidivism increases. Although this is a very simple item to score, it probably reflects a complex of psychological issues involving family stability, developmental harmony, and attachment issues. If these are disrupted, resulting in parental separation, risk increases. On the other hand, if parents have not separated before the individual is sixteen years of age, this acts as a mild protective variable. Again, this assessment is a purely empirical finding.

The VRAG and SORAG also include measures of childhood behavior problems—the greater the childhood disruption shown by the individual, the greater the risk of future recidivism. Again, this empirical finding attests to the importance of family and developmental stability. These findings do not mean that if individuals score positively on these items they are at high risk of future recidivism. Twelve items are on the VRAG and fifteen on the SORAG, therefore it is feasible that an individual will not feature on the other items and will not therefore be judged as a high or even medium risk of future offending. It is simply the case that these items, relating to family issues are shown empirically to increase risk. In addition, they have been validated on individuals with ID who show offending and challenging behavior.

A second group of assessments designed to assess risk for future offending are considered to be structured clinical judgments. These include the SVR-20 (Boer, Hart, Kropp, & Webster, 1997), which assesses twenty items in relation to risk for future sexual offense recidivism. Boer, Tough, & Haaven (2004) considered the assessment of future recidivism for sex offenders with developmental disabilities. They outlined a number of variables, which they consider to be important specifically in relation to this client group. The authors recommend the use of a static risk assessment such as the SORAG or the Rapid Risk Assessment for Sexual Offense Recidivism (RRASOR) (Hanson, 1997), which is a short actuarial assessment for sex offence recidivism that Boer et al. (2004) reported to have good predictive properties with this client group. The RRASOR includes four items: prior sex offenses, the gender of the victim, the relationship to the victim, and age of offender at time of the offense. This is an excellent predictor for future sexual offending with mainstream offenders in comparison to other risk assessments (Barbaree et al., 2001).

Boer et al. (2004) reviewed the dynamic/proximal variables that are supported by the evidence on clients with ID. These fall into four categories: stable dynamic (staff and environment), acute dynamic (staff and environment), stable dynamic (offenders), and acute dynamic (offenders). Risk factors fall into two broad categories: those on which actuarial predictions are made and which are historical and relatively unchangeable, and those that are more dynamic, changeable variables. The RRASOR reviews historical variables with a view-to-risk prediction. Proximal/immediate dynamic variables are further split into those that are stable (e.g., a history of alcohol abuse, a propensity toward violence) and those that are acute (e.g., resumption of alcohol abuse, being in an emotional/angry state).

Of particular interest from the point of view of families, the stable dynamic items include the attitudes of carers toward the sex offender, consistency of supervision, consistency of the environment, communication among supervisory staff and carers, and the knowledge of the client that supervisory staff may have. They comment specifically that family members or caregivers occasionally minimize the problems of the offender and as a result collude with him or her. Boer et al. also emphasize the importance of consistency of relationships. Under acute dynamic items (staff and environment) they include continued monitoring, victim access, environmental changes, and the introduction of new staff who may not know the client. Staff must not become complacent in relation to supervision since evidence is clear that the risk of further sexual offenses can continue over periods of up to twenty years (Cann, Falshaw, & Friendship, 2004). The stable dynamic items (offenders) include compliance with supervision, cognitive distortions, crime cycle and relapse prevention, self-management of sexuality, mental health problems, engagement in employment and activity, substance abuse, victim selection, self-efficacy, relationship skills, use of violence or threats toward others, impulsiveness, and family-related problems. By the latter they include neglect or abuse from parents or siblings. With reference to acute dynamic factors (offenders), they include changes in social support, increase in substance abuse, sexual preoccupation, changes in emotional state, changes in victim access, complacency on the part of the client (and carers), changes in ability to use coping strategies, changes to routine, and marital or family discord.

Lindsay, Elliot, & Astell (2004) found some empirical support for some of these variables. They followed up fifty-two sexual offenders and abusers and recorded recidivism over four years. They rated each participant on twenty-four variables taken from the literature on prediction of sex offense recidivism. The variables that comprised a significant predictive model were antisocial attitude, low self-esteem, lack of assertiveness, poor relationship with mother, staff complacency, poor response to treatment, offenses involving violence, attitudes tolerant of sexual crimes, denial of the crime, sexual abuse in childhood, unexplained breaks from routine/erratic attendance, deterioration in family attitudes toward the offenders regime, and unplanned discharge. This study has given empirical support to the importance of family/carer variables such as poor relationship with mother, allowances made by carers, carer/staff complacency, and deterioration in family attitudes toward supervision. Not only does this give empirical support to the structured clinical judgment outlined by Boer et al. (2004), it also stresses the importance of carer and family attitudes toward both sex offending and the offender.

ISSUES FOR FAMILIES

Patterson and Yoerger (1997) conducted an extensive series of studies reviewing a developmental model for the onset of delinquency and criminal behavior. They found that from as early as eighteen months, some families may promote a child's coercive behavior such as temper tantrums and hitting because these behaviors have functional value in terminating conflict. As these interactions are repeated, these behaviors are strengthened and firmly established. Other families promote behavior patterns that are quite distinct from those learned in distressed families. In other families, prosocial behaviors may be reinforced, the child learns that interaction such as talking and negotiating are followed by a termination of conflict and these children develop prosocial problem-solving and language skills. Parenting processes outlined by these authors are problem solving, positive parenting, discipline, and monitoring. Early in the child's life, parental discipline is more important in determining the emergence of coercive or prosocial skills. By early to middle adolescence, monitoring by parents emerges as a more important variable. In distressed family interactions, parental discipline reinforces coercive child behavior, prosocial interpersonal academic and work skills are encouraged less, and deviant problem solving is inadvertently taught which leads to the development of coercive behaviors in the termination of conflict. Such children are far less well adjusted and antisocial behavior patterns can be seen as early as age six or seven (Snyder & Patterson, 1995).

Farrington (1995) found that delinquency in early adolescence was significantly associated with troublesome behaviors at eight to ten years, an uncooperative family at eight years, poor housing at eight to ten years, poor parental behavior at eight, and low IQ at eight to ten years. Clearly family variables are significantly associated with the development of crime and deviance in later years. The best predictors of delinquency were invariably previous convictions from ten to thirteen years. For example, convictions at fourteen to sixteen years were predicted best by convictions at ten to thirteen years. Having convicted parents had an additional predictive effect. Adult criminal convictions at twenty-one to twenty-four years were best predicted by convictions in previous age ranges with low family income and a hostile attitude toward authority also making additional predictive contributions. This cycle begins with uncooperative families, poor parental behavior, parental convictions, troublesome behavior, poor housing, and low IQ at age eight. The higher the number of risk domains (families, childhood behavior, schooling, etc.) the higher the probability of later criminality (Stouthamer-Loeber, Loeber, Wei, Farrington, & Wikstrom, 2002).

Wilson (2004) notes the importance of the link between family, parenting, poverty, and education in the development of antisocial behavior. He also notes that 55 percent of those convicted between the ages of ten and sixteen are conviction free by the age of twenty-five and thirty-two. However, this means that 45 percent of those convicted will persist in their criminality over that period.

One study investigated the quality of relationships in sex offenders and non–sex offenders. Lindsay, Forrest, & Power (in press) use the Significant Others Scale (Power, Champion, & Aris, 1988) to review relationships to family members and friends in twenty-eight sex offenders and twenty-eight control subjects. They also employed the Life Experience Checklist (Ager, 1991) as a measure of quality of life in the participants. They found no differences between the groups in the number of times each significant other was mentioned (mother, father, sibling, best friend). The Significant Others Scale asks individuals about actual levels of support they do and have received and ideal levels of support they would like to receive. In regard to both mother and father, the actual and ideal levels of support reported by sex offenders was significantly lower than the control group. Not only did they see themselves as being more isolated from parental relationships, but they seemed not to seek an increase in emotional support. This suggested that the sex offenders with ID were a group of individuals who had been somewhat emotionally detached from important developmental relationships but who had adapted to such detachment to the extent that they were content for it to maintain.

Lindsay et al. also noted that with seven cases, respondents appeared to become angry when mothers, fathers, or siblings were mentioned, indicating that they never received support from them and certainly did not want it. Therefore, there was no discrepancy between actual and ideal measures of support although both were extremely low. For the sex offenders, almost half of the participants said that their father was not or never had been in the family and that they did not wish to establish a relationship with their father. This self-selection of relative isolation was emphasized by the results on the Quality of Life Assessment. No difference was found between the groups on the freedom section or the opportunities section of the assessment but, once again, the sex offenders' use of relationships and leisure was significantly lower than controls. Therefore, as a group, sex offenders with ID may have lower integration with family and community and a poorer attachment to significant relationships and control groups of individuals with ID.

Although little explicit information exists on family influences and relationships for sex offenders with ID, this chapter has managed to pull together a range of information that is implicitly contained in assessments and protocols. The risk appraisal guides include a number of family factors that are extremely important. Collusion with the sex offender, lack of compliance with the treatment regime, and attitudes tolerant toward sexual offending within the family all seem to serve as risk variables. As a group, sex offenders with ID may be more isolated from both family and community. Studies suggest that they are a relatively isolated group, several of whom have not had a great deal of contact with families and community and do not appear to wish to establish such relationships. Promotion of increased contact with family and community may be useful in future treatment development.

INTERVENTIONS

Three treatment approaches have been reported in the literature with reasonable frequency: pharmacological treatments, behavioral treatments, and, more recently, cognitive and problem-solving interventions. In regard to the importance of families, we shall see later that the fundamental issue is the extent to which families comply with treatment procedures and messages. This may take the form of continuing with monitoring and supervision arrangements or it may simply require family members to reinforce messages, which have been employed during treatment sessions. One sex offender treatment method in particular that specifically relies on the support of family members is relapse prevention. This is an amalgam of behavioral and cognitive techniques and will be reviewed later.

Antilibidinal medication is designed to act directly in reducing and suppressing sexual drive. Once it is administered, it does not require additional input from social or environmental influences. Therefore, beyond ensuring that the offender attends the appointment for an injection or continues to take medication, no active role for family members is required. However, if the family undermines the concept of sex offender treatment in the form of pharmacological treatment, the offender will not be encouraged to continue.

Behavioral Management

Two major texts in the area have reported behavioral management services for sex offenders with ID. Griffiths, Quinsey, & Hinsburger (1989) described a behavioral management program that included addressing deviant sexual behavior through education, training social competence and improving relationship skills, reviewing relapse prevention through alerting support staff, and training on issues related to responsibility. In a review of thirty cases, they reported no reoffending and they described a number of successful case studies to illustrate their methods.

Haaven, Little, & Pertre-Miller (1990) also described a behavioral management approach that included social skills training, sex education, and the promotion of self-control of aberrant sexual behavior in a residential setting. The main involvement of families and carers is in the monitoring and support of the treatment and management program. Family-related issues are common to all types of intervention.

Cognitive and Problem-Solving Techniques

Over the past fifteen years, major developments have been made in the use of cognitive and problem-solving techniques within sex offender treatment (Marshall, Anderson, & Fernandez, 1999). Treatment methods are based on the analysis that cognitive distortions set a personal cognitive framework that may be permissive of or consistent with sexual offending. Ward, Hudson, Johnston, & Marshall (1997) outlined an integrative theory designed to promote understanding of the way in which a range of cognitive structures might underpin the initiation, commission, and personal mitigation of sexual offenses. In this way a man may use the fact that a woman is wearing a short skirt to develop the mitigating cognition that she was dressing in a sexually provocative manner and therefore was complicit in his perpetration of a sexual offense. Similarly, he may use a rebuff from a woman, for example, in a bar to mitigate a sexual assault by reasoning that if she had not made him resentful, he would not have felt the urge to perpetrate the act.

A series of mitigating cognitions outlined by Kennedy and Grubin (1992) involve employing family stressors as excuses. Individuals reason that they would not have attempted to induce a child to have sex with them if their partner had been more willing to engage in sexual activity. Interestingly, this latter cognitive mitigation is probably less relevant to offenders with ID since relatively few remain in stable relationships.

Several reports have considered these cognitive processes during treatment. O'Conner (1996) developed a problem-solving intervention for thirteen adult male sex offenders. This involved consideration of a range of risky situations in which offenders had to develop safe solutions for both themselves and potential victims. She reports positive results from the intervention with most subjects achieving increased community access.

Lindsay, Marshall, Neilson, Quinn, & Smith (1998), Lindsay, Neilson, Morrison, & Smith (1998), and Lindsay and Smith (1998) reported a series of case studies on offenders against children, exhibitionists, and stalkers using cognitive interventions in which various forms of denial and mitigation of the offenses were challenged over treatment periods of up to three years. These treatments employed methods including disclosure of the offense, extensive analysis of mitigating and supporting cognitions, and frequent, persistent analysis of problem-solving scenarios. Most of the problem-solving scenarios would attempt to induce a degree of cognitive dissonance in the offender. Treatment would first allow the offender to express his or her firmly held cognitive distortion regarding mitigation or denial of the occurrence or seriousness of the offense. Treatment would then follow a process of Socratic questioning and inductive reasoning whereby the offender himself or herself would arise at a more socialized, acceptable cognition regarding the situation. For example, in one situation the cognition *"women laugh at being flashed at—it might turn them on"* was elicited. Through the treatment processes, the offenders in question would follow their own logical reasoning to arrive at alternative socialized cognitions such as *"she is just thinking about going home to cook her dinner, she doesn't want to be flashed at."* A process of reinforcing the socialized cognition and promoting the dissonance between the previously expressed statement and the socialized statement would then follow. The offender was encouraged to conclude that the previous statement was in fact a cognitive distortion and that the socialized statement is a realistic appraisal of a woman's thoughts regarding indecent exposure. Lindsay et al. reported changes in cognition during treatment and low reoffending rates four to seven years following initial conviction. Lindsay and Smith (1998) found that those treated for two or more years had significantly better outcomes on a range of measures than those treated for less than one year.

Rose et al. (2002) report a sixteen-week group treatment for five sex offenders with ID. They employed self-control procedures, consideration of the effects on victims, identifying emotions and motivations within oneself, sex education, appropriate assertiveness, and avoidance of risky situations. They assessed participants using a number of proximal measures including an attitude scale, a measure of locus of control, a victim empathy scale, and a scale to measure knowledge of sexual behavior and law. The only differences from baseline to posttreatment were found on the locus of control scale that indicated a more external locus of control after the intervention. Rose et al. reported that participants did not reoffend for one year. They felt that the changes in locus of control scores might have been due to a significant portion of treatment in which they emphasized the possible external consequences of any future offending behavior.

One of the most comprehensive and widely employed cognitive models in the treatment of sex offenders is that of relapse prevention (RP). This is developed from addiction models and reviews the cycle of offending and the importance of cognitive distortions and decision making in that process. The RP model highlights seemingly unimportant decisions or acts in regard to personal stress, boredom, leisure, family, etc., which might seem individually trivial and defendable, but taken together construct a clear cycle and pathway of offending. Intervention on this cycle provides the offender with the knowledge and capacity to alter and avoid these decisions, cognitions, and situations that might lead to lapses and relapses in the offense cycle. Offenders are provided with a relapse-prevention plan that is shared with family members and others in their life so that family members and others can identify salient aspects and support the offender in avoiding risky situations, personal and emotional distress, and other ways of entering into the offense cycle.

Although RP has been important in the development of a coherent model for sex offender treatment (Pithers & Gray, 1996; Laws, 1999), it has been criticized on both a theoretical and practical basis. Of particular relevance to this chapter is the issue that RP plans involve extensive postrelease supervision by family members and others in the offender's life. This may allow the sex offender to invoke others in excusing any relapse in that he or she can be blamed for insufficient vigilance and allowing the offender too much leeway in relation to their offence cycle. On the other hand, it assumes that family members will act in a manner that is consistent with sex offender treatment and will in fact promote the relapse prevention procedures. When this works it may act as an extremely powerful motivation and incentive to comply with treatment procedures. However, it also leaves the possibility that family members might undermine procedures through complacency, affection for their relative, a feeling of unfairness and so on. Therefore, family members and significant others become increasingly important in effective treatment for sex offenders.

Engagement with the Community

Lindsay (2004) has written that sex offender treatment should not only address issues of primary motivation such as sexual deviancy, but should also promote attachment, commitment, and engagement to the community including families. Based on control theory (Hirschi, 1969) and drawing on the evidence from Lindsay, Forrest, & Power (2004) he has argued that if the sex offender has an impoverished quality of life with lower levels of personal relationships, lack of prosocial influences, poor community integration, and impoverished housing, one would predict that it would increase his or her likelihood of sex offending and recidivism. Conversely, promotion of the involvement of significant others, and organization of occupational and educational placements are specific therapeutic techniques from which one would theoretically expect therapeutic gains through the mechanism of commitment to and engagement with society. This should occur through two mechanisms. First, with increasing occupational engagement with society (either through supported employment or another arranged placement), the individual will have less time to engage in any antisocial activities. Second, with increasing engagement and relationships, there will be a promotion of self-esteem and a realization that any relapse or recidivism would result in losing these esteem promoting activities. A further consequence of this would be to encourage self-restraint in relation to relapse. Lindsay makes the caveat that it is important to realize that while developing engagement and a sense of community, we do not promote dependence which might lead to others being blamed for an incident of offending. Care should also be taken that in the construction of a sense of commitment to society's conventions, the offender does not build in excuses for committing another offense because of lack of vigilance from others.

A further corollary of this model is that placing people in secure accommodation, away from society, will simply encourage disengagement and lack of commitment to society's conventions, functioning and activities. It may be that for a relatively small number of individuals, this is the only solution; however, it is the antithesis of any treatment model that purports family or societal engagement.

CASE EXAMPLE

Graham (forty-three years, WAIS IQ 60) was diagnosed as having epilepsy around age five. Subsequently, his behavior at home and school became extremely difficult and violent, leading to exclusion from school. As a teenager, he was involved in a major arson incident leading to attendance at the Children's Panel (juvenile court system in Scotland). He was then admitted to a special school, but was expelled once again for uncontrollable behavior. His father died when he was eight; consequently, his mother raised him, two elder, and two younger brothers. In 1977, he was referred to services because of indecent exposure to children and public masturbation. In the following five years, numerous incidents of public masturbation and indecent exposure occurred, all in the presence of young adult females and girls. His mother reportedly tried to do what she could with a very difficult situation, but was feeling that her son was now "a lost cause."

The incidents of indecent exposure and public masturbation continued, but through the 1990s, public tolerance of such behavior reduced dramatically. When he was thirty-four, after a further series of incidents, Graham went to court for the first time and was given a three-year probation order with a requirement to attend for treatment. At the time, his mother found the police attention and publicity extremely distressing but appeared to relax about the situation once treatment commenced. She reported becoming more confident about the future. Treatment was conducted according to the principles outlined by Lindsay et al. (1998) and reviewed earlier in this chapter. Graham disclosed a series of previous offenses, which he had committed against girls and one in particular against his niece. He explained (and his mother later confirmed this) that his mother told him to say nothing of what happened to the child's father (Graham's brother) because of the family upset that would ensue. Graham's mother made concerted efforts to keep the incident quiet and protect her son from his brothers.

Treatment

During treatment, we consistently tried to involve the family in supporting the main principles that are employed during sessions. Therefore, we endeavor to ensure that families do not minimize the incidents, maintain the messages of self-restraint toward the offender, persist in encouraging the offender to avoid risky situations, and adopt safe routines. One of the most difficult tasks can be to encourage the family to maintain a realistic relationship with the offender that is neither overprotective nor rejecting. To do this, community nursing staff and social workers who have knowledge of the treatment programs visit relatives to promote these messages. In Graham's case, initial visits did not have the desired effect as his mother attempted to downplay her son's assault on his niece, and appeared to refuse to accept this incident and previous incidents as being in any way serious. She did say that over the past few years she had stopped Graham from going to certain areas where children might be playing, but she maintained that she had stopped him because she did not like certain adults who he might meet there. Therefore, she adopted the personal cognitive distortion that the reason for restricting him was nothing to do with children. She also promoted this distortion with Graham himself, who understood that he did not go to certain areas because of adults he might meet. She attributed her son's offending behavior to confusion and the adverse effects of his medication. The sex offender treatment team began to think that one of the reasons why Graham's sexual difficulties were so pervasive and longstanding was the systematic underestimation of the seriousness by his mother. In addition, she had made energetic efforts to try to keep the issues within the family and had made strenuous efforts to supervise him herself. She consistently gave the impression that she was more worried about her son's behavior and the trouble it would lead him into rather than being concerned about the effects of his behavior on others.

Persistent work with Graham's mother eventually led to her becoming more accepting of the fact that his behavior was a danger to children. She began to be more realistic with Graham and accept the messages and information that underpinned sex offender treatment. She also informed his brothers of Graham's attraction to children so that the family could supervise him in a more realistic fashion when he was with his nieces.

Outcome with Graham has been reasonably positive. Following three years of treatment his attitudes toward stalking, public masturbation, exhibitionism, and offenses against children all improved. He became engaged with day placements in his local area and supervision at home and at day placements was much more appropriate. At one point his epilepsy deteriorated seriously and he was admitted to the hospital, where he perpetrated a violent attack on a female member of staff. Although there was a sexual component to the attack, it was felt to be so out of character and of such an unusual nature that it was related more to his epilepsy than any problems with sexual behavior. Apart from this, Graham has not offended for ten years. This is a remarkable reduction in offending since by the various accounts staff were able to piece together, Graham's frequency of offending was extremely high prior to his admission to sex offender treatment. In this case, progress could not have been achieved without considerable input into family interaction. The change in Graham's mother's approach to his sex offending behavior was a crucial element in his change and progress.

CONCLUSION

This chapter has reviewed prevalence issues, assessment, treatment, and family issues for sex offenders with ID. Knowledge in the field has increased considerably over the last ten years and there is every indication that these advances will continue in the future. Suggestions from various studies are that family issues may be important both in terms of the development of the offender and his or her inappropriate sexual behavior and also in terms of support for his or her current treatment and monitoring of attitudes, behavior and routines relevant to future sex offending. We hope that this chapter might point the way to some avenues of future research regarding families of sexual offenders with ID. Family support for the messages of sex offender treatment may be extremely important. The opposite is also suggested in that if families undermine the messages given during sex offender treatment, this might interfere with the progress and success of treatment. This is crucial since RP relies on family members becoming involved in identifying dangerous patterns of attitude and behavior that might lead to sexual offending. Given that this may have to continue over long periods, it is important to assess the extent to which families are able to persist in these procedures.

Another avenue for future investigation is the manner and amount of monitoring and supervision that families can reasonably be expected to provide. As the case studies have pointed out, such cooperation is extremely useful in organizing the regime to coordinate with sex offender treatment but we remain unaware of what are reasonable expectations. This is true in terms of the amount of monitoring, the complexity of the arrangements, the length of time that supervision arrangements should continue, and the degree of intrusion that might be legitimate. Clearly there is a potential that very intrusive monitoring of the offenders themselves may set up antagonism among family members. We suspect these issues are important but have little or no data to support this contention. If they are important, we need to investigate the limits that might be expected of the family's reasonable cooperation and the limits of their impact. Clearly, this work has to be conducted and there is no reason why it should not produce more effective systems of treatment and monitoring for this client group.

REFERENCES

Abel, G.G., Becker, J.V., & Cunningham-Rathner, J. (1984). Complications, consent and cognitions in sex between children and adults. *International Journal of Law & Psychiatry, 7,* 89-103.

Ager, A. (1991). *The life experience checklist.* Kidderminster: British Institute of Learning Disabilities.

Arscott, K., Dagnan, D., & Stenfert Kroese, B. (1999). Assessing the ability of people with a learning disability to give informed consent to treatment. *Psychological Medicine, 29,* 1367-1375.

Barbaree, H.E., Seto, M.C., Langton, C.M., & Peacock, E.J. (2001). Evaluating the predictive accuracy of six risk assessment instruments for adult sex offenders. *Criminal Justice & Behavior, 28,* 490-521.

Baroff, G.S. (1996). The mentally retarded offender. In J. Jacobsen and J. Mulick (Eds.), *Manual of diagnosis and professional practice in mental retardation* (pp. 311-321). Washington, DC: American Psychological Association.

Barratt, E.S. (1994). Impulsivity and aggression. In J. Monahan & H.J. Steadman (Eds.), *Violence and mental disorder* (pp. 61-79). Chicago: University of Chicago Press.

Beail, N. (2002). Interrogative suggestibility, memory and intellectual disability. *Journal of Applied Research in Intellectual Disabilities, 15,* 129-137.

Beail, N. & Warden, S. (1995). Sexual abuse of adults with learning disabilities. *Journal of Intellectual Disability Research, 39,* 382-387.

Blanchard, R., Watson, M., Choy, A., Dickey, R., Klassen, P., Kuban, N., & Feren, D.J. (1999). Pedophiles: Mental retardation, maternal age and sexual orientation. *The Archives of Sexual Behavior, 28,* 111-127.

Boer, D.P., Hart, S.D., Krop, P.R., & Webster, C.D. (1997). *Manual for the sexual violence risk—20: Professional guidelines for assessing risk of sexual violence.* Vancouver, British Columbia: British Columbia Institute on Family Violence & Mental Health, Law & Policy Institute, Simon Fraser University.

Boer, D.P., Tough, S., & Haaven, J. (2004). Assessment of risk manageability of developmentally disabled sex offenders. *Journal of Applied Research in Intellectual Disabilities, 17*(4), 275-283.

Broxholme, S. & Lindsay, W.R. (2003). Development and preliminary evaluation of a questionnaire on cognitions related to sex offending for use with individuals who have mild intellectual disability. *Journal of Intellectual Disability Research, 47,* 472-482.

Bucke, T. & Brown, D. (1997). In police custody: Police powers and suspects' rights under the revised P.A.C.E. codes of practice. *Home Office Research Study, 174.*

Cann, J., Falshaw, L., & Friendship, C. (2004). Sexual offenders discharged from prison in England and Wales: A 21-year reconviction study. *Legal & Criminological Psychology, 9,* 1-10.

Caparulo, F. (1991). Identifying the developmentally disabled sex offender. *Sexuality & Disability, 9,* 311-322.

Carson, D.R., Whitefield, E., & Lindsay, W.R. (2002). The uses and abuses of assessments of cognitions and attitudes. *Book of Abstracts. British Psychological Society Annual Conference 2002* (p. 10).

Dagnan, D. & Lindsay, W.R. (2004). Research issues in cognitive therapies. In E. Emerson, C. Hatton, T. Parmenter, & T. Thompson (Eds.), *The international handbook of applied research in intellectual disability* (pp. 517-530). Chichester: Wiley.

Day, K. (1993). Crime and mental retardation: a review. In K. Howells and C.R. Hollin (Eds.), *Clinical approaches to the mentally disordered offender* (pp. 111-143). Chichester: Wiley.

Day, K. (1994). Male mentally handicapped sex offenders. *British Journal of Psychiatry, 165,* 630-639.

Everington, C. & Fulero, S.M. (1999). Competence to confess: measuring, understanding and suggestibility of defendants with mental retardation. *Mental Retardation, 37,* 212-220.

Everington, C.T. & Luckasson, R. (1992). *Competence assessment for standing trial for defendants with mental retardation.* Worthington: International diagnostic systems, Inc.

Farrington, D.P. (1995). The development of offending and antisocial behavior from childhood: Key findings from the Cambridge study in delinquent development. *Journal of Child Psychology & Psychiatry, 36,* 929-964.

Farrington, D.P. (2000). Psychosocial causes of offending. In M.G. Gelder, J.J. Lopez-Ibor, & N. Andreasen (Eds.), *New Oxford Textbook of Psychiatry Volume 2* (pp. 2029-2036). Oxford, UK: Oxford University Press.

Finlay, W.M. & Lyons, E. (2001). Methodological issues in interviewing and using self-report questionnaires with people with mental retardation. *Psychological Assessment, 13,* 319-335.

Furey, E.M. (1994). Sexual abuse of adults with mental retardation: Who and where. *Mental Retardation, 32,* 173-180.

Glaser, W. & Deane, K. (1999). Normalization in an abnormal world: a study of prisoners with intellectual disability. *Journal of Offender Therapy and Comparative Criminology, 43,* 338-350.

Griffiths, D. & Lunsky, Y. (2003). *Sociosexual knowledge and attitudes assessment tool* (SSKAAT-R). Woodale, IL: Stoelting Company.

Griffiths, D.M., Fedoroff, P., Richards, D., & Cox-Lindenbaum, D. (in press). Sexual and gender identity disorders. In R. Fletcher, E. Loschen, & P. Sturmey (Eds.), *Diagnostic manual for people with intellectual disabilities.* Kingston, NY: National Association for Dual Diagnosis & American Psychiatric Association.

Griffiths, S.D.M., Quinsey, V.L., & Hingsburger, D. (1989). *Changing inappropriate sexual behavior: A community based approach for persons with developmental disabilities.* Baltimore: Paul Brooks Publishing.

Gross, G. (1985). *Activities of a development disabilities adult offender project.* Olympia, WA: Washington State Development Disabilities Planning Council.

Gudjonsson, G.H. (1992). *The psychology of interrogations, confessions and testimony.* New York: Wiley.

Gudjonsson, G.H. (1988). Interrogative suggestibility: Its relationship with assertiveness, social-evaluative anxiety, state anxiety, and method of coping. *British Journal of Clinical Psychology, 27*(2), 159-166.

Gudjonsson, G.H., Clare, I.C.H., Rutter, S., & Pearse, J. (1993). Persons at risk during interviews in police custody: the identification of vulnerabilities. *Research Study No. 12,* The Royal Commission on Criminal Justice. London HMSO.

Gudjonsson, G.H. & MacKeith, J. (1994). Learning disability and the police and criminal evidence act 1984. Protection during investigative interviewing: a video recorded false confession to double murder. *Journal of Forensic Psychiatry, 5,* 35-49.

Haaven, J., Little, R., & Petre-Miller, D. (1990). *Treating intellectually disabled sex offenders: A model residential program.* Orwell, VT: Safer Society Press.

Hanson, R.K. (1997). *The development of a brief actuarial risk scale for sex offense recidivism* (User report 1997-04). Ottawa: Department of the Solicitor General of Canada.

Hare, R.D. (1991). *The Hare psychopathy checklist—revised.* Toronto, Ontario: Multi Health Systems.

Harris, G. (2003). Men in his category have a 50 percent likelihood, but which half is he in? *Sexual Abuse: A Journal of Research & Treatment, 15,* 389-392.

Harris, G.T., Rice, M.E., Quinsey, V.L., Lalumiere, M.L., Boer, D., & Lang, C. (2003). A multi-site comparison of actuarial risk as instruments for sex offenders. *Psychological Assessment, 15,* 413-425.

Hayes, D. (1996). Recent research on offenders with learning disabilities. *Tizard Learning Disability Review, 1,* 7-15.

Hayes, S. (1991). Sex offenders. *Australia & New Zealand Journal of Developmental Disabilities (Journal of Intellectual & Developmental Disabilities), 17,* 220-227.

Hayes, S. (1994). The criminal law and the person with intellectual disability. *Australia & New Zealand Journal of Developmental Disabilities, 19*(4), 287-292.

Hingsburger, D., Griffiths, D., & Quinsey, V. (1991). Detecting counterfeit deviance: differentiating sexual deviance from sexual inappropriateness. *Habilitation Mental Health Care Newsletter, 10,* 51-54.

Hirschi, T. (1969). *Causes of delinquency.* Berkeley and Los Angeles: University of California Press.

Holland, A.J. (2004). Criminal behavior and developmental disability: an epidemiological perspective. In W.R. Lindsay, J.L. Taylor, & P. Sturmey (Eds.), *Offenders with developmental disabilities* (pp. 23-34). Chichester: John Wiley.

Kennedy, H.G. & Grubin, D.H. (1992). Patterns of denial in sex offenders. *Psychological Medicine, 22,* 191-196.

Kolton, D.J.C., Boer, A., & Boer, D.P. (2001). A revision of the Abel and Becker Cognition Scale for intellectually disabled sexual offenders. *Sexual Abuse: A Journal of Research & Treatment, 13,* 217-219.

Lambrick, F. (2003). Issues surrounding the risk assessment of sexual offenders with an intellectual disability. *Psychiatry, Psychology & Law, 10,* 353-358.

Laws, D.R. (1999). Relapse prevention: The state of the art. *Journal of Interpersonal Violence, 14,* 285-302.

Lindsay, W.R. (2002). Integration of recent reviews on offenders with intellectual disabilities. *Journal of Applied Research in Intellectual Disabilities, 15,* 111-119.

Lindsay, W.R. (2004). Sex offenders: Conceptualization of the issues, services, treatment and management. In W.R. Lindsay, J.L. Taylor, & P. Sturmey (Eds.), *Offenders with developmental disabilities* (pp. 163-187). Chichester, UK: John Wiley.

Lindsay, W.R. (2005). Model underpinning treatment for sex offenders with mild intellectual disability: Current theories of sex offending. *Mental Retardation, 43*(6), 428-441.

Lindsay, W.R., Elliot, S.F., & Astell, A. (2004). Predictors of sexual offence recidivism in offenders with intellectual disabilities. *Journal of Applied Research in Intellectual Disabilities, 17*(4), 299-305.

Lindsay, W.R., Forrest, D., & Power, M. (in press). Quality of life and relationships in sex offenders with intellectual disability. *Sexual Abuse: Research & Practice.*

Lindsay, W.R., Law, J., Quinn, K., Smart, N., & Smith, A.H.W. (2001). A comparison of physical and sexual abuse histories: Sexual and non-sexual offenders with intellectual disability. *Child Abuse & Neglect, 25,* 989-995.

Lindsay, W.R. & Lees, M. (2003). A comparison of anxiety and depression in sex offenders with intellectual disability and a control group with intellectual disability. *Sexual Abuse: A Journal of Research & Treatment, 15,* 339-346.

Lindsay, W.R., Marshall, I., Neilson, C.Q., Quinn, K., & Smith, A.H.W. (1998). The treatment of men with a learning disability convicted of exhibitionism. *Research on Developmental Disabilities, 19,* 295-316.

Lindsay, W.R., Michie, A.M., Martin, V., & Grieve, A. (in press). A test of counterfeit deviance: a comparison of sexual knowledge in sex offenders and non-offenders with intellectual disability.

Lindsay, W.R., Neilson, C.Q., Morrison, F., & Smith, A.H.W. (1998). The treatment of six men with a learning disability convicted of sex offences with children. *British Journal of Clinical Psychology, 37,* 83-98.

Lindsay, W.R. & Smith, A.H.W. (1998). Responses to treatment for sex offenders with intellectual disability: A comparison of men with 1 and 2 year probation sentences. *Journal of Intellectual Disability Research, 42,* 346-353.

Lindsay, W.R., Smith, A.H.W., Law, J., Quinn, K., Anderson, A., Smith, A., & Allan, R. (2004). Sexual and non-sexual offenders with intellectual and learning disabilities: a comparison of characteristics, referral patterns and outcome. *Journal of Interpersonal Violence, 19*(8), 875-890.

Lindsay, W.R., Smith, A.H.W., Law, J., Quinn, K., Anderson, A., Smith, A., Overend, T., & Allan, R. (2002). A treatment service for sex offenders and abusers with intellectual disability: characteristics of referrals and evaluation. *Journal of Applied Research in Intellectual Disability, 15,* 166-174.

Lindsay, W.R., Sturmey, P., & Taylor, J.L. (2004). Natural history and theories of offending in people with developmental disabilities. In W.R. Lindsay, J.L. Taylor & P. Sturmey (Eds.), *Offenders with developmental disabilities* (pp. 3-22). Chichester, UK: John Wiley.

Luiselli, J.K. (2000). Presentation of paraphilias and paraphilia related disorders in young adults with mental retardation: two case profiles. *Mental Health Aspects of Developmental Disabilities, 3,* 42-46.

Lund, J. (1990). Mentally retarded criminal offenders in Denmark. *British Journal of Psychiatry, 156,* 726-731.

Lyall, I., Holland, A.J., & Collins, S. (1995). Offending by adults with learning disabilities and the attitudes of staff to offending behavior: Implications of service development. *Journal of Intellectual Disabilities Research, 39,* 501-508.

Lyall, I., Holland, A.J., Collins, S., & Styles, P. (1995). Incidence of persons with a learning disability detained in police custody. *Medicine, Science & the Law, 35,* 61-71.

MacEachron, A.E. (1979). Mentally retarded offenders prevalence and characteristics. *American Journal of Mental Deficiency, 84,* 165-176.

Managed Forensic Care Network: Intellectual and Developmental Disabilities Sub-Committee (2004). *Report on offenders with intellectual and developmental disabilities.* Edinburgh: Scottish Executive.

Marshall, W.L., Anderson, D., & Fernandez, Y. (1999). *Cognitive behavioral treatment of sex offenders.* Chichester, UK: John Wiley & Sons.

Mason, J. & Murphy, G. (2002). Intellectual disability amongst people on probation: prevalence and outcome. *Journal of Intellectual Disability Research, 46,* 230-238.

McGillivray, J.A. & Moore, M.R. (2001). Substance use by offenders with mild intellectual disability. *Journal of Intellectual & Developmental Disability, 26,* 297-310.

Messinger, E. & Apfelberg, B. (1961). A quarter century of court psychiatry. *Crime & Delinquency, 7,* 343-362.

Meyer, F. (2003). *On the borderline: People with learning disabilities and autistic spectrum disorders in secure forensic and other settings.* Edinburgh: Scottish Executive.

Noble, J.H. & Conley, R.W. (1992). Toward an epidemiology of relevant attributes. In R.W. Conley, R. Luckasson, & G. Bouthilet (Eds.), *The criminal justice system and mental retardation* (pp. 17-54). Baltimore: Paul Brookes Publishing.

Novaco, R.W. & Taylor, J.L. (2004). Assessment of anger and aggression in male offenders with developmental disabilities. *Psychological Assessment, 16*(1), 42-50.

O'Conner, W. (1996). A problem-solving intervention for sex offenders with intellectual disability. *Journal of Intellectual and Developmental Disability, 21,* 219-235.

Parry, C. & Lindsay, W.R. (2003). Impulsiveness as a factor in sexual offending by people with mild intellectual disability. *Journal of Intellectual Disability Research, 47,* 483-487.

Patterson, G.R. & Yoerger, K. (1997). A developmental model for late onset delinquency. In D.W. Osgood (Ed.), *Motivation and delinquency* (pp. 119-177). Lincoln: University of Nebraska Press.

Pithers, W.D. & Gray, A.S. (1996). Utility of relapse prevention in treatment of sexual abusers. *Sexual Abuse: A Journal of Research & Treatment, 8,* 171-260.

Power, M., Champion, L., & Aris, S.J. (1988). The development of a measure of social support: the Significant Others Scale (SOS). *British Journal of Clinical Psychology, 27*(4), 349-358.

Quinsey, V.L., Book, A., & Skilling, T.A. (2004). A follow-up of deinstitutionalized developmentally handicapped men with histories of antisocial behavior. *Journal of Applied Research in Intellectual Disabilities, 17*(4), 243-253.

Quinsey, V.L., Harris, G.T., Rice, M.E., & Cromier, C.A. (1998). *Violent offenders: Appraising and managing risk.* Washington, DC: American Psychological Association.

Rose, J., Jenkins, R., O'Connor, C., Jones, C., & Felce, D. (2002). A group treatment for men with intellectual disabilities who sexually offend or abuse. *Journal of Applied Research in Intellectual Disabilities, 15,* 138-150.

Sequeira, H. & Hollins, S.A. (2003). Clinical effects of sexual abuse on people with learning disability. *British Journal of Psychiatry, 182,* 13-19.

Snyder, J.J. & Patterson, G.R. (1995). Individual differences in social aggression: A test of a reinforcement model of socialization in the natural environment. *Behavior Therapy, 26,* 371-391.

Stouthamer-Loeber, M., Loeber, R., Wei, E., Farrington, D.P., & Wikstrom, P.O.H. (2002). Risk and promotive effects in the explanation of persistent serious delinquency in boys. *Journal of Consulting & Clinical Psychology, 70,* 111-123.

Taylor, J.L., Novaco, R.W., Guinan, C., & Street, N. (2004). Development of an imaginal provocation test to evaluate treatment for anger problems in people with intellectual disabilities. *Clinical Psychology & Psychotherapy, 11*(4), 233-246.

Taylor, J.L., Thorne, I., & Slavkin, M.L. (2004). Treatment of fire setting behavior. In W.R. Lindsay, J.L. Taylor, & P. Sturmey (Eds.), *Offenders with developmental disabilities* (pp. 221-240). Chichester, UK: John Wiley.

Thompson, D. & Brown, H. (1997). Men with intellectual disabilities who sexually abuse: a review of the literature. *Journal of Applied Research in Intellectual Disabilities, 10,* 140-158.

Walker, N. & McCabe, S. (1973). *Crime and insanity in England.* Edinburgh: University Press.

Ward, T., Hudson, S.M., Johnston, L., & Marshall, W.L. (1997). Cognitive distortions in sex offenders: An integrative review. *Clinical Psychology Review, 17,* 479-507.

Wilson, M. (2004). The community and family context in understanding juvenile crime. In A. Needs & G. Towl (Eds.), *Applying psychology to forensic practice* (pp. 18-33). Oxford: British Psychological Society & Blackwell Publishing.

Xenitidis, K.I., Henry, J., Russell, A.J., Ward, A., & Murphy, D.G. (1999). An in-patient treatment model for adults with mild intellectual disability and challenging behavior. *Journal of Intellectual Disability Research, 43,* 128-134.

Chapter 7

Violent Sex Offenders

Devon L. L. Polaschek
Tony Ward
Theresa A. Gannon

INTRODUCTION

Survivors of serious sexual assault often describe the experience as violent, shocking, and degrading. Yet, in most offenses, the resulting level of physical injury to the recipient is low in comparison to the sexual and psychological impacts of sexual violation (Katz, 1991). Physically violent acts vary from restraint and threat, through slapping, punching, and kicking to strangling, smothering, choking, shooting, stabbing, mutilating, dismembering, and so on. Offenders often use physical violence in conjunction with sexual and psychological forms of violence during sexual assaults. However, the focus of this chapter is on the use of violence that has the potential to cause physical injury.

After defining the term *violent sex offender* we review research on the prevalence of violence and physical injury in sexual assault, before outlining what is currently known about the characteristics of violent sex offenders. Then we examine how offender typologies relate to offence violence, and the etiology of violent sex offending. In the second part of the chapter, we provide an overview of assessment, treatment and relapse-prevention issues, and end with a case example.

Our basic argument is that violent sex offenders are often difficult to discriminate from nonviolent sex offenders and general violent offenders. This partly is a function of the lack of relevant theory-directed research, and a tendency to rely on inadequate measures of violent dispositions and sadism. In view of these difficulties, we suggest that it is best to focus on the functional characteristics of sex offenders rather than derive treatment needs from poorly specified typologies.

THE NATURE OF VIOLENCE

Definition of Violent Offenders

The use of violence in sexual offenses is best understood as a continuous, not categorical variable (McConaghy, 1993). To distinguish such offenders from other sexual offenders, here we have defined *violent sex offender* as one who commits one or more violent sex offenses. A violent sex offense is defined to include the use of physical violence before, during, or after the commission of the sexual component of the offense, where that physical violence exceeds the level of force necessary to gain or maintain sufficient control of the victim to sexually assault her. In many low-violence sexual offenses, once the offender gains initial control of the victim, his or her sexual behavior toward the victim appears superficially similar to consenting heterosexual behavior. (Note that we are not suggesting that once the offender has control of the victim of rape, she or he behaves as if she or he is consenting, merely that many rapists carry out sexually common behaviors [e.g., penile-vaginal intercourse, male-superior position], once they have physical control of the victim.) Throughout the sexual assault literature violence that exceeds the force needed to gain that control is usually referred to as gratuitous (i.e., excessive or unnecessary) physical violence. However, when writers use such a term they reveal their assumption that the purpose of rape is simply to experience sexual gratification through pseudoconventional sex with an unwilling victim. As we will see later, this assumption is often not true of individuals who use significant amounts of physical violence. In other words, contrary to the implication in the term "gratuitous," we take the view that serious violence is not unnecessary, nor even puzzling, when the goals of the offender are understood. High levels of physical violence often occur in the service of goals additional to, or other than, sexual gratification.

Violent sex offenders can cause high levels of victim injury and even death. They generate understandable concern, but a minority of sexual assaulters commit extremely violent offenses. The empirical research base on these offenders is lean, and is almost exclusively concerned with male offenders and mainly with female victims. Although there have been high-profile cases in recent years of offenders who have raped and murdered children, the research literature on exceptionally violent offenders against children is almost nonexistent. Therefore, this chapter's focus is often on violent sex assaulters of adults.

Prevalence and Extent of Physical Violence in Sexual Assault

A variety of estimates are available of the prevalence of sexual assault against children and adults. These studies often describe a range of disparate sexual activities (e.g., fellatio, penile-vaginal penetration) but omit the more difficult task of documenting the violent aspects of offenses. Data on men who sexually abuse children suggest that the majority use threats or nonviolent means of gaining victim compliance. Kaufman, Wallace, Johnson, & Reeder (1995) found that children indicated that just 6 percent of perpetrators used physical force to get them to engage in sex, although threats were used in almost half of cases. Even when some form of force is used, children rarely experience serious physical injury as a result (Conte, Berliner, & Schuerman, 1986; Erickson, Walbek, & Seely, 1988).

Instead of grooming and psychological manipulation, overt physical force or threats accompanied by weapon presentation are commonplace in rape. Koss, Dinero, Seibel, & Cox (1988) found that 74 percent of strangers and 62 percent of acquaintance rapists twisted the victim's arm or held him or her down, according to victims' reports. More severe violence such as choking or beating occurred in 16 percent of stranger rapes and 7 percent of acquaintance assaults. Ullman and Knight (1991) found that over half of an exceptionally dangerous sample of rapists presented a weapon and two-thirds used a forceful "blitz"-style attack, with 76 percent using some form of physical violence. Despite this level of force, the average level of victim physical injury was judged to be just 2.8 on an 8-point scale, equivalent to being squeezed or slapped. Warren, Reboussin, & Hazelwood (1995) reported that on average, for 108 rapes minimal or no blunt force was used, weapons were displayed but not used, and overall victim injuries were either limited to minor cuts, scratches and abrasions, or victims were not injured at all. Canter, Bennell, Alison, & Reddy (2003) found that even single acts of violence (e.g., punching or slapping) occurred in a minority of rapes.

What proportion of rapes end in the death of the victim? Information about the frequency of homicide rapes versus nonfatal rapes is not readily available. Occasional studies report on the relative prevalence of fatal violence amongst rapists. These reports are usually methodological flawed by reliance on offender samples from local prisons, but they do suggest that fatal violence is quite rare. For example, Grubin and Gunn (1990) found that among forty-two imprisoned rapists, five had murdered their victims. Another three had subjected victims to severe nonfatal violence. In total about one-third had used some level of gratuitous violence.

OFFENDER CHARACTERISTICS

Information about violent sex offenders can be inferred from two types of studies, neither of which was designed specifically to compare offenders on the amount of violence used in their offenses. The first source is heterogeneous samples of rapists. Warren et al. (1995) reported no difference on age, number of rapes, or criminal history for more violent versus less violent serial rapists. Using Knight and Prentky's rapist classification scheme (see later section), Barbaree, Seto, Serin, Amos, & Preston (1994) reported that more violent and less violent rapist subtypes showed no differences on socioeconomic status, age or education, preoffense anger, or likelihood of weapon use. However, the more violent rapists reported less social alienation, offended more impulsively, and showed less arousal to rape stimuli than the less violent offenders.

The other main source of information on offender characteristics is sexual murderer research. When compared with rapists, sexual murderers appear to be more similar than different. Grubin (1994) found sexual murderers were older at the time of the offense, more likely to be of European ethnicity, and more socially and sexually isolated than rapists were. Proulx, Beauregard, & Nichole (2002) also compared sexual assaulters who had murdered their victims with a sample who had not, and found similarities on demographic and offense history variables, and on personality profiles using the Millon Clinical

Multi-Axial Inventory. However, sexual murderers were angrier, used alcohol and drugs more, and were more likely to use weapons than nonfatal assaulters. Milsom, Beech, & Webster (2003) analyzed interview data from sexual murderers and rapists, and found the murderers had higher levels of childhood grievance toward women, more adolescent peer group loneliness, and stronger endorsement of the "self-as-victim" stance in adulthood. However, they did not find differences on a raft of other developmental and psychological variables. Lastly, Beech, Fisher, & Ward (2005) compared the implicit theories of a sample of sexual murderers with previous research on implicit theories in rapists. Implicit theories are the underlying causal theoretical structures, or schemas that offenders use to make sense of the world around them and their own behavior. Cognitive distortions are thought to be generated from such schema. Beech et al. found strong similarities between the implicit theories of rapists and rapist-murderers.

The only published comparison of homicidal (HCM) and nonhomicidal (CM) extrafamilial child molesters found the two samples equivalent on a number of demographic and developmental history variables (Firestone, Bradford, Greenberg, Larose, & Curry, 1998). HCM were more likely to be strangers to the children and had more violent and sexual convictions. More CM than HCM had no previous involvement with the criminal justice system. HCM and CM obtained similar scores on inventories of hostility and sexual functioning. Compared to CM, HCM were significantly more psychopathic and more deviant on plethysmographic assessment. In particular, they obtained the highest scores on scenes depicting physical and sadistic assaults on children. More than half of HCMs and no CMs met diagnostic criteria for both sexual sadism and pedophilia.

The research on offender characteristics should be interpreted with caution at this stage. Sample sizes are small, and a lack of statistical power may obscure real differences. Local criminal justice system variables (e.g., sentencing and prison management practices) may explain differences when they are found. If force is a continuous variable, then dividing offenders into two groups on this variable is an artificial distinction anyway: some members of the high-violence group will always be very similar to some members of the low-violence group. Finally, difficulty in accurately establishing the actual level of force used may also cloud the picture.

RAPIST TYPOLOGIES AND VIOLENCE

Reliable and valid classificatory systems are essential to theory development, treatment design, and risk prediction. Typologies also shed light on links between the psychological life of an offender (e.g., motivations) and the behavior in the offense. Typologies for child molesters seldom have used level of violence or force as a classificatory variable, so we limit our discussion to typologies of rapists, a large number of which have been proposed since the 1950s. The amount of physical violence in the offense was recognized early for its taxonomic potential. However, taxonomists assumed a consistent relationship existed between the level of violence in an offense and the function of that violence. So, minimal violence was assumed to be force used by a sexually motivated offender to overcome victim resistance to having sex with him or her (i.e., instrumental violence). Violence exceeding this level was assumed to result from the offender expressing his or her rage at the victim (i.e., expressive violence). However, offense-related anger (Barbaree et al., 1994), and intentionality (i.e., instrumental versus expressive goals) cannot reliably be inferred from either the level of physical violence nor the victim's injuries (Rosenberg, Knight, Prentky, & Lee, 1988).

We describe two well-known typologies here, to illustrate how violent rape behavior has been related to offender motivation. The most scientifically robust of these is Knight and Prentky's (1990) MTC: R3 (i.e., the Massachusetts Treatment Center Rapist Typology Version 3), developed with sexually dangerous offenders at the Massachusetts Treatment Center in the United States (see also Prentky & Knight, 1991). There are nine subtypes, organized around four different types of primary motivation:

1. opportunistic (with high or low social competency),
2. pervasively angry, sadistic (overt or muted),
3. sexual nonsadistic (also with high or low social competency), and
4. vindictive (with moderate or low social competency).

Opportunistic refers to offending that is impulsive, driven primarily by the presence of a situational opportunity rather than an enduring, internally based offense goal. Such offenders are usually assumed to be seeking sexual gratification. *Pervasively angry* offenders evince "global and undifferentiated anger that pervades all areas of the offender's life" (Knight, 1999, p. 312), is directed toward both men and women, and causes significant victim injury.

Sexually motivated offenders rape in the context of extensive sexual fantasies that can be sadistic or nonsadistic. For the *sadistic* subtypes, the actual offense behavior may be *overtly sadistic,* or appear nonsadistic despite being fueled by sadistic fantasies (*muted* subtype). Last, are the *vindictive* offenders; men motivated to harm and humiliate by anger directed at women exclusively (Knight & Prentky, 1990).

The MTC: R3 suggests that physical violence and victim injury are most likely to be associated with the overtly sadistic sexual type, the pervasively angry type, and the vindictive (Ullman & Knight, 1995). However, the developers generally have not reported actual levels of violence and injury associated with each subtype (e.g., Knight, 1999; Knight & Prentky, 1990; Knight, Warren, Reboussin, & Soley, 1998). Contrary to some MTC:R3 predictions, with a community-based sample Barbaree et al. (1994) found that the vindictive and opportunistic committed the most violent and injurious offenses. However, their sample yielded no pervasively angry offenders, and they collapsed together the overt and muted sadistic subtypes, because of small numbers. Muted sadists should show low levels of violent behavior.

The other typology in widespread use is the psychodynamic classification system of Groth, Burgess, & Holmstrom (1977) also developed at the Massachusetts Treatment Center by comparing the accounts of 133 offenders and ninety-two victims. Groth et al. describe two types, power and anger rapists: each contains two subtypes.

According to Groth et al. (1977), *power rapists* use physical aggression and intimidation to overpower and force the victim into submission so that a sexual conquest can be effected. Raping reassures perpetrators of their mastery, strength, and dominance, thus assisting them in denying feelings of worthlessness, rejection, and vulnerability. Power rapists have no conscious interest in harming or degrading their victims.

Power rapists can be divided into two subtypes. The *power-assertive* rapist sees rape as expressing his virility and dominance. He feels entitled to force sex and to keep women "in line" in this manner. The *power-reassurance* rapist aims to get women into a controlled, helpless position in which rejection is not possible in order to resolve his doubts about his own masculinity and sexual adequacy.

By contrast, an *anger rapist* expresses rage, contempt, and hatred for his victim through sexual assault, forcing her to perform or submit to acts that he considers degrading, and displaying excessive physical and verbal violence. Sex itself is used as a weapon. Victims' injuries are predicted to be more numerous than for power rapists, and may be fatal. The *anger-retaliation* rapist expresses his hostility and rage toward women in his offenses. His main motive is revenge; hence, he degrades and hurts the victim. The *anger-excitation* rapist is the sexual sadist; he is sexually aroused by the victim's suffering and punishes, tortures, and injures the victim to ensure her suffering.

Research with Groth's typology reveals the rarity of sadistic rapes. In the 225 offenses studied in the combined sample (Groth et al., 1977), 35 percent were categorized as anger rapes. Anger-excitation rapes were very uncommon; making up 6 percent of the offenders' and 4 percent of the victim samples. Warren et al. (1995) found that just eleven of 108 serial rapists were categorized into either of Groth's anger types. However, they provided evidence that, compared to the sexual types, these eleven used more blunt force on victims, injured victims more, and were more likely to intentionally hurt the victim.

These two typologies show that violent sex offenses have been connected with two forms of offender motivation, vengeful (often referred to as "angry") and sadistic.

"Anger" Rapes

Here the expression of anger is often seen as driving the offense, and as explaining the physical violence in that offense. Although anger clearly can provide the impetus to assault someone, in making sense of rapes in which anger is prominent we still need to know (1) what the offender is angry about, since this is far more informative in explaining the offense behavior, than the fact that he is angry; and (2) why the assault is a sexual assault rather than simply a physical assault. In fact, Barbaree et al. (1994) found that regardless of type, on average rapists were very angry prior to committing their offenses. Therefore, being angry before the offense does not reliably predict the level of violence during the offense.

However, the cognitions driving the anger may affect the level of violence. Angry offenders who use excessive violence often seek to punish and harm the victim for some transgression or grievance. This sense of grievance can become temporally chronic, and can generalize to whole classes of victims; this process of generalization is captured in the MTC: R3 pervasively angry and vindictive subtypes. To make this point clear we think that offenses currently said to be motivated by anger should be renamed *grievance rape*. For example, Groth and Birnbaum (1979, p. 16) state that the anger rapist revenges himself for what he percevies to be wrong done to him by others, especially women.

> The common theme appeared to be one in which the offender felt that he had been wronged, hurt, put down, or treated unjustly in some fashion by some individual, situation or event. (p. 16)

Of course, this is the motivation for many violent offenses (Tedeschi & Felson, 1994). Grievance rapists understand that rape is the best way to hurt a woman, physically and psychologically. They may deny awareness of sexual arousal even though at the time they were sufficiently sexually functional to be able to violate the victim. Alternatively, they may not be sexually aroused at all and may use objects to violate. As with all violent offenses in which the intent is to harm and degrade the victim, postoffense grievance offenders can experience considerable satisfaction and a sense of achievement.

Sadism and Rape

Much has been made of the distinction between anger and sadism but in reality, so much confusion exists about what sadism is and how to diagnose it that the term has no clear utility at present. The confusion comes from a variety of sources. First, there is no clear definition of sexual sadism. Second, just as being angry does not predict the level of violence in rape, there is no close correspondence between sadistic fantasy and sadistic behavior.

Sexual sadism has attracted far more popular attention than scientific attention. A fundamental problem with its definition lies in determining exactly what it is that is sexually arousing to sadists. Authors writing about criminal sexual sadism (i.e., where the recipient of the sadist's actions does not consent) variously suggest that sexual arousal stems from having total control of the victim, the nonsexual violence itself, the victim's psychological or physical suffering, helplessness or fear, or the victim's humiliation. DSM-IV (American Psychiatric Association, 1994) lists physical and psychological suffering and humiliation. Prentky and Knight (1991) covered a variety of options in their definition: "violent sexualized fantasies, ritualized behavior, bizarre or peculiar sexual acts, or indications that the offender was aroused by seeing the victim in fear or pain" (p. 33). Langevin (1983) referred to the importance of enslavement and domination.

Some writers have used strictly behavioral definitions, thus categorizing all violent rapists, including grievance offenders as sadists. Ressler, Burgess, & Douglas (1993) implied that sadistic motivation is to be inferred from cruel and violent behavior toward animals and humans. Seto and Kuban (1996) similarly defined as sadists those whose offenses were characterized by the use of excessive force and degree of victim injury.

The DSM-IV diagnostic category called *sexual sadism* provides little evidence that it meets the requirements for a mental disorder. People ranging from those who only fantasize about tying their partners up through to rapist-murderers who have carried out mutilation and torture fantasies can meet diagnostic criteria, but only as long as they are distressed by their sadism or have impaired functioning as a result. As we have noted elsewhere, the scientific validity and clinical utility of this and other paraphilic diagnoses is not readily apparent (Polaschek, 2003a).

Consenting sadomasochistic fantasies and practices have been assumed to be related to sadistic sexual assault, but are they? Arguably, that relationship might be no closer than the relationship between consenting and nonconsenting sexual intercourse. The fact that the recipient consents could be argued to change completely the nature of the experience. In his review of sexual sadism, Hucker (1997) points out that sadists' partners are often treated with great care, in marked contrast to the recipients of the sexual practices of criminal sadists. The review suggests that fantasies of some "sadistic" practices such as bondage are quite prevalent in general samples but actually little research exists on sadistic fantasy and behavior in non-offenders (e.g., "bondage and discipline," or "S & M").

Another source of confusion comes from the related construct of (nonsexual) sadism. The DSM-III-R (APA, 1987) contained criteria for *sadistic personality disorder* (SPD) to acknowledge that some people show a pervasive history of sadistic behavior (i.e., cruel, demeaning, and violent) behavior across an array of life domains. SPD overlaps antisocial and narcissistic personality disorder, suggesting that it will be common in offender populations (Hucker, 1997).

Sexual sadists exist in many communities (Hucker, 1997). However, the case for the usefulness of the construct of sexual sadism in working with men who commit violent rapes has yet to be demonstrated convincingly. Currently, it is not possible to reliably detect sexual sadism unless offenders want to tell us about it (Marshall & Kennedy, 2003). However it is defined, it cannot be determined reliably from behavioral indices such as crime scene behavior (Knight et al., 1998), or the amount of force used (Knight & Prentky, 1990), nor from self-report measures of fantasy and preference.

The phallometric literature is no more helpful. The definitional difficulties previously noted have pervaded this research too, so that some samples simply include all violent rapists as sadists. Rapists whose offenses are higher in violence may respond sexually to more seriously violent stimuli, including nonsexual violence with women (Quinsey, Chaplin, & Upfold, 1984). However, in this study they did not show this preference to the same stimuli with men, which has led to the conclusion that it is *not* nonsexual violence per se that is arousing, but its occurrence in an implicitly sexual context (i.e., that it is against a woman). Seto and Kuban (1996) found no differences in responding between nonoffenders, low- and high-violence rapists (whom they called sadists) on arousal to nonsexual violence, non-violent rape, and violent, humiliating rape stimuli.

So how can we tell sadists and grievance offenders apart? Knight, Prentky, and Cerce (1994) have probably done the most detailed and sustained diagnostic work with seriously violent rapists, and have repeatedly found sexual sadism difficult to distinguish from other forms of motivation for violent sexual aggression. For example, Knight and Prentky (1990) suggest that overt sadists are "angry, belligerent rapists who except for their sadism and greater planning of their sexual assaults, look very similar to the pervasively angry types" (p. 45).

Knight (1999) found that pervasively angry and vindictive rapists scored higher than sadists on a self-report measure of sadistic fantasy, and were statistically indistinguishable from sadistic rapists on the variables of bondage behavior and synergism of sex and aggression. He has argued that it is a "lack of sexualization of their anger and aggression that distinguishes vindictive offenders from sadists" (Knight & Prentky, 1990, p. 312). Our research shows us that violent rapists are often able to sustain an erection and perform in a sexual manner through to ejaculation while vigorously assaulting the victim. Sexual and aggressive intent are clearly present simultaneously in such a person, as are sexual and angry arousal. At what point do we say that anger has become sexualized? When do we say that the simultaneous aggressive and sexual intents have fused? What internal processes actually distinguish him at that point, from a sexual sadist?

Whether sexually motivated or not, physically cruel and violent behavior is a problem with respect to risk and should be a treatment target. We think sadism (as captured in the criteria for SPD) underlies a variety of violent offending, including violent sex offending. Some offenders' violent sexual behavior may also sexually arouse them; they may be sexual sadists. However, no evidence as yet supports that *sexual* sadists should be managed or rehabilitated in a distinct manner from other types of sexual offenders. Given the profound problems with the scientific status of sadism at present, we would concur with Marshall and Kennedy (2003) in suggesting that we focus on applying general principles to the behavior itself for the moment.

ETIOLOGY OF VIOLENT SEX OFFENDING

Examining etiology in sexual offending reveals a confusing proliferation of offerings. The most inclusive of these, suggest that interplay between genetic predisposition, developmental, and cultural factors can explain the heterogeneity of sexual assault. At this point, no unique etiological pathways have been proposed to explain exceptionally violent sex offending. Some theories recognize the relevance of vengeful and sadistic motivation within their scope of explanation. For example, Marshall and colleagues' theory details many of the etiological elements that are likely to be relevant to violent sex offenders (Marshall & Barbaree, 1990; Marshall & Marshall, 2000), but these factors are not suggested to be uniquely relevant to the highly violent offenses. Indeed, many of the etiological factors proposed for sexual offending have some overlap with theories of violent and general offending.

CURRENT EMPIRICAL ASSESSMENT ISSUES WITH VIOLENT SEX OFFENDERS

Assessment of a sexual offender should always be organized around the goal of developing a case formulation of that offender and his or her offensive behavior. A case formulation is a conceptual model of an offender's characteristic strengths and deficits, their hypothesized underlying causes, and the relationships between all of these elements (Ward, Nathan, Drake, Lee, & Pathe, 2000). Individualized case formulations are particularly important with unusual or rare offense patterns (Polaschek, 2003a), in order to ensure that treatment planning covers all of the offender's areas of criminogenic deficit (i.e., risk-related treatable needs). With violent sex offenders, careful case formulation ensures the consideration of treatment targets that may otherwise be thought of as more relevant to violent offenders. However, there is little specific information on the assessment or treatment of violent sex offenders, and it is likely that they are best conceptualized as part of the heterogeneous sex offender population on which current practice is based. Hence, the general principles for empirically validated practice with sex offenders may provide the best guide for practice with violent sex offenders, although we argue that reviewing approaches to the treatment of violent offenders may also be informative.

Assessing the Offender

When collecting information about an offender and his or her offending, an important principle is to use as wide a range of information sources as possible. A range of different assessment methods is desirable, although often there is a heavy reliance on offender self-report from interviews and questionnaire administration (see Dougher, 1995; Ward, McCormack, Hudson, & Polaschek, 1997). Briefly, assessment areas should cover both offender and offense variables. Offender variables include developmental factors (e.g., family, educational, occupational, social, and sexual history), psychological characteristics (e.g., offense-related attitudes and beliefs, empathy, social competence, sexual preference, and psychopathology). Cultural and current social context factors should also be evaluated. Family and social networks are evaluated for the extent to which they support antisocial versus prosocial lifestyles. Cultural identity is the final area that may need remediation. Sometimes offenders have developed an identity that distorts aspects of their cultural background to their criminal behavior (Maynard, Coebergh, Anstiss, Bakker, & Huriwai, 1999).

Rapists should be evaluated and treated for risk of nonsexual violent recidivism (Polaschek & King, 2002) because of evidence that nonsexual convictions, especially convictions for violence, are common in such offenders. Therefore assessment targets should consider the best dynamic predictors for general and nonsexual violent recidivism: involvement in criminal social networks, generally criminal and violent attitudes, criminal personality, and a history of criminal behavior (Andrews & Bonta, 1994). Attitudinal measures with potential utility include the Criminal Sentiments Scale-Modified, the Pride in Delinquency Scale (both developed by Shields & Simourd, 1991), and the Criminal Attitudes to Violence Scale (Polaschek, Collie, & Walkey, 2004). The most widely researched measure of criminal personality currently would be one of Hare's psychopathy scales (e.g., the PCL-R: Hare, 1991, 2003).

Although initially thought to hold great promise as an indicator of sexual deviance, the assessment of sexual preference using the penile plethysmograph has turned out to be disappointing. In short, plethysmography does not reliably distinguish between rapists and nonrapists (Marshall & Kennedy, 2003) nor sadistic and nonsadistic offenders (Barbaree et al., 1994; Seto & Kuban, 1996).

Assessment of the Offense Process

Offense-related variables of interest include the cognitive, affective, and behavioral elements of the temporal sequence known as an *offense chain* or *offense process* (Polaschek, Hudson, Ward, & Siegert, 2001; Ward, Louden, Hudson, & Marshall, 1995). Part of an individual case formulation for a particular offender is the development of an offense chain for the current or a typical offense. Information about the offense chain is best obtained in individual interviews. Interviewers prepare for such interviews by accessing all of the available "objective" information about the offense of interest (e.g., victim statements, police summaries). Interview procedures for obtaining the oral narrative incorporate techniques used routinely in scientific clinical practice to enhance the reliability and validity of the data obtained (see Zamble & Quinsey, 1997). The interviewer begins with open-ended questions, gradually funneling in to establish fine details. Intentional redundancy is built into inquiries; the interviewer returns to key areas with questions in different forms, to assess accuracy, consistency, and the level of detail provided. When the offender's account differs from that of the file information, the discrepancy can be drawn to his attention, along with a nonjudgmental request for its resolution. Offenders often quite readily describe the events comprising their offense, but require prompting from the interviewer to include details of their thinking, affective responses and the volitional components. Such interviews often take from one to three hours to complete.

Looking simply at the topography of violent behavior (e.g., hitting, slapping, stabbing, pushing), gives very limited information about how to make sense of a particular offender's acts. The key to understanding violent sex offending lies in examining the offense chain, paying particular attention to the functions of the violence an offender perpetrates during a sexual assault, and how that violence interacts with sexual behavior. Function can change as the offense episode unfolds.

Risk Assessment

In addition to evaluating treatment needs, assessing risk, both before and after treatment, is the other major focus of assessment. A large body of research favors the use of statistically validated risk assessment instruments over clinical judgment in determining risk (see, for example, Quinsey, Harris, Rice, & Cormier, 1998, ch. 4). Several risk assessment instruments for sex offenders have been extensively validated for their predictive ability with both sexual and violent* recidivism (Barbaree, Seto, Langton, & Peacock, 2001; Harris et al., 2003). Currently the most promising measures appear to be the Violence Risk Appraisal Guide (VRAG; Harris, Rice, & Quinsey, 1993), the Sex Offender Risk Appraisal Guide (SORAG; Quinsey et al.,

---

*However, validity of prediction of violent recidivism using sex offender-specific scales such as the SORAG has mainly been demonstrated in jurisdictions where plea bargaining may result in a sexually motivated offense being officially recorded as a nonsexual violent offense.

1998), the Rapid Risk Assessment of Sexual Offense Recidivism (RRASOR; R. K. Hanson, 1997), and the Static-99 (R. K. Hanson & Thornton, 1999). These measures are all appropriate for use with violent sex offenders. Both risk of sexual and violent recidivism should be predicted since both have a major effect on community safety.

CURRENT EMPIRICALLY SUPPORTED INTERVENTIONS

Debate is ongoing about whether claims that sex offenders can be successfully rehabilitated are underpinned by empirical evidence (K. S. Hanson, 2000). For assaulters of children, this debate centers more on the methodological standards used in evaluations (e.g., choice of comparison group) than whether anyone appears to have demonstrated a decrease in recidivism following treatment. However, for rapists, Polaschek and King (2002) found that little evidence exists either way; few studies provide data specifically on rapists' outcomes, and when they do, they often have very small sample sizes. Disturbingly, Polaschek and King did find evidence that rapists' rates of nonsexual violent convictions were often at least as high as their sexual recidivism, and that program many not reduce violent recidivism. Note that studies in this review included all rapists, the bulk of whom as we noted earlier may have used little violence. We took the view, and we think it is even more justified here, that nonsexual violent treatment targets should also be incorporated into interventions for violent sex offenders. The failure of treatment providers to attempt to reduce violent recidivism in sex offenders may also explain why intervention with rapists in general may not yet be effective (Polaschek and King, 2002).

With these concerns in mind, the best current rehabilitation programs for sex offenders have a number of common components. Marshall (1996) suggested grouping the needs addressed by these components into *offense-specific* and *offense-related* treatment targets. He argued that this distinction is based on whether offenders need interventions for these particular targets or not: *specific* targets should be treated for all offenders but *offense-related* targets can be provided on an individual basis, depending on assessed need.

Common offense-specific targets include developing an understanding of the offense process, challenging offense-supportive attitudes and cognitive distortions, correcting deviant sexual interests, increasing victim empathy, improving social competence and sexual knowledge, and acquiring skills and plans for relapse prevention (Marshall & Serran, 2000). Programs for offense-related treatment include relationship/marital therapy, anger management, substance abuse, social skills and assertiveness training, and life-management skills (Marshall, 1996).

Violent sexual offenders may share etiology not just with sex offenders, but also with violent and generally criminal offenders. If so, a wider range of criminogenic needs should be considered. R. K. Hanson and Harris (2000) recently examined the stable dynamic predictors of sexual offender recidivism (i.e., the factors that could be targeted in treatment to reduce recidivism) and found that just two were sexual assault-specific. They included a lack of positive, or a preponderance of negative social supports, sexual assault-supportive attitudes, sexual preoccupation, antisocial lifestyle, poor avoidance of high-risk situations, and poor cooperation with supervision.

Non–sex offender rehabilitation programs focus more on attitudes supportive of antisocial behavior rather than just those associated with sexual offending, the influence of criminal associates, substance abuse, developing a noncriminal cultural identity (Maynard et al., 1999), and on a wider range of living skills such as employment and leisure skills (e.g., Polaschek & Dixon, 2001). Cognitive processing skills are common in general offender rehabilitation, but are rarely used with sex offenders, even though they may be effective (Robinson, 1995).

The responsiveness principle in offender rehabilitation refers to the need to accommodate service delivery to case characteristics and depends both on at least minimal motivation to take part and the development of some level of therapeutic alliance (Andrews, Bonta, & Hoge, 1990). Several features likely to be quite common in violent rapists will decrease their responsiveness to this tradition of intervention. Psychopathy, for example, is more prevalent in rapists than in child sexual offenders (Porter et al., 2000; Serin, Mailloux, & Malcolm, 2001; Seto & Barbaree, 1999), and may be more prevalent still in violent rapists.

Psychopathy is a complex disorder, part of which is a characteristic interpersonal style. Other interpersonal style factors associated with rape may also create responsivity barriers. *Dismissive attachment* is another example, characterized by a positive view of the self and a negative view of others causing the devaluation of attachment to others as an interpersonal goal, hostility toward others, and the overvaluing of independence and invincibility to negative feelings. Ward, Hudson, & Marshall (1996) found that one-third of a sample of rapists and half of a sample of nonsexual violent offenders described their predominant attachment style as dismissive. *Hostile masculinity* is similar, comprising "controlling, self-absorbed 'one-upmanship' personality characteristics" (Malamuth, Heavey, & Linz, 1996, p. 27).

A person with some of these characteristics is not easily caught up in the relationship ties that help foster treatment persistence, is more resistant to influence, disinterested in whether others similar to him, unmotivated to recognize personal deficiency and make change, and will tend to disrupt the development of a collaborative environment of effective group treatment. These characteristics suggest that violent rapists are less likely to willingly enter treatment, less likely to complete it, will tend to impede the progress of other group members and will be experiences as aversive by therapists. Recognition of these obstacles is important, and allows for the implementation of appropriate responses (e.g., therapist training in dealing with difficult clients the implementation of pretreatment motivational strategies).

RELAPSE PREVENTION

Relapse prevention (RP) was originally conceived of as a posttreatment or maintenance intervention (Laws, 1989; Laws & Marshall; 1990). In practice, many cognitive-behavioral sex offender programs use RP as the dominant framework, or organizing structure for the treatment enterprise (Polaschek, 2003b). We use the term RP to refer to endeavors to maintain change and prevent reoffending. Curiously, despite its great popularity, the existing empirical research has found no increase in intervention efficacy for sex offenders when RP is added to a standard cognitive-behavioral package (Marshall & Anderson, 2000). Yet, RP interventions are ubiquitous.

Violent sex offenders are often held in secure detention. When release is considered, preparing for that release and supporting the offender on release are important tasks if the offender is to succeed. Pithers (1990) distinguished two aspects of RP. The *internal self-management* dimension refers to the offender's own efforts to learn the principles of RP taught during the program, and to implement them himself. The *external supervisory* dimension (Pithers, 1990) refers to oversight from parole supervisors, family, and community treatment staff, after the offender completes the treatment program itself. For example, the offender informs family and staff of his specific risk factors and strategies, so that they can more effectively monitor him for signs of impending relapse. Before family can be involved in this way, it is important that they are prepared for the offender's release, understand and accept his responsibility for the offense, and understand the program philosophy and goals (e.g., control not cure, active management of risk).

CASE EXAMPLE

Throughout this chapter, we have emphasized that violent sex offenders are diverse; this diversity comprises part of the widely recognized heterogeneity of sex offenders. A very few violent sex offenders capture disproportionate media attention for the bizarreness and severity of their behavior. However, the behavior of most violent sex offenders is probably more ordinary. We have chosen a case example that we think is more like the majority of such offenders who will be encountered in routine practice.

Assessment Information

Mark is a forty-year-old European man referred for treatment while in prison for the rape and attempted murder of his ex-wife, then age twenty-nine. After ten years of marriage and three children, Mark's wife had an affair with a colleague at her work, she separated from Mark, taking the children with her. Mark made repeated attempts to contact them despite a legal protection order preventing him from doing so. Three months after the separation he was adjusting poorly: neglecting his business, sleeping and eating poorly, and consuming excessive alcohol. He reported being lonely and depressed and unable to understand why his relationship ended. One night he decided he just had to talk to his wife, so after consuming alcohol and marijuana, he traveled to his wife's new house, broke in through a window, and proceeded to hold her and the children hostage for three days. During this time, he raped his wife several times, and beat her severely with his son's baseball bat. Apparently, he did not assault the children, but did lock them in a room. One of them eventually escaped and called the police.

In outlining his offense chain, Mark described his former relationship in glowing terms but it is clear that he had little sense of his wife's needs, worked excessively long hours, took little interest in the children, and was sexually demanding and prone to angry outbursts. In the six months prior to the offenses, he painted a picture of escalating stress, anger, depression, and sleep difficulties. During the offense period itself, he alternated between fury at his wife for ending the relationship and betraying him by seeing another man, and tearful attempts to have sex with her, apparently in an attempt to form an emotionally meaningful connection with her.

Mark had some previous convictions for violent and nonviolent offenses but had not been imprisoned before. His wife reported a history of him assaulting her but had never called the police. He had his own business, but found it difficult to organize himself and solve problems. Consequently, he was in serious financial difficulty during the year before his offending. He had no close friends and was estranged from his family. In Mark's offense chain assessment, he stated that his offending was caused by stress that just built up, that he had no one to talk to, and that he just could not control himself. He could not explain how his wife was seriously injured; he reported that he only hit her a few times, though he might have "lost it" once. He agreed with file descriptions of his sexual behavior during the offending, but denied that it was rape, saying that he was "only trying to get close to [his] wife." He admitted that she had verbally and physically resisted but said he was used to this. When they were together, he often had to persuade her to have sex and she often said no at first. He appeared to have no awareness that his frequent angry outbursts and violence toward her made her often fearful of him, and he minimized the frequency with which he threatened her. Mark's plethysmography results showed no evidence of arousal to coercive sex, and adequate arousal to consenting sex. Mark stated that he was prepared to undertake treatment because he needs to get better control of his alcohol use and his temper. However, he did not expect to ever reoffend; from now on, he would avoid relationships with women because they cannot be trusted.

Treatment Plan

Short-Term Objectives

1. *Understanding his offense chain.* Although a preliminary description of the offense chain was obtained during assessment, going over it with Mark early in treatment will provide more detail, and begin the process of understanding his offense precursors. This understanding will lead Mark into identifying his own treatment needs, and help develop his motivation to continue in treatment.
2. *Reducing cognitive distortions about offending, and increasing victim empathy.* Mark holds some rape myths, and minimizes and denies the extensiveness and seriousness of his sexual and nonsexual violence toward his wife. He is also likely to falsely

think his violent behavior has had no effect on his children because he has not actually hit them. He is likely to blame both alcohol and anger for his offending. He may hold inappropriate views about his right to control others' actions and force them to meet his needs.
3. *Increasing anger control skills.* Initially Mark needs to learn to regulate his anger better, once he becomes aware of it. However, identifying and modifying the perceptions and interpretations that generate anger is the next step in reducing how often and how intensely he becomes angry.
4. *Developing a relapse-prevention plan,* and a range of other coping strategies for avoiding reoffending. Some long-term objectives comprise strategies that will be part of this plan.

Long-Term Objectives

1. *Assessing, and if necessary, treating alcohol and drug use problems.*
2. *Developing intimacy and relationship skills* and reducing his tendency to rely on sexual gratification as a substitute for emotional closeness. However, in order to motivate Mark in this domain, his apparent mistrust of and hostility toward women will need to be treated first.
3. *Improving lifestyle balance.* A number of separate needs are evident here, including (1) the development of a prosocial network to support him, and perhaps repairing relationships with his family of origin, and with his children if they desire it, and it is legally possible; (2) increasing Mark's leisure activities and decreasing his tendency to overwork; and (3) improving his business management skills.
4. On or near release, beginning *implementation of the relapse-prevention plan.*

CONCLUSION

In this chapter, we discussed the assessment and treatment of violent sex offenders. Their heterogeneity in conjunction with problems in adequately defining and measuring key constructs relating to sexual violence, mean that it is best to plan treatment on the basis of the functional characteristics of individual offenders. For one offender critical treatment targets might revolve around emotional regulation deficits, while for another, problems establishing and maintaining intimate relationships could be more important. Violent sex offenders are both violent and sex offenders. Therefore, they require interventions that straddle both types of problems. A research agenda that includes more empirical investigations as well as the development of better explanatory theories and typologies may help us to detect the mechanisms generating sexual violence and result in more fine-tuned (and effective) treatment strategies.

REFERENCES

American Psychiatric Association (1987). *Diagnostic and statistical manual of mental disorders* (3rd ed., rev.). Washington, DC: Author.

American Psychiatric Association (1994). *Diagnostic and statistical manual of mental disorders* (4th ed.). Washington, DC: Author.

Andrews, D. A. & Bonta, J. (1994). *The psychology of criminal conduct.* Cincinnati, OH: Anderson.

Andrews, D. A., Bonta, J., & Hoge, R. D. (1990). Classification for effective rehabilitation. *Criminal Justice and Behavior, 17,* 19-52.

Barbaree, H. E., Seto, M. C., Langton, C. M., & Peacock, E. J. (2001). Evaluating the predictive accuracy of six risk assessment instruments for adult sex offenders. *Criminal Justice and Behavior, 28,* 490-521.

Barbaree, H. E., Seto, M. C., Serin, R. C., Amos, N. L., & Preston, D. L. (1994). Comparisons between sexual and nonsexual rapist subtypes: Sexual arousal to rape, offense precursors, and offence characteristics. *Criminal Justice and Behavior, 21,* 95-114.

Beech, A., Fisher, D., & Ward, T. (2005). *Sexual murderers' implicit theories. Journal of Interpersonal Violence* 20(11), 1366-1389.

Canter, D. V., Bennell, C., Alison, L. J., & Reddy, S. (2003). Differentiating sex offences: A behaviorally based thematic classification of stranger rapes. *Behavioral Sciences and the Law, 21,* 157-174.

Conte, J. R., Berliner, L., & Schuerman, J. (1986). *The impact of sexual abuse on children: Final report.* Available from the first author at the School of Social Work, University of Washington.

Dougher, M. J. (1995). Clinical assessment of sex offenders. In B. K. Schwartz, & H. R. Cellini (Eds.), *The sex offender: Corrections, treatment and legal practice* (pp. 11.1-11.15). Kingston, NJ: Civic Research Institute.

Erickson, W. D., Walbek, N.H., & Seely, R. K. (1988). Behavior patterns of child molesters. *Archives of Sexual Behavior, 17,* 77-86.

Firestone, P., Bradford, J. M., Greenberg, D. M., Larose, M. R., & Curry, S. (1998). Homicidal and nonhomicidal child molesters: Psychological, phallometric, and criminal features. *Sexual Abuse: A Journal of Research and Treatment, 10,* 305-323.

Groth, A. N. & Birnbaum, H. J. (1979). *Men who rape: The psychology of the offender.* New York: Plenum.

Groth, A. N., Burgess, A. W., & Holmstrom, L. L. (1977). Rape: Power, anger, and sexuality. *American Journal of Psychiatry, 134,* 1239-1243.

Grubin, D. (1994). Sexual murder. *British Journal of Psychiatry, 165,* 624-629.

Grubin, D. & Gunn, J. (1990). *The imprisoned rapist and rape.* London: Institute of Psychiatry.

Hanson, K. S. (2000). Treatment outcome and evaluation problems (and solutions). In D. R. Laws, S. M. Hudson, & T. Ward (Eds.), *Remaking relapse prevention with sex offenders: A sourcebook* (pp. 485-499). Newbury Park, CA: Sage.

Hanson, R. K., (1997). *The development of a brief actuarial risk scale for sexual offense recidivism.* (User Report 1997-04.) Ottawa: Department of the Solicitor-General of Canada.

Hanson, R. K. & Harris, A. J. R. (2000). Where should we intervene? Dynamic predictors of sexual offence recidivism. *Criminal Justice and Behavior, 27,* 6-35.

Hanson, R. K. & Thornton, D. (1999). *Static 99: Improving actuarial risk assessments for sex offenders.* (User Report 1999-02.) Ottawa: Department of the Solicitor-General of Canada.

Hare, R. D. (1991). *The Hare Psychopathy Checklist-Revised.* Toronto, Ontario: Multi-Health Systems.

Hare, R. D. (2003). *The Hare Psychopathy Checklist-Revised* (2nd ed.). Toronto, Ontario: Multi-Health Systems.

Harris, G. T., Rice, M. E., & Quinsey, V. L. (1993). Violent recidivism of mentally disordered offenders: The development of a statistical prediction instrument. *Criminal Justice and Behavior, 20,* 315-335.

Harris, G. T., Rice, M. E., Quinsey, V. L., Lalumière, M. L., Boer, D., & Lang, C. (2003). A multisite comparison of actuarial risk instruments for sex offenders. *Psychological Assessment, 15,* 413-425.

Hucker, S. J. (1997). Sexual sadism: Psychopathology and theory. In D. R. Laws, & W. O'Donohue (Eds.), *Sexual deviance: Theory, assessment, and treatment* (pp. 194-209). New York: Guilford.

Katz, B. L. (1991). The psychological impact of stranger versus nonstranger rape on victims' recovery. In A. Parrot, & L. Bechhofer (Eds.), *Acquaintance rape: The hidden crime* (pp. 251-269). New York: Wiley.

Kaufman, K. L., Wallace, A. M., Johnson, C. F., & Reeder, M. L. (1995). Comparing female and male perpetrators' modus operandi: Victims' reports of sexual abuse. *Journal of Interpersonal Violence, 10,* 322-333.

Knight, R. A. (1999). Validation of a typology for rapists. *Journal of Interpersonal Violence, 14*(3), 303-330.

Knight, R. A. & Prentky, R. A. (1990). Classifying sexual offenders: The development and corroboration of taxonomic models. In W. L. Marshall, D. R. Laws, & H. E. Barbaree (Eds.), *Handbook of sexual assault: Issues, theories, and treatment of the offender* (pp. 23-52). New York: Plenum.

Knight, R. A., Prentky, R. A., & Cerce, D. D. (1994). The development, reliability, and validity of an inventory for the multidimensional assessment of sex and aggression. *Criminal Justice and Behavior, 21,* 72-94.

Knight, R. A., Warren, J. I., Reboussin, R., & Soley, B. J. (1998). Predicting rapist type from crime scene variables. *Criminal Justice & Behavior, 25,* 46-80.

Koss, M. P., Dinero, T. E., Seibel, C. A., & Cox, S. L. (1988). Stranger and acquaintance rape: Are there any differences in the victim's experience? *Psychology of Women Quarterly, 12,* 1-24.

Langevin, R. (1983). *Sexual strands: Understanding and treating sexual anomalies in men.* Hillsdale, NJ: Lawrence Erlbaum and Associates.

Laws, D. R. (Ed.). (1989). *Relapse prevention with sex offenders.* New York: Guilford.

Laws, D. R. & Marshall, W. L. (1990). A conditioning theory of the etiology and maintenance of deviant sexual preference and behavior. In W. L. Marshall, D. R. Laws, & H. E. Barbaree (Eds.), *Handbook of sexual assault: Issues, theories, and treatment of the offender* (pp. 209-229). New York: Plenum.

Malamuth, N. M., Heavey, C. L., & Linz, D. (1996). The confluence model of sexual aggression: Combining hostile masculinity and impersonal sex. *Journal of Offender Rehabilitation, 23,* 13-37.

Marshall, W. L. (1996). Assessment, treatment, and theorizing about sex offenders: Developments during the past twenty years and future directions. *Criminal Justice and Behavior, 23,* 162-199.

Marshall, W. L. & Anderson, D. (2000). Do relapse prevention components enhance treatment effectiveness? In D. R. Laws, S. M. Hudson & T. Ward (Eds.), *Remaking relapse prevention with sex offenders: A sourcebook* (pp. 39-55). Newbury Park: CA: Sage.

Marshall, W. L. & Barbaree, H. E. (1990). An integrated theory of the etiology of sexual offending. In W. L. Marshall, D. R. Laws & H. E. Barbaree (Eds.), *Handbook of sexual assault: Issues, theories, and treatment of the offender* (pp. 257-275). New York: Plenum.

Marshall, W. L. & Kennedy, P. (2003). Sexual sadism in sexual offenders: An elusive diagnosis. *Aggression and Violent Behavior, 8,* 1-22.

Marshall, W. L. & Marshall, L. E. (2000). The origins of sexual offending. *Trauma, Violence, and Abuse, 1,* 250-263.

Marshall, W. L. & Serran, G. A. (2000). Improving the effectiveness of sexual offender treatment. *Trauma, Violence, & Abuse, 1,* 203-222.

Maynard, K., Coebergh, B., Anstiss, B., Bakker, L., & Huriwai, T. (1999). Ki to arotu: Toward a new assessment—the identification of cultural factors which may predispose Maori to crime. *Social Policy Journal of New Zealand, 13,* 43-58.

McConaghy, N. (1993). *Sexual behavior: Problems and management.* New York: Plenum.

Milsom, J., Beech, A. R., & Webster, S. D. (2003). Emotional loneliness in sexual murderers: A qualitative analysis. *Sexual Abuse: A Journal of Research and Treatment, 15,* 285-296.

Pithers, W. D. (1990). Relapse prevention with sexual aggressors: A method for maintaining therapeutic gain and enhancing external supervision. In W. L. Marshall, D. R. Laws, & H. E. Barbaree (Eds.), *Handbook of sexual assault: Issues, theories, and treatment of the offender* (pp. 343-361). New York: Plenum.

Polaschek, D. L. L. (2003a). Classification. In T. Ward, D. R. Laws, & S. M. Hudson (Eds.), *Sexual deviance: Issues and controversies* (pp. 154-171). Thousand Oaks, CA: Sage.

Polaschek, D. L. L. (2003b). Relapse prevention, offense process models, and the treatment of sexual offenders. *Professional Psychology: Research and Practice, 34,* 361-367.

Polaschek, D. L. L., Collie, R. M., & Walkey, F. H. (2004). Criminal attitudes to violence: Development and preliminary validation of a scale for male prisoners. *Aggressive Behavior, 30*(6), 484-503.

Polaschek, D. L. L., & Dixon, B. G. (2001). The Violence Prevention Project: The development and evaluation of a treatment program for violent offenders. *Psychology, Crime, and Law, 7,* 1-23.

Polaschek, D. L. L., Hudson, S. M., Ward, T., & Siegert, R. J. (2001). Rapists' offense processes: A preliminary descriptive model. *Journal of Interpersonal Violence, 16,* 523-544.

Polaschek, D. L. L. & King, L. L. (2002). Rehabilitating rapists: Reconsidering the issues. *Australian Psychologist, 37,* 215-221.

Porter, S., Fairweather, D., Drugge, J., Hervé, J., Birt, A., & Boer, D. P. (2000). Profiles of psychopathy in incarcerated sexual offenders. *Criminal Justice and Behavior, 27,* 216-233.

Prentky, R. A. & Knight, R. A. (1991). Identifying critical dimensions for discriminating among rapists. *Journal of Consulting and Clinical Psychology, 59,* 643-661.

Proulx, J., Beauregard, É., & Nichole, A. (2002, October). *Developmental, personality and situation factors in rapists and sexual murderers of women.* Paper presented at the 21st annual conference of the Association for the Treatment of Sexual Abusers, Montreal, Canada.

Quinsey, V. L., Chaplin, T. C., & Upfold, D. (1984). Sexual arousal to nonsexual violence and sadomasochistic themes among rapists and non-sex-offenders. *Journal of Consulting and Clinical Psychology, 52,* 651-657.

Quinsey, V. L., Harris, G. T., Rice, M. E., & Cormier, C. A. (1998). *Violent offenders: Appraising and managing risk.* Washington, DC: American Psychological Association.

Ressler, R. K., Burgess, A. W., & Douglas, J. E. (1993). *Sexual homicide: Patterns and motives*. London: Simon and Schuster.

Robinson, D. (1995). *The impact of cognitive skills training on post-release recidivism among Canadian federal offenders*. Correctional Research and Development Report R-41. Ottawa, Canada: Correctional Service of Canada.

Rosenberg, R., Knight, R. A., Prentky, R. A., & Lee, A. (1988). Validating the components of a taxonomic system for rapists: A path analysis approach. *Bulletin of the American Academy of Psychiatry and the Law, 16,* 169-185.

Serin, R. C., Mailloux, D. L., & Malcolm, P. B. (2001). Psychopathy, deviant sexual arousal, and recidivism among sexual offenders. *Journal of Interpersonal Violence, 16,* 234-246.

Seto, M. C. & Barbaree, H. E. (1999). Psychopathy, treatment behavior, and sex offender recidivism. *Journal of Interpersonal Violence, 14,* 1235-1248.

Seto, M. C. & Kuban, M. (1996). Criterion-related validity of a phallometric test for paraphilic rape and sadism. *Behavior Research and Therapy, 34,* 175-183.

Shields, I. W. & Simourd D. J. (1991). Predicting predatory behavior in a population of young offenders. *Criminal Justice & Behavior, 18,* 180-194.

Tedeschi, J. T. & Felson, R. B. (1994). *Violence, aggression and coercive actions.* Washington, DC: American Psychological Association.

Ullman, S. E. & Knight, R. A. (1991). A multivariate model for predicting rape and physical injury outcomes during sexual assaults. *Journal of Consulting and Clinical Psychology, 59,* 724-731.

Ullman, S. E. & Knight, R. A. (1995). Women's resistance strategies to different rapist types. *Criminal Justice & Behavior, 22,* 263-283.

Ward, T., Hudson, S. M., & Marshall, W. L. (1996). Attachment style in sex offenders: A preliminary study. *Journal of Sex Research, 33,* 17-26.

Ward, T., Louden, K., Hudson, S. M., & Marshall, W. L. (1995). A descriptive model of the offence chain in child molesters. *Journal of Interpersonal Violence, 10,* 452-472.

Ward, T., McCormack, J., Hudson, S. M., & Polaschek, D. (1997). Rape: Assessment and treatment. In D. R. Laws & W. O'Donohue (Eds.), *Sexual deviance: Theory, assessment, and treatment* (pp. 356-393). New York: Guilford.

Ward, T., Nathan, P., Drake, C. R., Lee, J. K. P., & Pathe, M. (2000). The role of formulation-based treatment for sexual offenders. *Behavior Change, 17,* 251-264.

Warren, J., Reboussin, R., & Hazelwood, R. R. (1995). *The geographic and temporal sequencing of serial rape.* Washington, DC: National Institute of Justice.

Zamble, E. & Quinsey, V. L. (1997). *The criminal recidivism process.* Cambridge, UK: Cambridge University Press.

Chapter 8

Comorbid Psychopathology in Child, Adolescent, and Adult Sexual Offenders

David P. Fago

INTRODUCTION

During the past decade, the question of whether comorbidity of psychopathology is widely prevalent in human populations became an issue of intense theoretical and research interest (Kendall & Clarkin, 1992; Kessler, 1997; Kessler et al., 1994; Mineka, Watson, & Clark, 1998). This interest was preceded and perhaps catalyzed by a minor renaissance in the Kraepelinian model of discrete mental disorders, which was prominently displayed in the diagnostic exclusionary criteria published in the third edition of the *Diagnostic and Statistical Manual for Mental Disorders* (DSM-III, American Psychiatric Association, 1980). However, due to ensuing criticism on both conceptual and empirical grounds, these exclusionary criteria were subsequently eliminated from DSM-III-R and DSM-IV (American Psychiatric Association, 1987, 1994). Later research, particularly that reported in the National Comorbidity Survey (Kessler et al., 1994), eventually documented the extensive prevalence of comorbidity across the entire spectrum of psychopathology (Kendall & Clarkin, 1992), which prompted spirited debate over the meaning and implications of "comorbidity in psychopathology" (Mineka, Watson, & Clark, 1998). This debate has been largely absent from discussions of sex offenders and sexual offending, and recently some investigators have specifically argued that comorbidity is not commonly found in sex offender populations (Marshall, 1997; Purvis, Ward, & Devilly,

2002). However, the research and theory presented in this chapter offers a view that is more in keeping with the results of the National Comorbidity Survey (i.e., that comorbidity of psychopathology is a significant and prevalent phenomenon in sexual offenders). Furthermore, the literature presented here also suggests that these comorbidities may be variable, depending upon the age and developmental stage of the offender, as well as the type of offense that has been committed. Because different issues of developmental psychopathology may apply to child/adolescent and adult populations, the comorbidity data is presented separately for these age groups.

COMORBIDITY IN A DEVELOPMENTAL CONTEXT

Recent research in developmental psychopathology has confirmed two important findings with regard to human populations: (1) that comorbidity of psychopathology tends to be the rule and not the exception in both clinical and epidemiological samples, including samples of children and adolescents (Faraone, 2000; Fergusson, Horwood, & Lynskey, 1993; Kashani, Orvaschel, Rosenberg, & Reid, 1989; Kendall & Clarkin, 1992; VerHulst & van der Ende, 1993); and (2) that genetics and neurobiological/neurodevelopmental factors seem to be significant in the etiology of these comorbidities (O'Connor, McGuire, Reiss, Hetherington, & Plomin, 1998). Meanwhile, a recent review of the research literature on juvenile sexual offenders (Trivits & Reppucci, 2002) has noted a lack of information about this mostly adolescent population,

> The most consistent finding about JSOs [juvenile sexual offenders] is the lack of existing data about them and, in particular, the lack of prospective longitudinal data. . . . Much remains to be learned about JSOs, including the etiology of sexually deviant behavior, the progression of such behavior over time, and the different subgroups of offenders that may exist. Studies exploring sexual development need to be initiated to help identify pathways leading to normal versus deviant sexual behavior. (p. 701)

Despite this paucity of data on juvenile sex offenders, developmental researchers working in the broader area of "externalizing"/

antisocial-spectrum behaviors in children and adolescents have begun to make a distinction between "life-course persistent" and "adolescence-limited" antisocial behavior (Caspi & Moffitt, 1995; Moffitt, 1990, 1993, 2003). According to this developmental taxonomy, the antisocial behavior of life-course persistent offenders (1) has its origin in neurodevelopmental processes, (2) begins in childhood, and (3) continues worsening thereafter. In contrast, the antisocial behavior of adolescence-limited offenders has its origin in social processes, begins in adolescence, and desists in young adulthood. According to this theory, life-course persistent antisocial children are "few, persistent and pathological," while adolescence-limited antisocial youth are "common, relatively transient, and near normative" (Moffitt, 2003, p. 49). Although research is limited, the evidence available for child and adolescent sexual offenders appears to conform to this developmental taxonomy. Hence, there is an emerging developmental model of antisocial behavior, including sexual offending, that differentiates time-limited, episodic offending from more persistent, life-long offending that is associated with severe pathology and comorbidity. The accumulation of comorbidity data on sexual offenders at multiple life stages, and subsequent interpretation of this data within a developmental context, should allow for the refinement of this model, and should further our understanding of the etiology and probable trajectories of sexual offending behavior.

CHILD AND ADOLESCENT SEXUAL OFFENDERS

Although recent clinical and epidemiological research has amply documented the widespread prevalence of comorbidity in child and adolescent populations, relatively little research has documented the prevalence of comorbid psychopathology in juvenile sex offenders. Data from the few studies that have examined this issue are summarized in Table 8.1. A review of this data will reveal that, for many comorbid diagnoses, the range of reported incidence is broad. For example, probably the single most common comorbidity that has been identified in sex offenders of all ages is a history of previous sexual victimization. This finding is so intuitively reasonable that it has led to a general acceptance among clinicians and investigators that previous sexual victimization provides a primary pathway to future sexual

TABLE 8.1. Psychopathology Co-Occurring with Sexual Aggression in Juvenile Samples

Diagnosis	Range of reported comorbidity (percent)	References
Antisocial-Spectrum Disorders/Conduct Disorder (CD)	48 - 67	Kavoussi et al. (1998); McManus, Alessi, Grapentime, & Brickman (1984)
Sexual and/or Physical Abuse	19 - 60	Kavoussi et al. (1998); Becker, Kaplan, & Tenke (1992); Trivits & Reppucci (2002); Fago (2003)
Attention-Deficit/Hyperactivity Disorder	7 - 85	Kavoussi et al. (1998); Fago (2003); Miner, Siekert, & Ackland (1997)
Social Skill Deficits/Social Phobia/Peer Rejection	5 - 55	Kavoussi et al. (1998); Fago (2003); Schram, Milloy, & Rowe (1991)
Specific Learning Disability	37 - 53	Fago (2003); Ferrara & McDonald (1996); Langevin, Marentette, & Rosati (1996)
Mood Disorder/Depression/Bipolar Disorder	2 - 38	Kavoussi et al. (1988); Packard & Rosner (1985); McManus et al. (1984); Becker et al. (1992); Fago (2003)
Substance Abuse/Chemical Dependency	4 - 39	Kavoussi et al. (1988); Packard & Rosner (1985); McManus et al. (1984); Fago (2003); Hunter & Becker (1994)
Neurological Impairment	25 - 33	Ferrara & McDonald (1996)
Autism Spectrum and Related Disorders	21	Fago (2003)
Psychosis/Thought Disorder	2 - 18	Kavoussi et al. (1988); Packard & Rosner (1985)
Anxiety Disorder/OCD/Panic Disorder	0 - 10	Kavoussi et al. (1988); Fago (2003)

offending. Interestingly, however, the data summarized in Table 8.1 demonstrate that the rate of detected sexual abuse history in child and adolescent offenders is highly variable, ranging from 19 to 55 percent in different studies. Hence, it would seem that previous sexual victimization is not the only pathway to criminal sexual behavior; it may be a sufficient condition, but clearly is not a necessary condition for one to become a sex offender. To account for those offenders who have never been sexually victimized, the present author (Fago, 2003) has suggested that comorbid neurodevelopmental deficits may also act as catalysts to sexual offending. Still, the data for this latter type of comorbidity is also equivocal. For example, the diagnosis of comorbid attention-deficit/hyperactivity disorder (ADHD) is reported in one study of adolescent sex offenders (Kavoussi, Kaplan, & Becker, 1988) at only 7 percent of the sample, while in another study (Fago, 2003) it is reported at 82 percent. This disparity also holds for the reported incidence of social skill deficits, social phobia, and peer rejection, as well as that for mood disorder, substance abuse, and psychosis/thought disorder (with eight- to tenfold differences in magnitude). The only two comorbid diagnoses that approach consistency in the rates at which they have been reported tend to be at the extremes. The first, not surprisingly, is antisocial-spectrum disorders/conduct disorder (CD), which is consistently reported in half or more of all adolescent offender samples (one could reasonably argue that sexual offending and CD are one and the same disorder). The second is a subset of anxiety disorders that includes obsessive-compulsive disorder (OCD) and panic disorder (but not social anxiety disorder or PTSD), which consistently is reported at very low frequencies in adolescent sex offenders (10 percent or less).

The reasons for the disparities in reported comorbidities remain uncertain; however, they may be due to several methodological inconsistencies in the research. First, most of the studies summarized in Table 8.1 do not include children younger than age thirteen (even though sexually aggressive behavior is not uncommon in preteens); second, some studies use limited, unidimensional diagnostic processes (a symptom checklist or a brief clinical interview), which can result in the underdetection of comorbidity; and third, the studies vary significantly in their chosen diagnostic nomenclature and classification systems (e.g., DSM-III versus DSM-IV). Consequently, the available comorbidity data, while both useful and illuminating, is clearly limited and preliminary for children and adolescents. Future research will need to use consistent methodology with consistent diagnostic nomenclature and classification systems to further verify and specify the true extent of comorbidity in the population of child and adolescent sex offenders.

ADULT SEXUAL OFFENDERS

As with the data for children and adolescents, the comorbidity data for adult sexual offenders is rather sparse and inconsistent. Several early studies (Graber et al., 1982; Tarter et al., 1983) indicated, without providing incidence figures, that sexual offender populations frequently present a "history of learning problems" and "other neuropsychological impairments." Data from these studies are summarized in Table 8.2. The specific nature of these learning problems and neuropsychological impairments was not delineated and was not diagnosed with standard DSM diagnostic nomenclature. Other studies have described the characteristics of different offender types (e.g. "child molesters" versus "rapists"), but also have been nonspecific in describing their specific comorbid pathologies. For example, a 1992 summary of incarcerated sex offender characteristics (State of Ohio, 1992) describes "child molesters" as presenting a higher rate of "mental health problems" than was found for either "rapists" or "teen molesters" (46 percent versus 28 percent and 21 percent respectively).

TABLE 8.2. Psychopathology Co-Occurring with Pedophilic Sexual Aggression in Adult Samples

Diagnosis	Range of reported comorbidity (percent)	References
Mood Disorder/Depression/ Bipolar Disorder	42-72	McElroy et al. (1996); Raymond et al. (1999); Kafka & Hennen (2002)
Substance Abuse/Chemical Dependency	41-60	Kafka & Hennen (2002); Raymond et al. (1999)
History of Learning Disability	53	Langevin et al. (1996)
Attention-Deficit/Hyperactivity Disorder	43	Kafka & Hennen (2002)
Anxiety Disorder/OCD/Panic Disorder	38-64	Kafka & Hennen (2002); Raymond et al. (1999)
Social Skill Deficits/Social Phobia	22-38	Kafka & Hennen (2002); Raymond et al. (1999)
Neuropsychological Impairment	33	Langevin et al. (1996)
Antisocial/Narcissistic Personality Disorder	22	Raymond et al. (1999)

Recent studies provide specific diagnostic data on the comorbidities found in these different offender types. For example, Ahlmeyer, Kleinsasser, Stoner, & Retzlaff (2003) found, using the Millon Clinical Multiaxial Inventory (MCMI- III; Millon, 1997), that "child molesters," more often than "rapists," display features of dependent personality disorder, and were also found to be more "neurotic," "affective," and "socially impaired." Sexual offenders in general were found to present more varied personality disturbances than nonsexual offenders, and they were less frequently found to present the classical "antisocial, narcissistic, and sadistic" personality disturbances that are prevalent in general prison populations. The sexual offenders, on the other hand, were found to present more "affective pathology" in the form of anxiety, dysthymia, PTSD, and major depression. Meanwhile, the previously described Ohio study found a lower incidence of drug abuse history in the sex offender population, although "rapists" more closely approximated non–sex offenders on this dimension. The latter finding is further nuanced by the results of Barbaree, Seto, & Marie (2002), who found that incarcerated sex-offenders who refused treatment were more like non–sex offenders in their greater incidence of alcohol and drug abuse history and diagnosis of antisocial personality disorder. Other recent studies (McElroy, Pope, Keck, 1996; Raymond, Coleman, Ohlerking, Christenson, & Miner, 1999; Kafka & Hennen, 2002) replicated the findings of affect instability and mood dysregulation in adult sex offender populations. In fact, McElroy and collaborators found that a majority (61 percent) of male sex offenders suffered mood disorders and that more than half of those with mood disorder could be diagnosed with bipolar disorder. Similarly, Raymond et al. (1999), using the Structured Clinical Interview for DSM-IV Axis I Disorders (SCID-P), found a high incidence (42 percent) of mood disorder in a sample of adult "pedophilic offenders," and reported further that fully 92 percent of their sample had comorbid psychopathology. Social phobia (38 percent) and PTSD (33 percent) were the most common anxiety disorders reported, and 60 percent of the population reported a history of substance abuse.

ETIOLOGICAL IMPLICATIONS

The research evidence, gathered across different age and offender types, appears conclusive: comorbidity of psychopathology appears to be prevalent in sexual offender s of all ages. Despite inconsistencies in the data, some theoretical hypotheses are possible concerning the role and interacting properties of comorbid psychopathology in sex offending. First, the type of diagnosable comorbid psychopathology appears to differ among sexual offender types, as well as differentiate nonviolent sexual offenders from other offenders who do not commit sex crimes. For example, several studies have demonstrated that violent sex offenders ("rapists"), both adult and adolescent, more closely resemble the nonsexual offender population in their (1) higher incidence of diagnosed antisocial and narcissistic personality disorder, (2) higher incidence of substance abuse and chemical dependency history, and (3) lower incidence of social impairment and social incompetence. Hence, it seems that a distinction should be made between different types of sexual offenders, particularly on the dimension of overt violence, in discussing the role and prevalence of comorbid psychopathology in the development of their disordered behavior. The comorbidity profile is different for violent offenders, and presumably, the developmental and etiological pathways to violent offending also are different from those pathways for nonviolent offending. The distinction between adolescence-limited and life-course persistent behavior may be relevant to this discussion; however, these differences are not yet specifically known and need to be examined by future research. The following sections provide two additional hypotheses regarding the comorbidity-based etiological and developmental pathways associated with sexual offending.

MOOD DYSREGULATION AND THE "MONOAMINE HYPOTHESIS"

One of the more prevalent and consistently reported comorbidities for nonviolent sex offenders is that of mood disorder, including dysthymia, major depression, and bipolar disorder. Relatedly, a "monoamine hypothesis" for the pathophysiology of sexual disorders (paraphilias), including both sexually offending paraphilias as well as non-offending paraphilias, has been articulated by Kafka (2003). This hypothesis is based on four converging lines of empirical evidence:

1. the monoamine neurotransmitters, including dopamine, norepinephrine, and serotonin, have been found to serve a modulatory role in human and mammalian sexual motivation, appetitive and consummatory behavior, as well as mood regulation;
2. the pharmacological agents that regulate monoamine neurotransmitter function can have both significant facilitative and inhibitory effects on sexual behavior;
3. paraphilic disorders appear to have Axis I comorbid associations with nonsexual psychopathologies that are associated with monoaminergic dysregulation (e.g. mood disorders); and
4. pharmacological agents that enhance central serotonergic function in particular (the selective serotonin reuptake inhibitors, or SSRIs) have been reported to ameliorate paraphilic sexual arousal and behavior.

Therefore, the "monoamine hypothesis," as articulated by Kafka, suggests the possibility of a neurochemical pathway underlying the dysregulation of multiple human physiological functions, including mood, appetite, and sexual function and behavior. As explicated, this theory suggests that genetic or otherwise acquired disturbances to human monoamine function may contribute equally to significant dysregulation of mood, disruption to the acquisition of social skills, and impairment to the regulation and inhibition of sexual behavior.

THE "EXECUTIVE DYSFUNCTION" HYPOTHESIS

Current research and theory on neurodevelopmental disorders, which includes the continuum of "autism spectrum disorders" or ASD (autistic, Rett's, Asperger's, childhood disintegrative disorders, ADHD, and perhaps some mood disorders) indicate that many of these disorders' associated symptoms and deficits can be understood as deficits in "executive function" (Luria, 1966). The executive functions that are compromised in these disorders include the "higher," cortically mediated processes of

1. organizing and structuring activity,
2. planning and anticipating consequences,
3. regulating behavior and emotions,
4. controlling and inhibiting motor responses,
5. maintaining self-awareness and self-monitoring, and
6. achieving behavioral flexibility and adaptability.

In several respects, an etiological pathway between neurodevelopmental deficits and the emergence of sexually aggressive and assaultive behavior is intuitively reasonable. First, many children, adolescents and adults diagnosed with one of the ASD's, in combination with a comorbid conduct disorder, appear to share multiple characteristics with perpetrators of sexual aggression. These characteristics include

1. a frequent lack of interpersonal sensitivity and empathy, more generally demonstrated by a lack of emotional maturity,
2. vulnerability to chemical dependency and addictive behavior,
3. an attraction to dangerous, highly stimulating and high-risk behavior,
4. a tendency, in some, toward hypersexuality, and
5. difficulty or deficits in imposing limits, structure, and direction on their own behavior (Barkley, 1994, 1998; Biederman et al., 1993; Fehrenbach, Smith, & Monastersky, 1986; Fago, 2003; Moffitt, 1990; Nigg & Huang-Pollock, 2003).

The presence of executive function deficits (which also could be associated with monoamine dysregulation) may also help explain the occurrence of sexual aggression in children, adolescents, and adults who have never been previously victimized—sexually or otherwise—and who have not been exposed to sexual violence or other severe family dysfunction. Deficits in executive function, when coupled with exposure to sexual stimulation and accompanying social skill deficits, may be sufficient to evoke an imitative response that results in sexual aggression and misconduct.

Although deficits in executive function may be instrumental to a child's or adolescent's initial forays into sexual misconduct, particularly when other traumatic influences are absent, it is not likely to be the factor that propels this sexual behavior into a life-persistent pattern. In fact, it has been suggested that impulsivity (a central executive function deficit) may be a key variable in differentiating episodic, thoughtless acting out from the calculated, remorseless psychopathy frequently seen in more violent offenders (Hinshaw, 1994; White et al., 1994). As Ryan (1999), Moffitt (1993, 2003), and others have noted, a developmental perspective allows for the possibility that impulsive acts of sexual deviance can be replaced later by normative sexuality; just as some children may engage in delinquent behavior without continuing a criminal lifestyle as an adult, some also may become involved in sexually abusive behavior as children and not continue this behavior into adulthood. Conditions beyond a child's impulsivity may be necessary for childhood episodes of aggressive sexual behavior to develop into chronic patterns of planned, predatory behavior that persists into adulthood. One such condition, suggested by previous research and consistent with the previously described comorbidity profiles, is the presence of social anxiety and social deficits. These deficits might be described in part as deficits in emotional intelligence (Goleman, 1995) or personal intelligence (Gardner, 1983). If a child, adolescent, or adult is severely lacking in interpersonal and emotional understanding and skills, it may be unlikely that more appropriate and mature forms of sexual expression will subsequently develop, particularly if social-emotional competencies are never subsequently acquired. Instead, it may be likely that existing forms of sexual expression will become fixed and unchanging. It is certainly reasonable that these social/interpersonal deficits, if not ameliorated, could contribute to life-persistent problems with sexual intimacy and healthy sexual expression. In fact, the presence of cognitive deficits associated with the processing of social and emotional information may be instrumental to the creation of cognitive distortions that subsequently serve to maintain a chronic pattern of sexual misconduct. Hence, individuals with developmental deficits may be more vulnerable to imitating inappropriate sexual behavior during childhood and adolescence, and may be more likely to have this antisocial behavior persist into adulthood when they also lack the cognitive skills that are essential to their own social and emotional growth and development.

ASSESSMENT AND TREATMENT: A MULTIMODAL APPROACH

Assessment

In view of the reviewed comorbidity data, it is essential that evaluations of sexual offenders include clinical screenings for a broad range of psychopathology, particularly for the spectrum of disorders that display deficits in the regulation of mood, anxiety (particularly social), and executive function. Broad-based, multimodal assessment is essential to ensuring diagnostic accuracy and to avoiding clinical bias; research has demonstrated that clinicians tend to be biased in the direction of excessively weighting data that confirm existing clinical beliefs, and neglecting, or simply failing to collect, other types of data (Achenbach, 1985; Arkes, 1981). Employing a strategy of multimodal clinical as well as "actuarial" assessment (Beech, Fisher, & Thornton, 2003) helps to ensure (1) that risk and diagnostic data is collected from a variety of sources and informants, and (2) that the full range of etiologic and risk factors, including multiple or comorbid diagnoses, is given proper consideration in developing an intervention plan. Therefore, in addition to collecting actuarial data that can be used to predict the offender's risk for future offending and recidivism, "dynamic" clinical data should be collected to fully evaluate the offender's treatment requirements and relative capacity to benefit from various interventions. A sample list of standardized psychological instruments that can be used for dynamic assessment of comorbid psychopathology is provided in Table 8.3.

Treatment

Despite the popularity of sex offense-specific treatment models that borrow heavily from the relapse prevention model developed for alcoholism treatment (Pithers, Marques, Gibat, & Marlatt, 1983), there is little scientific evidence that relapse-prevention strategies actually work to reduce relapse and recidivism in sexual offenders (Marshall & Anderson, 2000; Polaschek, 2003). Specifically regarding the treatment of adolescent sexual offenders, Chaffin and Bonner (1998) and Weinrott (1996) observed that it is not possible to differentiate the superiority of one type of treatment intervention over another. One possible exception to this finding may be delinquency-focused

TABLE 8.3. Multimodal Assessment: Sample Instruments for Assessing Comorbid Psychopathology

Symptom/Pathology	Instrument	References
Children and Adolescents		
Multisymptom/Diagnoses	Achenbach Child Behavior Checklists (CBCL)	Achenbach (1985)
	Behavior Assessment System for Children	Reynolds & Kamphaus (1992)
Impulsivity/Hyperactivity/ADHD	Conners' Parent and Teacher Scales	Conners (1989, 1994)
Social Skill Deficits	Brown ADD Scales	Brown (1998)
Specific Learning Disability (SLD)	Achievement Tests (WIAT/Woodcock-Johnson)	Woodcock & Johnson (1989, 1990)
Dyslexia	Dyslexia Screening Test	Fawcett & Nicolson (1996, 1998)
Conduct Disorder/Delinquency Risk	Jesness Inventory	Jesness (1996)
Fine Motor/Visual/Motor Development	Bender Visual Motor Gestalt Test	Bender (1938)
	Beery-Buktenica Developmental Test (VMI)	Beery, Buktenica, & Beery (2003)
Antisocial/Psychopathic Deviance	Hare Psychopathy Checklist	Hare (1991)
	Millon Clinical Multiaxial Inventory	Millon (1997)
Other Disorders of Personality	Millon Clinical Multiaxial Inventory	Millon (1997)
Children/Adolescents and Adults		
Mood and Anxiety Disorders	Beck/Reynolds Inventories and Scales	Beck & Steer (1993); Reynolds (2000, 2002)
Social Anxiety/Impairment	Liebowitz Social Anxiety Scales	Liebowitz (1987)
Substance Abuse	Substance Abuse Subtle Screening Inventories	Miller (1996, 2001)
Trauma	Trauma Symptom Checklist/Inventory	Briere (1995, 1996)

TABLE 8.3 *(continued)*

Symptom/Pathology	Instrument	References
Attention/Executive and Cognitive Function	Wechsler Scales (WISC/WAIS)	Wechsler (1991, 1997)
	Delis-Kaplan Executive Function System	Delis, Kaplan, & Kramer (2001)
Distractibility/Inattention	Continuous Performance Tests (CPT)	

Note: This list of instruments is illustrative and not comprehensive.

multisystemic or multimodal treatment, which appears to be more effective than individual counseling with juveniles who have committed sex offenses (Chaffin & Bonner, 1998). Furthermore, as Weinrott (1996) has noted, no evidence supports the superiority of a "heavy-handed," coercive, and punitive correctional strategy with juvenile offenders. Similar research with adult offenders has demonstrated that treatment programs which achieve successful outcomes attend to more than just risk reduction by also focusing on the enhancement of offenders' personal strengths and ability to live healthy, more fulfilling lives (Marshall et al., 2003; Ward & Stewart, 2003). The following sections will therefore focus on issues related specifically to the treatment of comorbid psychopathology in offenders. This treatment is viewed as essential to offenders' healthy functioning as well as to their ability to make effective use of other risk-reducing treatment interventions.

Individual and Group Psychotherapy

Individual and group psychotherapy are cornerstone interventions in programs that treat sexual offenders, both young and old. For adults and older adolescents, traditional individual therapy can be useful and even necessary at the beginning of treatment, when the offender and family frequently are in crisis, often with symptoms of major depressive disorder and suicidal preoccupation. However, experience also has shown that traditional approaches to these therapies may not work well with this population after the initial crisis, largely because of the tendency, on the part of both clients and clinicians, to avoid material that readily evokes shame and disgust. Consequently, it has become standard practice to refer offenders to psychoeducational groups in which offense-specific interventions can be implemented. Although offense-specific group treatment can be particularly effective with adults and mature adolescents, it should be applied judiciously with adolescent offenders, and probably not at all with younger children, especially neurodevelopmentally compromised youngsters. This caution is based on recent research (Dishion, McCord, & Poulin, 1999; Levant, Tolan, & Dodgen, 2002), which has shown that peer treatment groups can have an iatrogenic effect in reinforcing rather than reducing psychopathology and aggressive behavior in conduct-disordered adolescents. Moreover, individuals with neurodevelopmental deficits may be particularly sensitive to this iatrogenic effect due to their emotional and social immaturity and their susceptibility to negative peer influence. In addition, psycho-educational group interventions can be particularly inappropriate for preadolescents who are not developmentally ready to cognitively or emotionally process and integrate such a program's informational content.

Family Interventions

Research on mental health treatments for children and adolescents with conduct disorders indicates that family therapy and parent training programs helpful contributors to the successful outcome of these interventions (Levant et al., 2002). Although it has not yet been demonstrated empirically, the importance of family involvement with nonviolent sex offenders of all ages is likely to be of equal importance. The importance of family treatment for child and adolescent offenders is based on several factors: these youngsters are likely to

1. display academic deficiencies and school failure,
2. display poor interpersonal and social skills and heightened levels of peer rejection, and
3. live in families where there is frequent history of psychiatric disturbance, marital and family distress, dysfunctional communication, and high levels of parental stress (Kazdin, 2003).

Family and marital therapy for adult offenders is obviously essential to the successful treatment of incest offenders, but may be less appropriate to child molesters and violent offenders who have not previously functioned in adult partnerships or adult family relationships. Instead, chronic, fixated pedophiles may require interventions focused on the development of adult social and emotional skills, while violent offenders will more frequently require interventions specific to the treatment of antisocial personality deficits and perhaps chemical dependency.

Cognitive and Emotional Training

Most sexual offender treatment programs emphasize the importance of (1) cognitive distortions in the etiology of sexual aggression, and (2) cognitive retraining as a means for correcting these distortions (Murphy, 1990). These programs also emphasize that offenders should develop empathy for their victims. However, psychotherapeutic work with impulsive, neurodevelopmentally compromised individuals is more frequently concerned with cognitive deficits than cognitive distortions. These individuals, rather than acting because of distorted perceptions or beliefs, tend to act and react impulsively, without thinking about the consequences of their behavior. The relevant therapeutic task, therefore, is not to alter these offender's pathological perceptions or beliefs, but rather to train them to stop and think before acting. Focusing solely on cognitive distortions may be developmentally inappropriate and largely ineffective because the essential therapeutic task is to create thinking rather than to simply alter it. These very different tasks require entirely different interventions with different developmental assumptions. Similarly, empathy training is frequently beyond the developmental competency of young children and those individuals with significant neurodevelopmental deficits. If an individual is not yet developmentally ready to think about, understand, and manage his or her own behavior and emotional reactions, he or she stands little chance of abstractly understanding these emotional states in others.

Psychopharmacology

Finally, psychopharmacological agents play an important role in a multimodal treatment plan. The "monoamine hypothesis" and the frequent comorbidity of mood dysregulation in sexual offenders have been previously described. This hypothesis and finding suggest that the agents used for treating mood disorders, problems of impulse control, and deficits in executive function may offer dramatic improvement for offenders in their emotional, social, and sexual functioning. Such improvements may in turn enhance their ability to profit from other treatments aimed at risk reduction. Medications that may be helpful for this population include

> serotonin reuptake inhibitors—fluoxetine (Prozac), sertraline (Zoloft), and paroxetine (Paxil),
> atypical antidepressants—buproprion (Wellbutrin),
> mood stabilizers—carbamazepine (Tegretol) and valproic acid (Depakote),
> psychostimulants—methylphenidate (Ritalin) and dextroamphetamine sulfate (Dexedrine), and possibly also
> the older tricyclic antidepressants—immipramine (Tofranil) and desipramine (Norpramin), or
> a combination of these.

Through their psychoactive effects, these medications may enhance mood and emotional resiliency as well as improve an offender's ability, when otherwise impulsive and undercontrolled, to impose better limits and direction on behavior. With these enhanced abilities, better use can be made of other interventions that are part of a comprehensive treatment plan.

CASE EXAMPLE

John is a thirty-year-old male who was evaluated at the request of his attorney from the Federal Public Defender's Office. At the time of initial evaluation, he had been incarcerated in a federal corrections center for approximately nine months, subsequent to a criminal conviction for possession of child pornography. John came into possession of this material through his work with a federal agency, where he was responsible for constructing video evidence that was to be used in the prosecution of federal crimes. Up until the time of his criminal conviction, John had an unblemished work history with several commendations for his conscientious and proficient work. He also had no previous criminal arrests or convictions. John's sexually related problems began when he was assigned the task of organizing and assembling videographic evidence for the prosecution of child pornography cases. In the process of assembling this evidence, he began to save selected video files to his own laptop computer for personal use. Subsequently, one of his co-workers became aware of these files and reported them to the appropriate authorities. John was subsequently terminated from his employment and referred for criminal prosecution under federal statutes related to possession of child pornography. Although John displayed obvious and overt pedophilic interests, and had been working with children in a church group, no evidence was found that he had ever acted on these interests in committing a sexual assault.

John was born after a full-term pregnancy and an essentially uncomplicated vaginal delivery. His biological mother presented a history of chronic alcohol abuse that eventually culminated in her premature death. John's success in achieving expected developmental milestones is uncertain, as he lived with his biological mother until age three and received minimal supervision and care. His biological father and stepmother subsequently took custody. At the time of the change in custody, he was found to be suffering from malnutrition, with retarded physical development and rickets/scurvy-like symptoms associated with chronic vitamin deficiency. He responded quickly to proper nutrition and reached near-normal height and weight by the time he entered kindergarten. Throughout childhood, and well into adolescence and young adulthood, he experienced recurrent problems with enuresis and encopresis, which was presumed to be associated with prolonged immaturity in his neurological development. He otherwise was physically healthy as a child and required no hospitalizations, surgeries, or prolonged medical care. He is described by his stepmother as having been a very pleasant and well-behaved child who displayed no temper tantrums or other behavioral problems.

In kindergarten, John was immediately identified as having significant learning difficulties, as he was unable to memorize the alphabet or learn simple counting. Unfortunately, the family moved after his kindergarten year, and he subsequently did not receive special educational services until he reached the sixth grade. Despite the fact that other students persistently teased him about his learning problems, he reportedly liked school and was noticeably motivated and hard working. He was not required to repeat any grades following first grade, and he eventually successfully graduated from a vocational-technical high school program. Although teachers frequently commented on his memory and attention problems, no diagnosis was made of attention-deficit/hyperactivity disorder (ADHD) or minimal brain dysfunction (an earlier and now discarded diagnosis that prevailed during most of his early school years). However, he was diagnosed at age twelve (sixth grade) with a developmental reading disorder (dyslexia), and problems with "language capability, auditory processing, memory . . . and distractibility." Some of these problems have persisted into adulthood, as he continues to have difficulty with reading, spelling, and some word pronunciations. During high school, he experienced multiple episodes of mild seizure in which he briefly lost consciousness; however, follow-up neurological evaluation did not yield a diagnosis or result in a regimen of treatment.

Assessment

John was found to be friendly and cooperative, and presented himself with a social ease that was not expected, given his history of significant learning and developmental deficits. Similar to the reported impressions of his attorney and correctional officers, John impressed his evaluators with his sincerity, honesty, and diligent work ethic. All of the information he provided was consistent with information that was available from previous criminal investigation and mental health evaluations. At the initial evaluation, John presented as well-oriented, with no evidence of thought disorder or other evidence of psychotic process or illness. His clinical presentation, history, and the results of psychological testing provided no evidence of antisocial/psychopathic personality features or impulsive, uncontrolled, antisocial behavior. Previous evaluations had noted symptoms of clinical depression, and there was continued evidence for this diagnosis.

John presented an extensive and well-documented history of neurodevelopmental immaturity with multiple associated learning deficits. His neurodevelopmental immaturity was also thought to have contributed to several noncognitive, emotional and social deficits in personality. These deficits included a pattern of dependency and passivity, an assiduous avoidance of interpersonal conflict, a determination to please and conform to the wishes of others, and a reliance on daydream and fantasy as primary coping mechanisms. These characteristics, in addition to the noted cognitive deficits, prevented John from making a successful social and emotional transition into adulthood, and into successful adult sexual functioning. Although ostensibly functioning as an adult, particularly in regard to career and church responsibilities, John had struggled socially, emotionally, and sexually, and in these respects was seen as functioning at a level more consistent with middle adolescence.

Results from both previous and current psychological testing, in addition to the clinical and academic record, suggested the presence of an additional diagnosis of ADHD, inattentive type. This diagnostic finding was seen as consistent with the specific problems in learning that John displayed over a twenty-year period, and with the classic symptoms of executive dysfunction displayed throughout John's history. It was further concluded that John's neurodevelopmental deficits were likely associated with his preoccupation with and collecting of child pornography, and with other compulsive, hoarding behaviors that he had displayed throughout the course of his life.

In addition to the contributing influences of the identified neurodevelopmental deficits, John's involvement with child pornography was likely influenced by other factors as well. These include

1. his responsibilities at work, which included the reconstruction of child pornography evidence, and which enabled him to believe (via cognitive limitations and distortions) that it was both appropriate and legal to possess this material,
2. his conscientious conformity to the tenets of his religious beliefs, which instructed that he not engage in premarital, adult sexuality, and
3. his chronic difficulty with setting appropriate limits and boundaries on himself and on the demands made of him by others.

Consequently, it was thought to be inappropriate to describe John as having exclusive or chronic pedophilic interests. His long-term interest in marriage, as well as a previous marital engagement, was not viewed as life events common in the developmental history of fixated pedophiles (Groth, 1979, 1982). Rather, John was viewed as an emotionally, socially, and cognitively immature young man who acted-out sexually during a period of developmental stress and conflict. These dynamic factors, in addition to multiple static, actuarial factors, were thought to make John a low risk for committing future sexual offenses.

Treatment

Because John was evaluated as not presenting a significant or continuing risk to the community, a recommendation was made to transfer him from criminal confinement to supervised community probation. In addition to the advantage of having access to offender treatment while residing in the community (which was not available in this federal corrections center), long-term incarceration was also seen as having the disadvantage of further reinforcing John's dependency and immaturity. Hence, there was concern that continued long-term incarceration might actually enhance the likelihood that he would develop long-term, chronic problems in sexual adjustment and maturity.

John was also referred to multimodal outpatient treatment. This treatment was seen as critical in addressing multiple issues and concerns, specifically:

1. John's need for education related to healthy and appropriate adult sexual functioning,
2. his pathological avoidance of conflict and attendant difficulties in setting and enforcing appropriate personal and physical boundaries,
3. his tendency to engage in compulsive overactivity and work to compensate for other areas of life where he had greater difficulty functioning successfully,
4. his unmet needs for emotional and physical intimacy, and the conflicts these needs created for his religious beliefs and practices, and
5. issues associated with a diagnosis of chronic depression and John's likely need for psychotropic medication to treat this mood disorder.

John was seen as demonstrating a strong motivation to succeed. He presented a lengthy history of conscientious compliance with rules and expectations, and it was thought that there was a high likelihood that John would successfully comply with treatment. These recommendations were subsequently implemented, and several years later John had successfully returned to community living without further reported incidents of sexual criminal behavior.

REFERENCES

Achenbach, T.M. (1985). *Assessment and taxonomy of child and adolescent psychopathology.* Beverly Hills: Sage.
Ahlmeyer, S., Kleinsasser, D., Stoner, J., & Retzlaff, P. (2003). Psychopathology of incarcerated sex offenders. *Journal of Personality Disorders, 17*(4), 306-318.
American Psychiatric Association. (1980). *Diagnostic and statistical manual of mental disorders* (3rd ed.), Washington, DC: Author.
American Psychiatric Association. (1987). *Diagnostic and statistical manual of mental disorders* (3rd ed., Revised). Washington, DC: Author.
American Psychiatric Association. (1994). *Diagnostic and statistical manual of mental disorders* (4th ed.) Washington, DC: Author.

Arkes, H.R. (1981). Impediments to accurate clinical judgment and possible ways to minimize their impact. *Journal of Consulting and Clinical Psychology, 49,* 323-330.

Barbaree, H.E., Seto, M.C., & Marie, A. (2002). Sex offender characteristics, response to treatment, and correctional release decisions at the Warkwith Sexual Behaviour Clinic. Ottawa, Ontario: Department of the Solicitor General of Canada.

Barkley, R.A. (1994). Impaired delayed responding: A unified theory of attention-deficit hyperactivity disorder. In D.K. Routh (Ed.), *Disruptive behavior disorders in childhood: Essays honoring Herbert C. Quay* (pp. 11-57). New York: Plenum Press.

Barkley, R.A. (1998). *Attention deficit hyperactivity disorder: A handbook for diagnosis and treatment.* New York: Guilford Press.

Beck, A.T. & Steer, R.A. (1993). *Beck Depression Inventory: Manual.* San Antonio, TX: The Psychological Corporation.

Becker, J.V., Kaplan, M.S., & Tenke, C.E. (1992). The relationship of abuse history, denial, and erectile response profiles of adolescent sexual perpetrators. *Behavior Therapy, 23,* 87-97.

Beech, A.R., Fisher, D.D., & Thornton, D. (2003). Risk assessment of sex offenders. *Professional Psychology: Research and Practice, 34*(4), 339-352.

Beery, K.E., Buktenica, N.A. & Beery, N.A. (2003). *Beery-Buktenica Developmental Test of Visual-Motor Integration,* 5th ed. Odessa, FL: Psychological Assessment Resources.

Bender, L. (1938). *A visual motor gestalt test and its clinical use.* New York: American Orthopsychiatric Association.

Biederman, J., Farone, S.J., Spencer, T., Wilens, T., Norman, D., Lapey, K.A., Mick, E., Lehman, B.K., & Doyle, A. (1993). Patterns of psychiatric comorbidity, cognition, and psychosocial functioning in adults with attention-deficit disorder. *American Journal of Psychiatry, 150,* 1792-1798.

Briere, J. (1995). *Trauma Symptom Inventory (TSI) professional manual.* Odessa, FL: Psychological Assessment Resources.

Briere, J. (1996). *Trauma Symptom Checklist for children professional manual.* Odessa, FL: Psychological Assessment Resources.

Brown, T.E. (1998). *Brown attention deficit disorders scales.* San Antonio, TX: The Psychological Corporation.

Caspi, A. & Moffitt, T. (1995). The continuity of maladaptive behavior: From description to explanation in the study of antisocial behavior. In D. Cicchetti, & D. Cohen (Eds.), *Developmental psychopathology* (Vol. 2, pp. 472-511). New York: Wiley.

Chaffin, M. & Bonner, B. (1998). Don't shoot, we're your children: Have we gone too far in our response to adolescent sexual abusers and children with sexual behavior problems? *Child Maltreatment 3*(4), 314-316.

Conners, C.K. (1989). *Conners Rating Scale manual.* Toronto: Multi-Health Systems.

Conners, C.K. (1994). *Attention deficit hyperactivity disorder: Assessment and treatment for children and adolescents.* Toronto: Multi-Health Systems.

Delis, D., Kaplan, E., & Kramer, J. (2001). *Delis-Kaplan Executive Function System (D-KEFS).* San Antonio, TX: The Psychological Corporation.

Dishion, T.J., McCord, J., & Poulin, F. (1999). When interventions harm: Peer groups and problem behavior. *American Psychologist, 54,* 755-764.

Fago, D.P. (2003). Evaluation and treatment of neurodevelopmental deficits in sexually aggressive children and adolescents. *Professional Psychology: Research and Practice, 34*(3), 248-257.

Faraone, S.V. (2000). Genetics of childhood disorders: XIX. ADHD, Part 4: Is ADHD genetically heterogeneous? *Journal of the American Academy of Child and Adolescent Psychiatry, 39,* 1201-1205.

Fawcett, A.J. & Nicolson, R.I. (1996). *The dyslexia screening test.* London: The Psychological Corporation.

Fawcett, A.J. & Nicolson, R.I. (1998). *The adult dyslexia screening test.* London: The Psychological Corporation.

Fehrenbach, P.A., Smith, W., & Monastersky, C. (1986). Adolescent sexual offenders: Offender and offense characteristics. *American Journal of Orthopsychiatry, 56,* 225-233.

Fergusson, D.M., Horwood, L.J., & Lynskey, M.T. (1993). Prevalence and comorbidity of DSM-III-R diagnoses in a birth cohort of 15 year olds. *Journal of the American Academy of Child & Adolescent Psychiatry, 32,* 1127-1134.

Ferrara, M.L. & McDonald, S. (1996). *Treatment of the juvenile sex offender: Neurological and psychiatric impairments.* Northvale, NJ: Jason Aronson.

Gardner, H. (1983). *Frames of mind: The theory of multiple intelligences.* New York: Basic Books.

Goleman, D. (1995). *Emotional intelligence.* New York: Bantam Books.

Graber, B., Hartmann, K., Coffman, J.A., Huey, C.J., & Golden, C.J. (1982)., Brain damage among mentally disordered sex offenders. *Journal of Forensic Science, 27*(1), 125-134.

Groth, A.N. (1979). Sexual trauma in the life histories of rapists and child molesters. *Victimology: An International Journal, 4,* 10-16.

Groth, A.N. (1982). The incest offender. In S.M. Sgroi (Ed.), *Handbook of clinical intervention in child sexual abuse* (pp. 215-239). Lexington, MA: Heath & Co.

Hare, R.D. (1991). *The Hare Psychopathology Checklist—Revised (PCL-R).* Toronto, Ontario: Multi Health Systems.

Hinshaw, S.P. (1994). Conduct disorder in childhood: Conceptualization, diagnosis, comorbidity, and risk status for anti-social functioning in adulthood. In D. Fowles, P. Sutker, & S. Goodman (Eds.), *Psychopathy and antisocial personality: A developmental perspective* (pp. 3-44). New York: Springer.

Hunter, J.A. & Becker, J.V. (1994). The role of deviant sexual arousal in juvenile sexual offending: Etiology, evaluation, and treatment. *Criminal Justice and Behavior, 21*(1), 132-149.

Jesness, C.F. (1996). *Jesness Inventory—Revised*. Palo Alto, CA: Consulting Psychologists Press.

Kafka, M.P. (2003). The monoamine hypothesis for the pathophysiology of paraphilic disorders: An update. *Annals of New York Academy of Science, 989,* 86-94; discussion 144-153.

Kafka, M.P. & Hennen, J. (2002). A DSM-IV Axis I comorbidity study of males (n = 120) with paraphilias and paraphilia-related disorders. *Sex Abuse, 14*(4), 349-366.

Kashani, J.D., Orvaschel, H., Rosenberg, T.K., & Reid, J.C. (1989). Psychopathology in a community sample of children and adolescents. *Journal of the American Academy of Child & Adolescent Psychiatry, 28,* 701-706.

Kavoussi, R.J., Kaplan, M., & Becker, J.V. (1988). Psychiatric diagnoses in adolescent sex offenders. *Journal of the American Academy of Child and Adolescent Psychiatry, 27,* 241-243.

Kazdin, A.E. (2003). Problem-solving skills training and parent management training for conduct disorder. In A.E. Kazdin & J.R. Weisz (Eds.), *Evidence-based psychotherapies for children and adolescents* (pp. 241-262). New York: Guilford.

Kendall P.C. & Clarkin, J.F. (1992). Introduction to special section: Comorbidity and treatment implications. *Journal of Consulting & Clinical Psychology, 60,* 833-834.

Kessler, R.C. (1997). The prevalence of psychiatric comorbidity. In S. Wetzler & W.C. Sanderson (Eds.), *Treatment strategies for patients with psychiatric comorbidity* (pp. 23-48). New York: Wiley.

Kessler, R.C., McGonagle, K.A., Zhao, S., Nelson, C.B., Hughes, M., Eshelman, S., Weltchen, H.-U., & Kendler, K.S. (1994). Lifetime and 12-month prevalence of DSM-III-R psychiatric disorders in the United States: Results from the National Comorbidity Survey. *Archives of General Psychiatry, 51,* 8-19.

Langevin, R., Marentette, D., & Rosati, B. (1996). Why therapy fails with some sex offenders: Learning difficulties examined empirically. *Journal of Offender Rehabilitation, 23,* 143-155.

Levant, R.F., Tolan, P., & Dodgen, D. (2002). New directions in children's mental health policy: Psychology's role. *Professional Psychology: Research and Practice, 33,* 115-124.

Liebowitz, M.R. (1987). Social phobia. *Modern Problems of Pharmacopsychiatry, 22,* 141-173.

Luria, A.R. (1966). *Higher Cortical Functions in Man.* New York: Basic Books.

Marshall, W. (1997). Pedophilia: Psychopathology and theory. In R.D. Laws, & W. O'Donohue (Eds.), *Sexual deviance: Theory, assessment and treatment* (pp. 152-174). New York: Guilford Press.

Marshall, W.L. & Anderson, D. (2000). Do relapse prevention components enhance treatment effectiveness? In D.R. Laws, S.M. Hudson, & T. Ward (Eds.), *Remaking relapse prevention with sex offenders: A sourcebook* (pp. 39-55). Newbury Park, CA: Sage.

Marshall, W.L., Fernandez, Y.M., Serran, G.A., Mulloy, R., Thornton, D., Mann, R.E., & Anderson, D. (2003). Process variables in the treatment of sexual offenders: A review of the relevant literature. *Aggression and Violent Behavior, 8,* 205-234.

McElroy, S.L., Pope, H.G., Keck, P.E. (1996), Are impulse-control disorders related to bipolar disorder? *Comprehensive Psychiatry, 37*(4), 229-240.

McManus, M., Alessi, N.E., Grapentime, W.L., & Brickman, A. (1984). Psychiatric disturbance in serious delinquents. *Journal of the American Academy of Child and Adolescent Psychiatry, 139,* 1194-1196.

Miller, G.A. (1996). *Substance Abuse Subtle Screening Inventory (SASSI-3).* Springville, IN: The SASSI Institute.

Miller, G.A. (2001). *The Adolescent Substance Abuse Subtle Screening Inventory (SASSI-A2).* Springville, IN: The SASSI Institute.

Millon, T. (1997). *The Millon inventories: Clinical and personality assessment.* New York: Guilford.

Mineka, S., Watson, D., & Clark, L.A. (1998). Comorbidity of anxiety and unipolar mood disorders. *Annual Review of Psychology, 49,* 377-412.

Miner, M.H., Siekert, G.P., & Ackland, M.A. (1997). *Evaluation: Juvenile sex offender treatment program, Minnesota Correctional Facility-Sauk Centre. Final report-Biennium 1995-1997.* Minneapolis, MN: University of Minnesota, Department of Family Practice and Community Health, Program in Human Sexuality.

Moffitt, T. E. (1990). Juvenile delinquency and attention deficit disorder: Boys developmental trajectories from age 3 to age 15. *Child Development, 61,* 893-910.

Moffitt, T. E. (1993). "Life-course persistent" and "adolescence-limited" antisocial behavior: A developmental taxonomy. *Psychological Review, 100,* 674-701.

Moffitt, T. E. (2003). Life-course persistent and adolescence-limited antisocial behavior: A ten year review and a research agenda. In B.B. Lahey, T.E. Moffitt, & A. Caspi (Eds.), *Causes of conduct disorder and juvenile delinquency* (pp. 49-75). New York: Guilford Press.

Murphy, W.D. (1990). Assess mane and modification of cognitive distortions in sex offenders. In W. Marshall, D.R. Laws, & H.E. Barbaree (Eds.), *Handbook of sexual assault: Issues, theories, and treatment of the offender* (pp. 331-342). New York: Plenum Press.

O'Connor, T. G., McGuire, S., Reiss, D., Hetherington, E. M., & Plomin, R. (1998). Co-occurrence of depressive symptoms and antisocial behavior in adolescence: A common genetic liability. *Journal of Abnormal Psychology, 107,* 27-37.

Packard, W.S. & Rosner, R. (1985). Psychiatric evaluation of sex offenders. *Journal of Forensic Science, 30,* 715-720.

Pithers, W.D., Marques, J.K., Gibat, C.C., & Marlatt, G.A. (1983). Relapse prevention with sexual aggressives: A self-control model of treatment and maintenance of change. In J.G. Greer, & I.R. Stewart (Eds.), *Handbook of sexual assault: Issues, theories, and treatment of the offender* (pp. 214-239). New York: Plenum Press.

Polaschek, D.L.L. (2003). Relapse prevention, offense process models, and the treatment of sexual offenders. *Professional Psychology: Research and Practice, 34*(4), 361-367.

Purvis, M., Ward, T., & Devilly, G.G. (2002). Community corrections officers' attributions for sexual offending against children. *Journal of Sexual Abuse, 11*(4), 101-123.

Raymond, N.C., Coleman, E., Ohlerking, F., Christenson, G.A., & Miner, M. (1999). Psychiatric comorbidity in pedophilic sex offenders. *American Journal of Psychiatry, 156,* 786-788.

Reynolds, C.R. & Kamphaus, R. (1992). *Behavior Assessment System for Children: Manual.* Circle Pines, MN: American Guidance Service.

Reynolds, N.M. (2000). *Adolescent Psychopathology Scale.* Odessa, FL: Psychological Assessment Resources.

Reynolds, N.M. (2002). *Reynolds Adolescent Depression Scale-2.* Odessa, FL: Psychological Assessment Resources.

Ryan, G. (1999). Treatment of sexually abusive youth: The evolving consensus. *Journal of Interpersonal Violence, 14,* 422-436.

Schram, D.D., Milloy, C.D., & Rowe, W.E. (1991). *Juvenile sex offenders: A follow up study of reoffense behavior.* Olympia, WA: Washington State Institute for Public Policy, Urban Policy Research and Cambie Group International.

State of Ohio (1992). *Summary of sex offender characteristics: 1992 intake sample population.* Columbus: Ohio Department of Justice.

Tarter, R.E., Hegedus, A.M., Alterman, A.I., & Katzgarris, L. (1983). Cognitive capacities of juvenile violent, nonviolent, and sexual offenders. *Journal of Nervous & Mental Disease, 171*(9), 564-567.

Trivits, L.C. & Reppucci, N.D. (2002). Application of Megan's Law to juveniles. *American Psychologist, 57,* 690-704.

Verhulst, F.C. & van der Ende, J. (1993). "Comorbidity" in an epidemiological sample: A longitudinal perspective. *Journal of Child Psychology & Psychiatry, 34,* 767-783.

Ward, T. & Stewart, C.A. (2003). The treatment of sex offenders: Risk management and good lives. *Professional Psychology: Research and Practice, 34*(4), 353-360.

Wechsler, D. (1991). *Wechsler Intelligence Scale for children* (3rd ed.). San Antonio, TX: Psychological Corporation.

Wechsler, D. (1997). *Wechsler Adult Intelligence* (3rd ed.). San Antonio, TX: Psychological Corporation.

Weinrott, M. (1996). *Juvenile sexual aggression: A critical review.* Boulder, CO: University of Colorado, Institute for Behavioral Sciences, Center for the Study and Prevention of Violence.

White, J.L., Moffitt, T.E., Caspi, A., Bartusch, D., Needles, D., & Stouthamer-Loeber, M. (1994). Measuring impulsivity and examining its relationship to delinquency. *Journal of Abnormal Psychology, 103,* 192-205.

Woodcock, R.W. & Johnson, M.B. (1989, 1990). *Woodcock-Johnson Psycho-Educational Battery—Revised.* Allen, TX: DLM Teaching Resources.

Index

Page numbers followed by the letter "e" indicate exhibits; those followed by the letter "t" indicate tables.

AASI, 52
ABC model, 116
Abel and Becker cognition scale, 145
Abel Assessment for Sexual Interest (AASI), 52
Abuse settings, 104-107
Abused to abuser hypothesis, 139
Abuser, fear of becoming, 80-81
Ackerman, M.J., 38
Actuarial assessment, 204
ADHD, 5, 28, 197
Adolescent adjustment reaction, 22
Adolescent Cognition Scale, 38
Adolescent sex offenders, 21-22
    assessment of, 31-40
    case example, 41-42
    characteristics, sexual behavior, 24-27
    cognitive characteristics of, 28-29
    comorbidity, 195-197, 196t
    demographics, 23-24
    environmental dynamics, 29-30
    psychiatric characteristics of, 28-29
    social dynamics, 29-30
    treatment for, 40-41
    victimization, history of, 27-28
Adolescent Sexual Interest Card Sort (ASIC), 36
Adolescent-limited antisocial behavior, 195
Adult male sex offenders, 47
    assessment, 51-54
    case example, 59-64

Adult male sex offenders *(continued)*
    characteristics, 48-49
    comorbidity, 198-199, 198t
    etiology, 49-50
    interventions, 54-55
    offense, consequences of, 50
    prevalence, 48
    risk factors, 51
    therapy groups, 55
    treatment, 55-58
Age, adolescent sex offender, 23
Aggressive sexual behavior, 2
Allen, C.M., 76
Anal penetration, 25
Anderson, B., 79
Anger rapist, 174-175
Antilibidinal medication, 152
Approach goal abusers, 121
Araji, S.K., 3
Arousal, female sex offenders, 90
ASD, 201
ASIC, 36
Assessment
    adolescent sex offenders, 31-40
    adult male sex offenders, 51-54
    child sex offenders, 8-12
    comorbidity, 204, 205t-206t
    female sex offenders, 82-86
    ID sex offenders, 142-149
    perpetrators within professions, 112, 113e-116e, 116-117
    violent sex offenders, 179-182

Attention-deficit/hyperactivity disorder (ADHD), 5, 28, 197
Autism spectrum disorders (ASD), 201
Avoidant goal offenders, 121
Awad, G.A., 26

Babysitter, adolescent sex offender, 25-26
Barbaree, H.E., 170, 173
Baroff, G.S., 138-139
Barratt Impulsiveness Scale, 143
Beck Anxiety Inventory, 143
Beck Depression Inventory, 143
Becker, J.V., 24-25, 30, 39-40
Beech, A., 102, 108, 110, 171
Behavioral management, 152
Berliner, L., 2
Berry, J., 104
Birnbaum, H.J., 175
Blanchard, R., 141-142
Blitz-style attack, 169
Bonner, B., 204
Brackenridge, C.H., 107
Brannan, C., 101
Briere, J., 79
Brown, D., 135
Brown, G.R., 79
Browne, K., 106
Bucke, T., 135
Burkhart, B., 76
Burton, D.L., 28

Canadian Centre for Justice Statistics, 75
Case examples
    adolescent sex offender, 41-42
    adult male sex offenders, 59-64
    child sex offenders, 13-17
    comorbidity, 209-213
    female sex offenders, 92-94
    ID sex offenders, 156-158
    perpetrators within professions, 122-126
    violent sex offenders, 185-187

Catholic Church, 105-106
CD, 197
Cellini, H.R., 30
Chaffin, M., 204
Chambers, H.J., 30
Characteristics
    adolescent sex offenders, 24-27
    adult male sex offenders, 48-49
    child sex offenders, 4-6
    ID sex offenders, 133-136
    violent sex offenders, 170-171
Child care institution, abuse setting, 104
Child Protection in Sport unit, UK, 107
Child sex offenders, 1-2
    assessment of, 8-12
    case example, 13-17
    characteristics of, 4-6
    comorbidity, 195-197, 196t
    etiology, 7-8
    family of, 6
    interventions, 12-13
    the offense, 6-7
    prevalence of, 3-4
Church, abuse setting, 104-105
Clement, M., 104
Clinical interview, adolescent sex offender, 32-33
Coercive sexual behavior, 2
Cognitive behavioral therapy, 117-118
Cognitive characteristics
    adolescent sex offenders, 28-29
    child sex offenders, 5-6
Cognitive Distortions Scale, 115e
Cognitive restructuring, 120, 152-155
Community involvement, ID sex offenders, 155-156
Comorbidity, 193-194
    adolescent sex offenders, 195-197, 196t
    adult sex offenders, 198-199, 198t
    assessment, 204, 205t-206t
    case example, 209-213
    child sex offenders, 195-197, 196t
    development of, 194-195
    etiology, 200
    "executive dysfunction" hypothesis, 201-203

Comorbidity *(continued)*
    medications, 209
    "monoamine hypothesis," 200-201
    treatment, 204, 206-209
Competency assessment, 144
Conduct disorder (CD), 197
Conley, R.W., 135-136
Consequences, sexual offending, 50, 77-82
Consent, 144
Consistency, relationships, 148
Control conditions, lack of, 140
Coping, female sex offenders, 88-89
Counterfeit deviance, 138
Cultural issues, adolescent sex offender, 34

Davis, G.E., 28
Decision chain, 117
DeLuca, R.V., 82
Demographics, adolescent sex offending, 23-24
Denial, 34
Denov, M., 78-82
Depression, 79
Developmentally precocious sexual behavior, 2
Deviant fantasy, female sex offenders, 90
Dhaliwal, G., 79
Diagnostic and Statistical Manual of Mental Disorders, 75, 176-177, 193
Dismissive attachment, 183-184
DSM, 75, 176-177, 193
Dynamic risk factors, 51
Dysfunctional family, 6

Education
    adolescent sex offenders, 29-30
    perpetrators within professions, 120
Eldridge, H., 88, 90, 91

Emotional Identification with Children Scale, 115e
Emotional intelligence, deficit, 203
Emotional regulation, female sex offenders, 87-88
Emotional training, 208
Empathy, 58
English, D.J., 27-28
Entrapment, 109
Environmental dynamics, adolescent sex offenders, 29-30
Ethnicity, adolescent sex offender, 24
Etiology of abuse
    adult male sex offenders, 49-50
    child sex offenders, 7-8
    comorbidity, 200
    female sex offenders, 72-74
    perpetrators within professions, 107-109
"Executive dysfunction" hypothesis, 201-203
Exhibitionism, 25
External barriers, precondition of sexual abuse, 53
    treatment, 57
External supervision, violent sex offenders, 185

Faller, K.C., 102
Family
    of adolescent sex offenders, 28
    of child sex offenders, 6, 13
    ID sex offenders, 143, 149-151
Family assessment
    adolescent sex offenders, 36-37
    child sex offenders, 11
Family therapy, 57, 207-208
Federal Bureau of Investigation, 22, 24
Fehrenbach, P.A., 25
Female sex offenders, 71-72
    abuse of, 7, 24
    assessment, 82-86
    case example, 92-94
    etiology, 72-74

Female sex offenders *(continued)*
  offense consequences, 77-82
  prevalence, 74-77
  treatment, 86-91
Finkelhor, D., 51-54, 103
Folkman, S., 88
Foster care, abuse setting, 106
Four Preconditions of Sexual Abuse, 51-54
Freund, K., 74
Friedrich, W.N., 6, 7
Fritz, G.S., 76
Fromuth, M., 76
Frottage, 25

Gender
  adolescent sex offenders, 23-24
  child sex offenders, 5
Genesis II Female Sex Offenders Program, 73
Genital fondling, 25
Gil, E., 2
Grayston, A.D., 82
Grievance rape, 175
Griffiths, S.D.M., 137
Groth, A.N., 173, 175
Groth, N., 76-77
Group therapy, 206-207
Groze, V., 103
Grubin, D., 170
Gudjonsson suggestibility scales, 144
Gunn, J., 170
Gust-Brey, K.L., 26

Hagan, M.P., 26
Hanson, R.K., 183
Hare Psychopathy Checklist, 141
Harris, A.J.R., 183
Harter Self-Esteem Questionnaire, 38
Hayes, S., 135
HCM, 171
High-deviancy abusers, 112
Holland, A.J., 137

Homicidal child molester (HCM), 171
Horton, C.B., 2
Hostile masculinity, 184
Hucker, S.J., 176
Hunter, J.A., 27, 39-40, 79

ID sex offenders, 133
  assessment, 142-149
  case example, 156-158
  characteristics, 133-136
  families, 149-151
  interventions, 151-56
  prevalence, 133-136
  typology of, 137-142
Inappropriate sexual behavior, 2
Incarceration, 50
Intellectual disabilities (ID), 133. *See also* ID sex offenders
Interindividual approach, 88
Internal barriers, precondition of sexual abuse, 52-53
  treatment, 56
Internet, 110, 126
Interventions
  adult male sex offenders, 54-55
  ID sex offenders, 151-156
  perpetrators within professions, 117-120
  violent sex offenders, 182-184
Intimacy, fear of, 80-81
Intraindividual approach, 88
IQ scores, 5-6

Johnson, T.C., 2, 6

Kafka, M.P., 201
Kahn, T.J., 30
Kaufman, K.L., 169
Keenan, T., 108
King, L.L., 182
Knight, R.A., 169, 176, 177, 178
Koss, M., 169

Lanyon, R.I., 31
Lazarus, R.S., 88
Learned behavior, abuse as, 49
Lichtenberg, H., 28
Life Expectancy Checklist, 150
Life-course persistent behavior, 195
Low-deviancy abusers, 112, 116
Luecke, W.J., 6, 7
Lyall, I., 134-135
Lynch, M.A., 106

Male sex offenders. *See* Adult male sex offenders
Male-accompanied, female sex offender, 73-74
Male-coerced, female sex offender, 73-74
Mandated therapy, 50
Marshall, W.L., 90, 182
Math Tech Sex Education Test, 36
Mathews, J.K., 72
Mathews, R., 73-74
Mathis, J.L., 71
McFadden, E.J., 104
Medications, sex offenders, 152, 209
Meezan, W., 28
Mendel, M.P., 75, 76
Mental illness, 140
Mental Status Examination (MSE), 35
Millon Clinical Multi-Axial Inventory, 170-171
Milsom, J., 171
Model, offender assessment, 9-10
Moffitt, T.E., 203
"Monoamine hypothesis," 200-201
Mood dysregulation, 200-201
Motivation, precondition of sexual abuse, 51-52
  treatment, 56
Motivation for treatment, adolescent sex offender, 40
MSE, 35
MSI, 52, 114e
MSI: Justifications Scale, 115e

MSI: Sexual Obsessions, 115e
MTC: R3, 172-173
Multiphasic Sex Inventory (MSI), 52, 114e
Multiple perpetrators, 111
"Multiply entrapped," 6

Nathan, P., 82
National Society for the Prevention of Cruelty to Children study, 102-103
"New Me" model, 91
Nicholaichuk, T., 84
Noble, J.H., 135-136
Nonhomicidal child molester, 171
Nonsadistic offenders, 173
Normal sexual behaviors, 1, 2
Nowicki-Strickland Locus of Control Scale, 114e
Nunno, M.A., 103

Obsessive-compulsive disorder (OCD), 197
Offense chain, 180
Offense characteristics
  adolescent sex offenders, 24-25
  child sex offenders, 6-8
Offense consequences
  female sex offenders, 77-82
  perpetrators within professions, 109-112
Offense-specific targets, 182-183
O'Hagan, K., 75
Opportunistic, 172
Orchard, J., 33

Paraphilia, 75
Perpetrators within professions, 101-102
  abuse settings, 104-107
  assessment, 112, 113e-116e, 116-117
  case example, 122-126
  etiology, 107-109

Perpetrators within professions
  (continued)
  interventions, 117-120
  offense, consequences of, 109-112
  prevalence, 102-104
  relapse prevention, 120-121
Perry, G.P., 33
Personal Distress Scale, 113e-114e
Personal intelligence, deficit, 203
Pervasively angry offenders, 172-173
Peterson, K.D., 84
Phallometric assessment, 36
Phone call, obscene, 26
Physical abuse, children, 7
Physiological measurement, adolescent sex offenders, 39
Pierce, L., 75
Pierce, R., 75
Pithers, W.D., 6
Polaschek, D.L.L., 182
Power rapist, 173-174
Preassessment, adolescent sex offender, 34
Predisposed, female sex offender, 74
Prentky, R.A., 176, 177, 178
Prevalence
  adult male sex offenders, 48
  child sex offenders, 3-4
  female sex offenders, 74-77
  ID sex offenders, 133-136
  perpetrators within professions, 102-104
Problem-solving techniques, ID sex offenders, 152-155
Proulx, J., 170
Psychiatric evaluation
  adolescent sex offenders, 38
  child sex offenders, 12
Psychological characteristics
  adolescent sex offenders, 28-29
  child sex offenders, 5-6
Psychological evaluation
  adolescent sex offenders, 37-38
  child sex offenders, 11-12
Psychopharmacology, 208-209

Psychosocial assessment
  adolescent sex offenders, 35-036
  child sex offenders, 10

Rabb, J., 1-3
Rage, 79-80
Rapid Risk Assessment for Sexual Offense Recidivism (RRASOR), 147
Rapist. *See* Violent sex offenders
Rapist classification scheme, 170
Rawlings, L., 2
Ray, J.A., 27-28
Recidivism
  adolescent sex offenders, 26-27
  adult male sex offenders, 48, 50, 58
  female sex offenders, 83-84
  ID sex offenders, 154-155
  perpetrators within professions, 120-121
  violent sex offenders, 184-185
Reframing, 56
Reinhart, M., 75-76
Relapse prevention. *See* Recidivism
Relapse Prevention Questionnaire, 116e
Relationship needs, female sex offenders, 87
Relationships with women, victims of female sex offenders, 80
Reppucci, N.D., 194
Rich, P., 31-32, 41
Rindfleisch, N., 103
Risk assessment
  adolescent sex offenders, 39-40
  child sex offenders, 12
  violent sex offenders, 181-182
Risk factors, adult male sex offenders, 51
Roane, T., 76
Rose, J., 154
RRASOR, 147
Rubbing bodies, 25
Ryan, G., 203
Ryan, P., 104

Sadism, rape and, 175-178
Sadistic offenders, 173
Sadistic personality disorder (SPD), 177
Saradjian, J., 87, 88, 90, 91
Saunders, E.B., 26
SCID-P, 199
Self-as-victim, 171
Self-concept, 81-82
Self-injury, 78-79
Self-management
  female sex offenders, 91
  violent sex offenders, 184-185
Self-regulation deficiencies, 121
Sex Offender Needs Assessment Rating (SONAR), 52
Sex Offender Risk Appraisal Guide (SORAG), 146-147
Sexual scripts, 71
Sexual terrorists, 104
Sexually reactive, 2
School, adolescent sex offenders, 29-30
Scotland, 135
Short Self-Esteem Scale, 113e
Significant Others Scale, 150
Smith-Magenis syndrome, 137
Social dynamics, adolescent sex offenders, 29-30
Socio-Sexual Knowledge and Attitudes Assessment Tool—Revised, 138
Socratic questioning, 120
SONAR, 52
SORAG, 146-147
SPD, 177
Sports settings, abuse in, 107
Static risk factors, 51
Stein, R.M., 30
STEP measures, 113e-116e
Stewart, C.A., 87, 90, 91
Stinnett, R.D., 48
Structured Clinical Interview for DSM-IV Axis I Disorders (SCID-P), 199
Substance abuse
  adolescent sex offenders, 30
  sex abuse victims, 78
Suicide, 79
Sullivan, J., 102, 110

Teacher/lover, female sex offender, 73
Templeman, T.L., 48
Therapy groups, 55, 206-207
Thinking patterns, female sex offenders, 89-90
Tourette's syndrome, 137
Treatment
  adolescent sex offenders, 40-41
  adult male sex offenders, 55-58
  comorbidity, 204, 206-209
  female sex offenders, 84-91
Trivits, L.C., 194
Typology
  ID sex offenders, 137-142
  rapist, and violence, 172-178

UCLA Emotional Loneliness Scale, 113e
Ullman, S.E., 169
Underassertiveness Scale, 113e
Uniform Crime Report, FBI, 3
United Kingdom, 135
U.S. Department of Justice, 75
Utting, W., 111-112

Victim Empathy Distortions Scale, 114e
Victim resistance, precondition of sexual abuse, 53-54
Victimization, history of
  adolescent sex offenders, 27-28
  child sex offenders, 7
Victims, adolescent sex offender, 25
Vindictive offender, 173
Violence, nature of, 168-170
Violence Risk Appraisal Guide (VRAG), 146-147
Violent sex offenders, 167-168
  assessment, 179-182
  case example, 185-187

Violent sex offenders *(continued)*
  characteristics, 170-171
  definition of, 168-169
  etiology, 178
  interventions, 182-184
  prevalence, 169-170
  relapse prevention, 184-185
  typology, 172-178
Voluntary settings, abuse in, 106
Voyeurism, 25, 26
VRAG, 146-147

WAIS-R, 11
Ward, T., 82, 87, 90, 91, 108

Warning signs, relapse, 120
Warren, J., 169-170
Weinrott, M., 206
Weschler Adult Intelligence Scale-Revised (WAIS-R), 11
Westcott, H., 104, 111
Will, D., 33
Williams, S.M., 84
Wolvercote Clinic, 118-119, 119t
Women as sex offenders. *See* Female sex offenders

Yokley, J., 30

Order a copy of this book with this form or online at:
http://www.haworthpress.com/store/product.asp?sku=5260

COMPREHENSIVE MENTAL HEALTH PRACTICE WITH SEX OFFENDERS AND THEIR FAMILIES

_____ in hardbound at $49.95 (ISBN-13: 978-0-7890-2542-5; ISBN-10: 0-7890-2542-6)

_____ in softbound at $29.95 (ISBN-13: 978-0-7890-2543-2; ISBN-10: 0-7890-2543-4)

Or order online and use special offer code HEC25 in the shopping cart.

COST OF BOOKS_____	☐ **BILL ME LATER:** (Bill-me option is good on US/Canada/Mexico orders only; not good to jobbers, wholesalers, or subscription agencies.)
POSTAGE & HANDLING_____ (US: $4.00 for first book & $1.50 for each additional book)	☐ Check here if billing address is different from shipping address and attach purchase order and billing address information.
(Outside US: $5.00 for first book & $2.00 for each additional book)	Signature_____
SUBTOTAL_____	☐ **PAYMENT ENCLOSED:** $_____
IN CANADA: ADD 7% GST_____	☐ **PLEASE CHARGE TO MY CREDIT CARD.**
STATE TAX_____ (NJ, NY, OH, MN, CA, IL, IN, PA, & SD residents, *add appropriate local sales tax*)	☐ Visa ☐ MasterCard ☐ AmEx ☐ Discover ☐ Diner's Club ☐ Eurocard ☐ JCB
	Account #_____
FINAL TOTAL_____ (If paying in Canadian funds, convert using the current exchange rate, UNESCO coupons welcome)	Exp. Date_____
	Signature_____

Prices in US dollars and subject to change without notice.

NAME_____
INSTITUTION_____
ADDRESS_____
CITY_____
STATE/ZIP_____
COUNTRY_____ COUNTY (NY residents only)_____
TEL_____ FAX_____
E-MAIL_____

May we use your e-mail address for confirmations and other types of information? ☐ Yes ☐ No
We appreciate receiving your e-mail address and fax number. Haworth would like to e-mail or fax special discount offers to you, as a preferred customer. **We will never share, rent, or exchange your e-mail address or fax number.** We regard such actions as an invasion of your privacy.

Order From Your Local Bookstore or Directly From
The Haworth Press, Inc.
10 Alice Street, Binghamton, New York 13904-1580 • USA
TELEPHONE: 1-800-HAWORTH (1-800-429-6784) / Outside US/Canada: (607) 722-5857
FAX: 1-800-895-0582 / Outside US/Canada: (607) 771-0012
E-mail to: orders@haworthpress.com

For orders outside US and Canada, you may wish to order through your local
sales representative, distributor, or bookseller.
For information, see http://haworthpress.com/distributors

(Discounts are available for individual orders in US and Canada only, not booksellers/distributors.)
PLEASE PHOTOCOPY THIS FORM FOR YOUR PERSONAL USE.
http://www.HaworthPress.com   BOF06